Shaped by the West

VOLUME 1

SHAPED BY THE WEST

VOLUME 1

A History of North America to 1877

William Deverell and Anne Hyde

UNIVERSITY OF CALIFORNIA PRESS

University of California Press, one of the most distinguished
university presses in the United States, enriches lives around
the world by advancing scholarship in the humanities, social
sciences, and natural sciences. Its activities are supported by the
UC Press Foundation and by philanthropic contributions from
individuals and institutions. For more information, visit
www.ucpress.edu.

University of California Press
Oakland, California

Library of Congress Cataloging-in-Publication Data

Names: Deverell, William F., 1962- author. | Hyde, Anne Farrar,
    1960- author.
Title: Shaped by the West / William F. Deverell and Anne F. Hyde.
Description: Oakland, California : University of California Press,
    [2018] | Includes bibliographical references and index. |
Identifiers: LCCN 2017060975 (print) | LCCN 2018002204 (ebook) |
    ISBN 9780520964372 (ebook) | ISBN 9780520290044 (v. 1 ; pbk. :
    alk. paper) | ISBN 9780520964372 (v. 1 ; ebook) |
    ISBN 9780520291416 (v. 2 ; pbk. : alk. paper) |
    ISBN 9780520965201 (v. 2 ; ebook)
Subjects: LCSH: West (U.S.)—History. | Frontier and pioneer life—
    West (U.S.) | United States—History. | Indians of North
    America—Great Plains—History.
Classification: LCC F591 (ebook) | LCC F591 .D395 2018 (print) |
    DDC 978—dc23
LC record available at https://lccn.loc.gov/2017060975

Manufactured in the United States of America

27   26   25   24   23   22   21   20   19   18
10   9   8   7   6   5   4   3   2   1

Contents

Preface

These two volumes on the history of the American West first came about because of a really good idea that did not work. Twenty years ago, the two of us agreed to sign up for an innovative project aimed at tying regional history to the broadest sweeps of US history. The elegant intention for a two-volume annotated reader on the West was that it would supplement American history survey courses taught at colleges and universities *in* the West.

Broad-brush national issues—war, slavery, conquest, labor, gender and the family, cities, etc.—would be elaborated upon by documents and images drawn from, and interpreted within, western settings. Students learning about Prohibition, for example, would address that topic and its long history by reading temperance and Prohibition sources alongside stories from western places: Colorado, California, Wyoming, Oregon, and others. Specific settings would shed light on the overriding topic, and students in the West would get to know their region's history better and more broadly.

Good idea, right? It was. And the first edition of these two volumes offered the two of us, friends and colleagues now for half our lives, a great opportunity to work on something together.

So what happened? The easy answer is that, for whatever reason or reasons, the survey courses on campus in the US West did not much bend to the regional illumination our books offered. Maybe the survey-course instructors did not want to alter the way they taught their courses. Maybe a textbook-driven syllabus could not easily accommodate two additional volumes of readings and exercises. Maybe the innovative idea required a bit more public relations energy than a busy publisher could be expected to provide.

But the books did not fail. They just hit a different target than the one we first imagined. Not long after they were published in 2000, we began to hear from our western history colleagues all over the country, who told us that our two volumes were a hit in their courses. Not their US survey courses but their western, or various versions of regional, history courses. The documents and images brought the West's complex, chaotic history to life and to the ground. Voices of real people could be heard in the primary source records we had mined for the books. And our brief annotations and introductions helped our colleagues by adding context and scholarly perspective to history's themes, moments, and episodes.

The "hook" was unintended, but no less gratifying because of it. The books got out there, they got taught, and our colleagues told us that they liked using them.

So here we are, two decades later, launching them again. We're different, our students are different, the concerns of historians who focus on the West have changed, so these books are different. With a new publisher, everything had to be rethought, reorganized, and revised in light of how much the field of western history has changed in this century.

It still makes sense to pull the long history of the West apart, to make this a two-volume reader. There is an early West and a later West, though the dividing line is a slippery concept. We opted, once again, for a division deep into the American period, roughly at the Civil War moment. We expect that the books will be taught apart and together. One aspect of western history that has invigorated the field in recent times has been the brilliant scholarship illuminating the indigenous histories of the West, before and after Spanish contact, before and after American conquest. We have been careful to bring much of that work to bear in our documents, short essays, and bibliographies, which close each chapter in both volumes.

The West has grown since we wrote the first edition of these books. Western historians who were once pretty content with the continental and national outlines of the American West must now, thanks again to bold, new scholarship, look beyond conventional boundaries of the West as a trans-Mississippi or trans-Rockies terrestrial place. Our West, and our students' West, is capacious and boundary-breaking, because the human beings who lived there and the ideas they carried with them crossed borders. We incorporate a West that is not defined by terra firma but is instead oceanic. The rise of transnational and Pacific histories within the western historical canons of scholarship has added much to our field. Now we ask how the West looked, and how people lived their lives, in and around "the great Ocean" that borders the western edges of a West we ought no longer delimit at high tide.

There are other ways in which the West has grown richer as a field of historical inquiry. Our field's embrace of environmental history, long strong, has only gotten more ambitious and interesting, and those prisms of analysis and those stories are reflected in these pages. Western history has long been a field in which breakthrough scholars have helped us better understand such concepts as gender and masculinity. Researchers whose work addresses sexuality have added magnificently to those foundations, and we are indebted to them here, just as we are to historians and others who address LGBTQ histories in the archives and narratives of western America. They bring us a stunningly human West, where people learned new things about themselves, did awful things to each other, and sometimes took great care. Throughout this project, our aim has been to make these books speak to a new western audience, using up-to-date scholarship, and simultaneously to relay to students just how exciting it is to be working in western history at this moment in American historical writing. Our archives grow, the people in them change, and our access to that knowledge gets easier every day. The stories and puzzles they yield have never been more compelling.

We also find obligation in opportunity. We have tried to bring contemporary concerns and problems into sharper view by way of context and history. The West is a troubled place in early twenty-first-century America. It is a place where many of the nation's uncertainties and tensions seem to get wrestled with first out in the open, in ways both inspiring and repulsive. Our West, and the West of the students who will read these volumes, has—as it always has—problems atop possibilities, troubles atop triumphs. But the stakes seem, to us, higher now. What the West will do or not do, what the West will collectively say to the nation and to the world, matters greatly. Think of challenging issues in contemporary America: immigration, the environment, the carceral state, native sovereignty, global change, race and racism, gender and power. These are not just western issues—of course not. But they have western valences, they have western contexts, and that particular history ought to help us all to better understand them.

So in a way we have come full circle. We're still friends, we still disagree about aspects of the West and its history, but we care about it deeply. This little two-volume project about the history of the region reflects our passion and experience. We still believe, as we did twenty years ago, that the West provides a sharply focused lens to view national and international issues. And it remains a distinctive region because of its physical setting and particular histories. We hope that in learning about that region and its wild history you will be shaped by the West. We hope you take that knowledge far beyond your classrooms.

ACKNOWLEDGMENTS

Because western history and the West have not grown simpler over the years, it took us a while to reimagine these volumes and to wrestle them into useful shape and size. We are very grateful to Niels Hooper at the University of California Press for thinking these volumes were a good idea and for not saying too much when they took longer than we ever thought they would. Bradley Depew, Niels's able assistant, has shaped these volumes and corralled the authors.

Copyeditors Ann Donahue and Lindsey Westbrook did wonderful work in correcting errors, finding inconsistencies, and making the volumes look terrific.

We owe a lot to reviewers, who looked at initial proposals and then first and second drafts of both volumes. As experienced teachers and western scholars, they gave us excellent and detailed advice that pushed us to reconfigure these volumes. Susan L. Johnson, from the University of Wisconsin; Adam Arenson of Manhattan College; Greg Hise from the University of Nevada, Las Vegas; and Shana Bernstein of Northwestern University all read carefully and convinced us to make significant changes. We can't thank them enough, and we hope these volumes begin to represent their efforts. In Southern California, Bill would like to thank Taryn Haydostian, Elizabeth Logan, Brian Moeller, Erin Chase, and Aaron Hodges for their efforts in tracking down images, rekeying documents, and getting permissions. In Oklahoma, Anne would like to thank the staff at the Western History Collection, Laurie Scrivener, Curtis Foxley, and History 1493, for test driving documents and ideas.

William Deverell, University
of Southern California
Anne Hyde, University of Oklahoma

Introduction

This document collection is many years, we might say hundreds of years, in the making. It is the product of centuries of historical change and upheaval, triumph and tragedy, in the region we now call the American West. It offers hundreds of voices from the past to represent a range of human beings that enable you to see both glimmers of yourself in the past and worlds and ideas that are breathtakingly different.

As we think about how these will be used in classrooms, by you and your classmates, we are confident in two major ideas. The first is that you, your classmates, and your instructors will shape these volumes by your collective ideas, wrapped around history and region. We know also that reading and thinking about the history of the West is best done if you can sit with the words and images of the people who are no longer around. Some of these are written documents that have been translated many times, but some are objects, photographs, maps, or buildings. We have an obligation as historians to guide you in that work, almost to sit alongside you as you read.

The West we take you through is far more than what eventually becomes the US West. Those borders and that idea of a region didn't always exist. Some of your experiences will tilt earlier, to a West not yet conquered by Anglo-America, to a West of overlapping claims, global ambitions, and Native systems of governance, both roving and rooted in western places and spaces. Other classes, other students of the West, will find more to grapple with in a "later West," when conquest morphed into the colonialism of taking gold, oil, coal, or water on unprecedented scales, when cities arose to marshal commodities, people, and capital. And some of you will focus more attention on the West of the most recent vintage, the West of your own lifetimes, a West of roiling demographic and political change (not so new, actually), a West at the center of some of the most vexing and divisive issues in contemporary American life.

So we take you to places where different ideas about how people should live and who should control resources bump up against each other. Sometimes that makes a border, sometimes a frontier, sometimes a war zone, or sometimes a place of peaceful diplomacy. In moving through these zones of contention or collaboration, the people actually there do the speaking. Our job is to ask you to think about this or think about that as you read. We frame the documents and pictures within the context of their making, and we introduce you to the circumstances that led to that letter or that law or that photograph.

The real meaning of all this is in the exchanges you have with the western past. If we know what we are talking about, our annotations, captions, and miniessays will help you as you move through western time and space. But it is your give and take with the actual sources of history that we hope this book inspires. The past is both like and utterly unlike the present we inhabit. Listen to the voices of the West. See how language is the same, yet different. Understand the circumstances people, groups, and nations found themselves in, how they made decisions, what those decisions ultimately meant. Ask questions of these sources—why did this happen? What might have happened differently? How can two people see the same moment so divergently? What were the best ideas of the past? What were the worst? How does the past, and all those decisions made by people who came before us, still influence the present and the future?

Where does the past stop, and where does the present begin? And what is our present other than the future's past?

History offers fascinating terrain to exercise your ideas and come up with new ones. It is hard work, the answers are never easy to come by, and history has neither a neat beginning nor a neat end. The West, only one of an infinite number of ways in which to carve up the past, is a place that has fascinated us for the entirety of our careers. We hope that this same excitement, along with ideas we haven't even thought of, accompanies you as you think your way through these volumes.

Peñasco Blanco, the White House. Built around 1000 CE, in what is now northwestern New Mexico, this is an example of the complex world that indigenous Americans built in North America. This large structure, housing hundreds of people, was constructed in a place with little water and little wood. Peñasco Blanco, which its residents abandoned around 1300, was part of a great flowering of ancestral Puebloan culture on the Colorado Plateau. How it was built and why the people left remains a mystery, but its presence reminds us of the range of peoples, their human gifts, and their brilliance in adapting to a challenging place.

A Vast Native World

1

Societies and cultures as diverse as Asia or Africa or Europe developed on the American land mass long before European explorers stumbled upon the Americas. What Europeans found was not empty land but places long settled, farmed, and fought over. Many peoples, upwards of eighteen million, lived in what is now North America. Some lived in large cities, others in small villages, and whether we call them indigenous, native, or Indian, they inhabited every part of North America. They traded with each other across enormous distances and spoke thousands of different languages.

Anthropologists, historians, and Native experts disagree about when these people settled on the North American landscape. It could be as recently as twelve thousand or as long as fifty thousand years ago. Experts continue to debate whether they came across the Bering Land Bridge, whether they came on ships or rafts, or whether they emerged here, on this continent, as humans, for the first time. The most ancient is called the Paleo-Indian period, encompassing hunting cultures who developed survival strategies to meet the challenging conditions of late Ice Age times. This is followed by the Archaic period, a long era of relatively stable hunter-gatherer ways of living. In North America this included several regionally defined cultures of seminomadic peoples. By thirteen thousand years ago, nomadic hunters of the Clovis culture (or cultures) had spread far and wide across much of North America. Their sudden appearance over such vast spaces meant that they either swiftly migrated into previously unpopulated lands or other peoples adapted their stone tool technology and transformed their own landscapes. The issue is still hotly debated.

More radical changes characterize the third era, termed Formative, when corn-based farming replaced foraging among a number of North America's Native peoples, who now inhabited warmer places with better soil for planting. Finally, the Historic period describes the era when non-native explorers and settlers—mostly coming from the south and east—left their imprint on the continent's landscape and eventually displaced the native tribes in sometimes violent encounters.

How do archaeologists define and label cultures of the distant past such as Clovis? Without having access to written languages, we have no idea what names they used to identify themselves or other people, nor how they defined their own cultural or political boundaries, using some kind of "us vs. them" notion. Cultural anthropologists use tools, boundary-setting, and evidence of language and religion to define culture as a set of shared behaviors passed down from generation to generation.

Few of the people who lived in North America before Columbus arrived were literate in the way we understand that now. They didn't leave texts written in European languages in familiar forms like books or photographs that recorded literal snapshots of the past. But they left lots of evidence of their presence behind in different kinds of materials and objects. Great monuments that still stand, ruins of villages that we can reconstruct, and vast trash heaps where we find jewelry, pottery, clothing, and human and animal bones enable scholars to estimate populations, their health, and their wealth. Drawings and picture-writing, called pictographs, show us historical events, individual people, details about daily life, religious ceremonies, mathematical equations, and weather predictions. Once scholars in the present knew how to look, they found tax records, census materials, and legal codes that organized these complex societies.

People organized their households and personal lives in many ways. Many Native American societies acknowledged three to five genders—*female, male, Two-Spirit female, Two-Spirit male, and transgendered*—but these terms come from modern ways of thinking about sexuality. LGBTQ Native Americans adopted the term *Two Spirit* from the Ojibwe language in Winnipeg, Manitoba, in 1989. Each tribe has their own specific language for a range of sexualities, but later more universal terms that modern people could understand became useful. The Navajo refer to Two Spirits as *Nádleehí* (one who is transformed), the Lakota as *Winkté* (a male who wants to behave as a female), the Ojibwe as *Niizh Manidoowag* (two spirit), and the Cheyenne as *Hemaneh* (half man, half woman), to name a few.

Before Columbus, at least five hundred Native nations flourished in North America. They included great powerful empires like the Mississippian mound builders, who ruled the center of the continent. A thousand years ago, about the year 1050 CE, a "big bang" of culture and power erupted in the center of the continent. A great planned capital city arose near where St. Louis, Missouri, is now, and it radically shifted politics, religion, art, and economics. The new city, marked by giant ceremonial mounds that sprang up for hundreds of miles, represented a powerful and attractive new way of life. Up and down the Mississippi River, communities got the protection of a powerful kingdom, new trade connections, and consumer goods in return for loyalty, as well as slavery and taxes. Why these cultures disappeared remains a huge historical mystery.

At about the same time, another cultural flowering emerged on the Colorado Plateau. A group of cities, linked by highways and water aqueducts linked peoples we now call the Ancestral Puebloans. Their great cities—built by slaves— are now ruins like Chaco Canyon, Mesa Verde, and Canyon de Chelly. They once housed hundreds of people and hosted extensive ceremonies in a region where water is so scarce it is difficult to imagine how urban life evolved there. For more than a thousand years, the Ancestral Puebloans built great structures; filled them with spectacular pottery, carvings, and weaving; and then, around 1300 CE, abandoned their cities. While much debate remains about why the Ancestral Puebloans left, Native experts and scholars agree that a prolonged drought was a central factor. People resettled in smaller cities, towns, and villages along the Rio Grande and Gila Rivers, where water was more secure, and on top of great mesas, where their enemies could not reach them.

Other powerful alliances linked peoples along the Atlantic seaboard from what is now Newfoundland to Georgia. The Iroquois Confederacy formed in the 1570s and included many New England nations. As many as fifty tribes created a confederation based on a system that used voting, representation, and a constitution. Because they wanted to build a powerful alliance to protect the region from hostile Native groups, these nations created a common council that gave each tribe one vote and required unanimity for decisions. They used elaborate rituals, including wampum belts and peace pipes, to choose leaders, to make decisions, and to allow people to disagree.

Before Columbus, along the West Coast of North America, from what is now Baja in Mexico to British Columbia in Canada, hundreds of small, independent tribes flourished. They spoke dozens of languages, lived in large wooden structures and tiny brush shelters, and fed themselves without agriculture because of the wealth of their landscape. From the famous totem poles of northern British Columbia to elaborate grass weavings from Southern California, coastal peoples made the most of their resources. They carved every size of boat to fish on rivers and in the ocean and had rich artistic traditions in carving wood; weaving baskets; and fashioning armor, shoes, and traps for fish and animals.

None of these nations, peoples, or societies lived in isolation. The need and desire for more and different foods or goods and curiosity about other worlds and new places brought people into contact across wide distances. Trade, war, and captivity created contact and relationships between these groups. Larger, more complex societies often needed laborers, soldiers, and personal servants, roles that people who were captured in war could fill. But whether people captured others or borrowed their technologies, North Americans knew about many different peoples and ways of doing things.

AS YOU READ: The "documents" in this chapter are not all written texts but rather a range of things left behind and passed down to us over many centuries. How does the interpretation of these materials differ from written descriptions of places and people? What might we miss in our assumptions about how lives could and should be organized?

1. ORIGIN STORIES FROM THE SOUTHWEST, PACIFIC COAST, AND GREAT LAKES

These three pieces, translated from Native languages or taken orally, come from Native peoples who lived in different places and times. All three emphasize the centrality of a place of origin and how people emerged in a specific spot. In this important location, either in the desert southwest, the Pacific Northwest, or the Great Lakes, human beings simply emerged from their earlier animal forms or made an arrangement with the gods to take a new form. Such important cultural stories have been handed down from generation to generation by storytellers, who cherish these stories but also change them as new situations require new stories. What patterns and qualities are shared by all three stories? Which details make them specific to a place? What is the role of a higher being in each of these stories? Does it matter who collected the story and when?

Zuni

"Sun and Moon in a Box"[1]

Coyote and Eagle were hunting. Eagle caught rabbits. Coyote caught nothing but grasshoppers. Coyote said: "Friend Eagle, my chief, we make a great hunting pair."

"Good, let us stay together," said Eagle.

---

1. Alfonso Ortiz and Louise Erdoes, eds. *American Indian Trickster Tales* (New York: Penguin, 1999), 4–6.

They went toward the west. They came to a deep canyon. "Let us fly over it," said Eagle.

"My chief, I cannot fly," said Coyote. "You must carry me across."

"Yes, I see that I have to," said Eagle. He took Coyote on his back and flew across the canyon. They came to a river. "Well," said Eagle, "you cannot fly, but you certainly can swim. This time I do not have to carry you."

Eagle flew over the stream, and Coyote swam across. He was a bad swimmer. He almost drowned. He coughed up a lot of water. "My chief," he said, "when we come to another river, you must carry me." Eagle regretted to have Coyote for a companion.

They came to Kachina Pueblo. The Kachinas were dancing. Now, at this time, the earth was still soft and new. There was as yet no sun and no moon. Eagle and Coyote sat down and watched the dance. They saw that the Kachinas had a square box. In it they kept the sun and the moon. Whenever they wanted light they opened the lid and let the sun peek out. Then it was day. When they wanted less light, they opened the box just a little for the moon to look out.

"This is something wonderful," Coyote whispered to Eagle.

"This must be the sun and the moon they are keeping in that box," said Eagle. "I have heard about these two wonderful beings."

"Let us steal the box," said Coyote.

"No, that would be wrong," said Eagle. "Let us just borrow it."

When the Kachinas were not looking, Eagle grabbed the box and flew off. Coyote ran after him on the ground. After a while Coyote called Eagle: "My chief, let me have the box. I am ashamed to let you do all the carrying."

"No," said Eagle, "you are not reliable. You might be curious and open the box and then we could lose the wonderful things we borrowed."

For some time they went on as before—Eagle flying above with the box, Coyote running below, trying to keep up. Then once again Coyote called Eagle: "My chief, I am ashamed to let you carry the box. I should do this for you. People will talk badly about me, letting you carry this burden."

"No, I don't trust you," Eagle repeated. "You won't be able to refrain from opening the box. Curiosity will get the better of you."

"No," cried Coyote, "do not fear, my chief, I won't even think of opening the box." Still, Eagle would not give it to him, continuing to fly above, holding the box in his talons. But Coyote went on pestering Eagle: "My chief, I am really embarrassed. People will say: 'That lazy, disrespectful Coyote lets his chief do all the carrying.'"

"No, I won't give this box to you," Eagle objected. "It is too precious to entrust to somebody like you."

They continued as before, Eagle flying, Coyote running. Then Coyote begged for the fourth time: "My chief, let me carry the box for a while. My wife will scold me, and my children will no longer respect me, when they find out that I did not help you carry this load."

Then Eagle relented, saying: "Will you promise not to drop the box?"

"I promise, my chief, I promise," cried Coyote. "You can rely upon me. I shall not betray your trust."

Then Eagle allowed Coyote to carry the box. They went on as before, Eagle flying, Coyote running, carrying the box in his mouth. They came to a wooded area, full of trees and bushes. Coyote pretended to lag behind, hiding himself behind some bushes where Eagle could not see him. He could not curb his curiosity. Quickly he sat down and opened the box. In a flash, Sun came out of the box and flew away, to the very edge of the sky, and at once the world grew cold, the leaves fell from the tree branches, the grass turned brown, and icy winds made all living things shiver.

Then, before Coyote could put the lid back on the box, Moon jumped out and flew away to the outer rim of the sky, and at once snow fell down from heaven and covered the plains and the mountains.

Eagle said: "I should have known better. I should not have let you persuade me. I knew what kind of low, cunning, stupid creature you are. I should have remembered that you never keep a promise. Now we have winter. If you had not opened the box, then we could have kept Sun and Moon always close to us. Then there would be no winter. Then we would have summer all the time."

Pullayup
"The Story of the Changer"[2]

"Star husbands" is a favorite theme in Native mythology. It occurs in tribal tales from Nova Scotia to the Washington coast. Among the tribes of the Puget Sound and Olympic Peninsula areas, it is usually linked with the birth of the Changer, but it is used in another way in "The Earth People Visit the Sky People." A Puyallup variant of the following Puyallup myth was related in August 1952 by Jerry Meeker.

Two sisters, working together, dug the fern roots for their family. Often when they were digging roots at some distance from home, they would camp over night. One evening as they lay looking at the sky, the girls wondered what kind of people the Stars were and how they lived up in Star Land.

"Which star would you like to marry?" asked the younger sister. "The big bright one or the little red one?"

"Oh, don't be foolish!" answered the older sister. "Why do you talk that way?"

But her sister was not silenced. "I want to marry the big bright star. You may have the little red one."

---

2. Ella Clark, ed. *Indian Legends of the Pacific Northwest* (University of California Press, 1963), 143–46.

Thus the Changer traveled over the land, helping the people and getting rid of evil creatures. He taught the people how to make all the things they needed, how to play games, how to cure the sick. He showed them how to get power from the spirits.

One day as he was traveling along a river, he became hungry. He saw a salmon jumping, called it to him, put it on a spit, and placed it beside his fire. While it was cooking, the Changer fell asleep. A wandering creature came and ate all the salmon. Before he slipped away, he rubbed some grease on the lips and fingers of the sleeping Changer, and put some bits of fish between his teeth and lips. When the sleeper awoke, he knew that he had been tricked. He followed the tracks of the creature and soon found him looking at himself in the water. The Changer transformed him into a coyote.

When he went to the home of his blind grandmother, Toad, he saw a mountain of rock. The mountain had been formed from the coils of cedar rope which his mother and aunt had made in Star Land. As he looked up at the sky, the Changer thought that there should be more light. So he went up to the Sky World and traveled across it by day in the form of the sun.

But he made the days so hot that the people could not stand the heat. He called his brother, who had been made from the cradleboard, and made him the sun.

"I will be the night sun," said the Changer. "And I will take with me as my wife the maiden who can lift and carry this great bag of things which I have made."

Only the daughter of Frog could carry such a load, and so she went up to the sky with him. Today the Changer, the Frog, and the bag she carried can be seen in the full moon.

Ojibwe
"An Allegory of the Seasons"[3]

An old man was sitting alone in his lodge, by the side of a frozen stream. It was the close of winter, and his fire was almost out. He appeared very old and very desolate. His locks were white with age, and he trembled in every joint. Day after day passed in solitude, and he heard nothing but the sounds of the tempest, sweeping before it the new-fallen snow.

One day, as his fire was just dying, a handsome young man approached and entered his dwelling. His cheeks were red with the blood of youth, his eyes sparkled with animation, and a smile played upon his lips. He walked with a light and quick step. His forehead was bound with a wreath of sweet grass, in place of a warrior's frontlet, and he carried a bunch of flowers in his hand.

---

3. Henry Schoolcraft, ed. *Algic Researches: Indian Tales and Legends,* vol. 1 (Michigan: Clearfield Company 1839), 84–86.

"Ah, my son," said the old man, "I am happy to see you. Come in. Come, tell me of your adventures, and what strange lands you have been to see. Let us pass the night together. I will tell you of my prowess and exploits, and what I can perform. You shall do the same, and we will amuse ourselves."

He then drew from his sack a curiously-wrought antique pipe, and having filled it with tobacco, rendered mild by an admixture of certain leaves, handed it to his guest. When this ceremony was concluded they began to speak.

"I blow my breath," said the old man, "and the streams stand still. The water becomes stiff and hard as clear stone."

"I breathe," said the young man, "and flowers spring up all over the plains."

"I shake my locks," retorted the old man, "and snow covers the land. The leaves fall from the trees at my command, and my breath blows them away. The birds get up from the water, and fly to a distant land. The animals hide themselves from my breath, and the very ground becomes as hard as flint."

"I shake my ringlets," rejoined the young man, "and warm showers of soft rain fall upon the earth. The plants lift up their heads out of the earth, like the eyes of children glistening with delight. My voice recalls the birds. The warmth of my breath unlocks the streams. Music fills the groves wherever I walk, and all nature rejoices."

At length the sun began to rise. A gentle warmth came over the place. The tongue of the old man became silent. The robin and bluebird began to sing on the top of the lodge. The stream began to murmur by the door, and the fragrance of growing herbs and flowers came softly on the vernal breeze.

Daylight fully revealed to the young man the character of his entertainer. When he looked upon him, he had the icy visage of *Peboan*. Streams began to flow from his eyes. As the sun increased, he grew less and less in stature, and anon had melted completely away. Nothing remained on the place of his lodge fire but the *miskodeed*, a small white flower, with a pink border, which is one of the earliest species of Northern plants.

2. DEBATES OVER ANCESTRAL PUEBLOANS: DROUGHT, WAR, OR MIGRATION

Petrograph of 1054 Crab Nebula Supernova, Alex Marentez, 2006 *(see p. 11)*

Interpreting what people leave behind is challenging, especially with no common words or detailed written descriptions. The puzzle of the great cliff dwellings has still not been solved, though people living there have left us some clues. In Chaco Canyon, Arizona, just outside the great house called Peñasco Blanco (see image at the opening of this chapter), is a drawing contain-

Petrograph of 1054 supernova. Photo by Alex Marentez, 2006.

ing three symbols carved in stone: a large star, a crescent moon, and a hand-print. Ethnoastronomers, or people who study the ancient sky, believe that this petroglyph represents a unique celestial event that occurred in 1054 CE. A supernova is the explosion of a very large star, much larger than our sun. The star that created the Crab Nebula was vast and after it exploded and the light of the explosion traveled to earth, it looked like a very bright star. On July 4, 1054, 4000 years after the Crab Nebula supernova actually occurred, a star six times brighter than Venus appeared in the sky. It was visible on Earth at noon and stayed visible for 23 days. The Chinese and Japanese recorded the appearance of a very bright "guest star" around this time. People living in Chaco Canyon, in a culture highly attuned to how the sky moved, surely noticed it and likely recorded it.

The petroglyph and Chaco Canyon still have things to tell us. Every 18.5 years, the moon and earth return to approximately the same positions they took on July 4, 1054. The ancient diagram enables us to position a telescope so that you will see the Crab Nebula. Why would people living in Chaco Canyon then care about movement of the stars? Why would an explosion in the sky be recorded by so many different people? Why would the Chacoan residents leave such an elaborate home?

3. FINDING MISSISSIPPIAN KINGDOMS: CAHOKIA MOUNDS *(SEE P. 13)*

About a thousand years ago, just across the Mississippi River from where St. Louis is now, a city called Cahokia sprang up in the rich bottomlands. By 1050 CE, a series of chiefdoms had built large communities that flourished there for hundreds of years. They designed calendars, armaments, religious buildings, and stored tons of food that they traded up and down the river. The most distinctive and long-lasting parts of this culture, however, were the great mounds they created out of dirt, brick, stones, and grass. Soaring several hundred feet up, they signaled power and influence to all who could see them. However, by about 1300, this stunning landscape had been abandoned. Whether war, disease, famine, or too much demand on resources drove people away, by the time European explorers arrived in the 1600s, the sites were empty. St. Louis, also called "Mound City" because of the seventy-two mounds that covered its riverfront, emerged in an old native spot, but few St. Louisans had any idea of the value of these mounds that interfered with their efforts to build docks and ports. Slowly, every one of these great mounds was dug out and bulldozed down, though some still exist across the river in Cahokia, Illinois. The images you see here are reconstructions of what Cahokia might have looked like in 1100 and early nineteenth-century photographs taken by St. Louis citizens. What does the scale of these structures tell you about the people who built them? How could these giant buildings represent a shift in power in the region?

4. VARIETIES OF NATIVE LIFE: SEEING TWO-SPIRIT PEOPLE IN THE INDIGENOUS PAST[1]

In 1528, a Spanish soldier named Alvar Núñez Cabeza de Vaca found himself shipwrecked along the coast of Texas. He had planned to be part of a grand invasion of Florida, involving dozens of ships and hundreds of men and horses, but everything had gone wrong. Instead, along with three other survivors, Cabeza de Vaca spent eight years traveling across the Gulf Coast, into the interior of what is now the US Southwest, in his effort to find Mexico City and a way home. Forced to be a slave, a healer, and a merchant, he had contact with dozens of different Indian nations and peoples. He viewed everything through his own cultural lens—that of an elite Spanish Catholic soldier—and was amazed by the variety of who and what he saw. Military expertise, sophisticated weaponry, and hunting skills impressed him, but the lack of interest in Christianity and the unwillingness to farm concerned him. He recorded an enormous range

---

1. Cabeza de Vaca (1529). "Chronicle of the Narvaez Expedition," trans. David Frye, chapter 26 (New York: W. W. Norton, 2013), 59–60.

View of a mound near St Louis.

Cahokia mounds. *Top,* UNESCO World Heritage Site, East St. Louis, Illinois. Photo by Ko Hon Chiu Vincent; *bottom,* "Riverfront Mounds, St. Louis, 1852," Missouri History Museum, St Louis. Artist unknown.

of households, from single families to large kinship groups to groups of single men or single women, all living peaceably. Cabeza de Vaca provides us with one of the first accounts of what we would call same-sex unions or transgender behaviors among Native Americans. We have to read this carefully: through the lenses of our own modern definitions, taking account of what the first Catholic translators of this account might have thought, and through Cabeza de Vaca's own agenda. How might categories of men and women be different in other times and places? What are the challenges of viewing cultures in the past, looking for evidence of our own definitions in the present?

Cabeza de Vaca
"Chronicle of the Narvaez Expedition"
1528

I also want to enumerate their nations and languages that exist from the Island of Ill Fate to the last ones,+++ {the Cuchendados}. On the Island of Ill Fate there are two languages: one group is called Capoques, the other is called Han. On the mainland, facing the island, there are others called Charruco, and they take their name from the woods where they live. Farther on, along the seacoast, are others called Deaguanes, and in front of them others named the people of Mendica. Farther on, on the coast, are the Quevenes, and in front of them, within the mainland, the Mariames. And following along the coast, there are others called Guaycones, and in front of them, within the mainland, the Iguaces. After these are others called Atayos, and behind them are others, Acubadaos, and there are many of these farther on in this direction. On the coast live others called Quitoles, and in front of them, within the mainland, the Chavavares. These are joined by the Maliacones, and others, Cultalchuches, and others called Susola and others who are called Comos. And farther along the coast are the Camolas; and on the same coast, farther along, are others whom we call the people of the figs.

All those peoples have dwellings and pueblos and diverse languages. Among these, there is a language in which, when they call men, for "look here" they say *arre acà,* and they call dogs by saying *shoh.*

All over the land they get drunk on a certain smoke, and they will give everything they have for it. They also drink another thing that they extract from the leaves of trees like live oaks, which they toast in jars over the fire; after they have toasted them, they fill the jar with water and then keep it on the fire, and when it has boiled twice they pour it into a vessel, and they work to cool it down, using a gourd cut in half. And when it is full of foam, they drink it as hot as they can stand it. And from the time they pour it out of the jar until they drink it, they keep shouting out, "Who wants to drink?" And when the women hear these shouts, they immediately stand still, not daring to move; even if they are carrying a very heavy load they do not dare to do anything else. If one of the women should happen to move, they dishonor her and thrash her, and in a great rage they spill the water that they were about to drink, and they spit up what they have already drunk, which they do very easily and without any embarrassment. The reason they give for this custom is that, when they want to drink that water, if the women move from the spot where they first hear the shouts, then an evil thing gets into their bodies from that water, and not long afterward it causes them to die. And the whole time the water is boiling, the jar has be covered. If it happens to be uncovered and some woman passes by, they pour it out and do not drink that water. It is yellow, and they drink it for three days without eating. And each day, each person drinks an arrob and a half of it.

And when women have their periods, they only gather food for themselves, because no other person else will eat any of what they bring.

During the time I was thus among them, I saw one devilry which is that I saw one man married to another man, and these are womanish, impotent men. They go about covered up like women, and they do the duty of women, and they {do not} use the bow and they carry great loads. Among these people we saw many such men—womanish, as I have said; and they are stouter than other men, and taller; they can bear up under very heavy loads.

FURTHER READING

Calloway, Colin G. *One Vast Winter Count: The Native American West Before Lewis and Clark.* Lincoln: University of Nebraska Press, 2004.

Fagan, Brian Fagan. *Chaco Canyon: Archaeologists Explore the Lives of an Ancient Society.* New York: Oxford University Press, 2005.

Fenn, Elizabeth R. *Encounters at the Heart of the World: A History of the Mandan People.* New York: Hill and Wang, 2014.

Munn, Charles C. *1491: New Revelations of the Americas Before Columbus.* New York: Alfred A. Knopf, 2005.

Nabokov, Peter. *A Forest of Time: American Indian Ways of History.* New York: Cambridge University Press, 2002.

Pauketat, Timothy R. *Cahokia: Ancient America's Great City on the Mississippi.* New York: Penguin Books, 2009.

Rifkin, Mark. *When Did Indians Become Straight? Kinship, the History of Sexuality and Native Sovereignty.* New York: Oxford University Press, 2011.

Van Dyke, Ruth M. *The Chaco Experience: Landscape and Ideology at the Center Place.* Santa Fe: School for Advanced Research, 2007.

Young, Biloine Whiting, and Melvin Fowler. *Cahokia: The Great Native American Metropolis.* Urbana: University of Illinois Press, 2000.

Zolbrod, Paul G. *Dine Bahane: The Navajo Creation Story.* Albuquerque: University of New Mexico Press, 1984.

An Aztec view of Cortés's arrival, c. 1520. This image, from a manuscript written and illustrated by Indians in the sixteenth century, is one of the few existing pictures showing us how Native peoples perceived the arrival of Europeans. The drawing depicts what happened when Aztec soldiers greeted Hernán Cortés. *Top,* the Indians present Cortés with gifts; *bottom,* Cortés threatens the Aztecs and puts them in chains. How might the Spanish and the Aztecs each have explained this event?

Arthur J. O. Anderson and Charles E. Dibble, *The War of Conquest: How It Was Waged Here in Mexico* (Salt Lake City: University of Utah Press, 1978), 14.

First Encounters

2

Expectation and Cultural Difference

When the people we now might label Indians and Europeans met in the Western Hemisphere after Columbus's first voyage in 1492, each group met worlds and perspectives entirely new to them. All of these people carried with them assumptions, both good and bad, about the lands and the people they met. Indigenous people in the Western Hemisphere, who had lived in North America for at least forty thousand years, had developed a variety of religious and cultural practices that affected the way they viewed and understood Europeans. Even before Columbus, people in Europe and Asia disagreed about what to call the people who lived in North America. Native people had names for their own groups and for others, but early European explorers rarely heard those names and often adopted the wrong names or lumped people together who had very different ways of living. This remains a linguistic and political challenge as native groups reform and change in the present. Most native people would prefer to be called by their traditional tribal names, for example, Diné, rather than Navajo, or Anishnabeg, rather than Chipewa. Powerful, urbanized nations like the Aztecs in Mexico, who had succeeded in bringing huge numbers of people under their control, assumed that the Europeans represented a new but manageable nation they could handle politically or militarily.

Less densely populated communities of farmers, traders, and hunters to the north, where the United States would develop, had long histories of constant change and movement. They flourished by adapting their economies and customs to new situations. They assumed that the new arrivals would bring a few useful ideas and then simply be absorbed into North American Native cultures, as had earlier visitors.

For the European explorers and conquistadors who came after Columbus, expectations about easy riches, fertile lands, and, especially, their own superiority colored everything they saw and did. The recent success of Spain in reconquering Europe from the Islamic Moors, who had taken over much of southern Europe in the thirteenth and fourteenth centuries, gave merchants and explorers great conviction about the strength of their religion and society and about the justice of military conquest. This confidence, combined with burgeoning scientific innovation, which allowed more accurate navigation, enabled ambitious sailors like Columbus to expand their horizons beyond Europe. Because Columbus had stumbled upon the New World while looking for the Orient, a place of fabled riches, he assumed that these newly discovered lands would offer the same kinds of wealth. These assumptions, carried first by the Spanish and the Portuguese, and later by the English and the French, had their most important impact on European relations with Indians.

Europeans also brought misconceptions about geography to the New World. Confidence and experience led many European explorers to assume that they knew all about the world and its peoples. Although today we have evidence of fishing expeditions from a variety of places in Europe, Viking exploration in North America, African voyages to South America, and Chinese ventures to the West long before 1492, Western European explorers like Columbus did not know that the Western Hemisphere existed. Because Columbus sailed west hoping to find the East Indies and a trade route to Asia, he believed that the Bahamian and Caribbean islands he landed on were a part of "the Indies" and thus assumed that the people he met were "Indians." His geographical and cultural error has echoed throughout the past five hundred years. How Columbus and the explorers who followed him treated these Indians also reflected the culture from which they came. Traditions of violent conquest, expectations of easy wealth, and a trail of deadly germs and invasive European plants and animals became part of a Columbian legacy that continues to affect us in the present.

The story of European conquest was never simple. Native peoples resisted conquest in a myriad of ways: they fought Europeans on the battlefield quite successfully, they refused to work, and they opposed the new European cultures in ways often invisible to Europeans. On the European side, various interests disagreed about the purposes and methods of conquest. A small but powerful minority opposed the violence of military conquest and the greedy motives behind it, arguing that the primary goal of conquest should be the conversion of Native peoples to Catholicism. In fact, the pope and the kings of Spain and France made conversion the official policy, and priests and other clerics accompanied explorers and settlers to the New World in order to minister to the Indians. Many complained that the desire for riches and status had undermined the central role of religion.

The story of Hernán Cortés and his conquest of Mexico illustrates both the desire for wealth and how cultural preconceptions affected what people saw and did. Lured by the reports of earlier explorers, Cortés and his soldiers arrived on the coast of Central America in 1519. The Aztec leader Montezuma (more correctly spelled Mocteczuma), not knowing who or what had appeared on the coast, acted with caution and escorted the newcomers to his capital. Because Montezuma proceeded cautiously and carefully, instead of immediately displaying his military power, Cortés took that moment to gain control over the Aztecs. Using a combination of surprise, political manipulation, military strategy, and the silent ally of epidemic disease, Cortés managed to conquer the Spanish empire. Almost immediately, Spanish galleons laden with Aztec gold traveled across the Atlantic, transforming Spain into a world power and fueling a European contest for the wealth of the New World.

Because of Cortés's success, numerous other conquistadors dreamed of finding another Mexico but instead found failure and disappointment. One of the most famous involved the tales of riches from the legendary Seven Cities of Cíbola. Because Mexico had proved to be so wealthy, many Spanish officials and explorers assumed that the lands to the north must have similar riches. Rumors about other cities filled with gold, fueled by inaccurate reports from priests and military leaders, convinced the leadership of New Spain to mount several expeditions.

For most Europeans, however, the New World presented dangerous Native peoples and land with few obvious riches. The French started late in the imperial endeavors of the sixteenth century. They were driven out of Florida by the Spanish in the 1580s and were harassed along the Atlantic coast by the English, so they headed north to what is now Canada. Samuel de Champlain, an agent of the Royal Canadian Company, organized a New World settlement specifically to trade furs with the Indians. Quebec, founded by Champlain in 1608, became the center of the Canadian fur trade. The French pursuit of fur fostered a working relationship between French traders, priests, and Native Americans. Champlain recognized his dependence on the Indians for success in the fur trade and developed a complex set of alliances with the tribes of the Great Lakes region. He also relied on Jesuit priests, who first arrived in 1611, to learn Indian languages and to act as mediators between the French and various Indian tribes. Yet even though the French empire spread thinly across North

America, it had a devastating impact. Epidemic disease killed nearly 75 percent of some Native nations.

The documents in this chapter, written by both Native and Spanish peoples during the 1500s and 1600s to inform their rulers about conditions in the New World, show the complexities conquest. The Catholic faith stood at the center of the Spanish world and priests, soldiers, and settlers believed a Christian God stood behind their actions. An Aztec account describes the confusion and fear that Cortés and his soldiers created on their arrival, while a letter from Fray Bartolome de Las Casas paints a graphic picture of violent conquest. Another selection is a description of the legendary city of Cíbola, one by Fray Marcos de Niza, who insisted on its existence. The final two selections, written by a French priest and a Micmac elder demonstrate cultural misperceptions around religion and social life in early New France.

AS YOU READ: Think about what these documents tell you about the people who produced them. How did expectations filter what these writers actually saw? What surprised the Spanish? Native Americans? Are there similarities between Indian and European accounts? Where does the word *Indian* come from, and what are the challenges of using it to describe indigenous Americans? Did Spanish ideas about the Native peoples change between the Cortés descriptions in 1519 and those of Coronado in 1542?

5. ENFORCING CHRISTIANITY ON ANOTHER WORLD

The rulers of Europe, especially those of Portugal and Spain, who were the first to send soldiers and explorers west, viewed themselves as servants of a Catholic God. Part of everyone's goal in the new world was to create a model of Catholic Christian society in every place they found. They believed there was only one true religion ruled by the Catholic pope in Rome and that any other religion was false. Soldiers and priests who arrived in Native communities in the Americas carried with them a document that they read aloud to everyone they met.

This Requerimiento, written by Spanish lawyers, explained that the Spanish had a legal right to conquest and that all Native people were now required to submit to Spanish rule and the Catholic pope. Whether or not Native people understood the Spanish document, just reading it gave conquistadors and priests a legal right to attack, enslave, or kill Native people who didn't submit. How does this document lay out a Spanish worldview? How does it mix legal and religious languages? How does the document combine threat and promise? What might Native people have made of such a first meeting and this formal reading, given that they didn't speak Spanish?

Palacios Rubios

The Requerimiento

1513[1]

On the part of the King, Don Fernando, and of Doña Juana, his daughter, Queen of Castile and León, subduers of the barbarous nations, we their servants notify and make known to you, as best we can, that the Lord our God, Living and Eternal, created the Heaven and the Earth, and one man and one woman, of whom you and we, all the men of the world, were and are descendants, and all those who came after us. But, on account of the multitude which has sprung from this man and woman in the five thousand years since the world was created, it was necessary that some men should go one way and some another, and that they should be divided into many kingdoms and provinces, for in one alone they could not be sustained.

Of all these nations God our Lord gave charge to one man, called St. Peter, that he should be Lord and Superior of all the men in the world, that all should obey him, and that he should be the head of the whole human race, wherever men should live, and under whatever law, sect, or belief they should be; and he gave him the world for his kingdom and jurisdiction.

And he commanded him to place his seat in Rome as the spot most fitting to rule the world from; but also he permitted him to have his seat in any other part of the world, and to judge and govern all Christians, Moors, Jews, Gentiles, and all other sects. This man was called Pope, as if to say, Admirable Great Father and Governor of men.

The men who lived in that time obeyed that St. Peter and took him for Lord, King, and Superior of the universe; so also they have regarded the others who after him have been elected to the pontificate, and so has it been continued even till now and will continue till the end of the world. One of these Pontiffs [popes] who succeeded that St. Peter as Lord of the world, in the dignity and seat which I have before mentioned, made donation of these isles and Tierra-firme to the aforesaid King and Queen and to their successors, our lords, with all that there are in these territories, as is contained in certain writings which passed upon the subject as aforesaid, which you can see if you wish.

So their Highnesses are kings and lords of these islands and land of Tierra-firme by virtue of this donation: and some islands, and indeed almost all those to whom this has been notified, have received and served their Highnesses, as lords and kings, in the way that subjects ought to do, with good will, without any resistance, immediately, without delay, when they were informed of the aforesaid facts. . . .

---

1. Juan López de Palacios Rubios, "The Requirimiento" 1513, English Translation, http://en .wikipedia.org/wiki/Requerimiento#Requerimiento_translation

If you do so, you will do well, and that which you are obliged to do to their Highnesses, and we in their name shall receive you in all love and charity, and shall leave you, your wives, and your children, and your lands, free without servitude, that you may do with them and with yourselves freely that which you like and think best, and they shall not compel you to turn Christians, unless you yourselves, when informed of the truth, should wish to be converted to our Holy Catholic Faith, as almost all the inhabitants of the rest of the islands have done. And, besides this, their Highnesses award you many privileges and exemptions and will grant you many benefits.

But, if you do not do this, and maliciously make delay in it, I certify to you that, with the help of God, we shall powerfully enter into your country, and shall make war against you in all ways and manners that we can, and shall subject you to the yoke and obedience of the Church and of their Highnesses; we shall take you and your wives and your children, and shall make slaves of them, and as such shall sell and dispose of them as their Highnesses may command; and we shall take away your goods, and shall do you all the mischief and damage that we can, as to vassals who do not obey, and refuse to receive their lord, and resist and contradict him; and we protest that the deaths and losses which shall accrue from this are your fault, and not that of their Highnesses, or ours, nor of these cavaliers who come with us. And that we have said this to you and made this Requisition, we request the notary here present to give us his testimony in writing, and we ask the rest who are present that they should be witnesses of this Requisition.

6. AN AZTEC VIEW OF EUROPEANS

When Montezuma, the ruler of the Aztecs, heard rumors that strange white men had arrived on the coast, he immediately sent soldiers out to investigate. Such rumors were not good news for Montezuma, who ruled over a complex alliance of nations. According to the Aztec calendar, they had reached the end of an important ritual cycle, a period of uncertainty filled with omens and predictions. The strangers could be gods, according to some visionaries, or simply a new group of people to be brought under Aztec control. The reports brought back by Aztec soldiers had a great impact on Montezuma's decision about how to deal with this threat.

Although no firsthand Aztec accounts of this first encounter survive, this document, which is part of a history of the conquest written by a Spanish priest in the 1550s, is as close to an Aztec point of view as we can get. The priest, Bernardino de Sahagún, learned Indian languages, collected documents, and interviewed people who remembered the conquest. This selection first describes the initial meeting between Cortés and Montezuma's messengers and then Montezuma's reaction to the report given by the messengers on their return. What surprised the Aztecs most about the Spanish? Why did Montezuma tell his men to treat the strangers like gods? How did the Aztec religion affect Montezuma's decisions? In view of how this document was written, how might it be biased?

Bernardino de Sahagún
Aztec Messengers Report to Montezuma
1519[1]

Fifth Chapter, Where It Is Said What Happened When Moteucçoma's (Montezuma) Messengers Went into Don Hernando Cortés's Boat

Then they climbed up, carrying in their arms the goods. When they had gotten up into the boat, each of them made the earth-eating gesture before the Captain. Then they addressed him, saying,

"May the god attend: his agent Moteucçoma who is in charge in Mexico for him addresses him and says, 'The god is doubly welcome.'"

Then they dressed up the Captain. They put on him the crown and the green-stone serpent earplugs. And they put the sleeveless jacket on him, and around his neck they put the plaited green-stone neckband with the golden disk in the middle. On his lower back they tied the back mirror, and also they tied behind him the cloak called a *tzitzilli.* And on his legs they placed the green-stone bands with the golden bells. And they gave him, placing it on his arm, the shield with gold and shells crossing, on whose edge were spread quetzal feathers, with a quetzal banner. And they laid the obsidian sandals before him.

And the other three outfits, the gods' appurtenances, they only arranged in rows before him.

When this had been done, the Captain said to them, "Is this everything you have by way of greeting and rapprochement?"

They answered, "That is all with which we have come, o our lord."

Then the Captain ordered that they be tied up; they put irons on their feet and necks. When this had been done they shot off the cannon. And at this point the messengers truly fainted and swooned; one after another they swayed and fell, losing consciousness. And the Spaniards lifted them into a sitting position and gave them wine to drink. Then they gave them food, fed them, with which they regained strength and got their breath back.

When this had been done the Captain said to them, "Do listen, I have found out and heard that by what they say these Mexica are very strong, great warriors, able to throw others down. Where there is one of them he can chase, push aside, overcome, and turn back his enemies, even though there should be ten or twenty. Now I wish to be satisfied, I want to see you, I want to try out how

1. Bernardino de Sahagún. *Florentine Codex: General History of the Things of New Spain* (1585). Reprinted in *We People Here: Nahuatl Accounts of the Conquest of Mexico,* ed. James Lockhart (Berkeley: University of California Press, 1993), 70–76, 80–84.

strong and manly you are." Then he gave them leather shields, iron swords, and iron lances. [He said,]

"Well now, very early in the morning, as dawn is about to come, we will struggle against each other, we will challenge each other, we will find out by comparison who will fall down first."

They answered the Captain, saying, "May the lord pay heed, this is not at all what his agent Moteucçoma ordered us. All we came to do was to greet and salute you. We were not charged with what the lord wishes. If we should do that, won't Moteucçoma be very angry with us because of it, won't he destroy us for it?"

Then the Captain said, "No indeed; it is simply to be done. I want to see and behold it, for word has gone to Spain that you are very strong, great warriors. Eat while it is still before dawn, and I will eat then too. Outfit yourselves well."

Sixth Chapter, Where It Is Said How Moteucçoma's Messengers Came
Back Here to Mexico to Tell Moteucçoma What They Had Seen

Then [Cortés] let them go. [The Spaniards] lowered them into their boat, and when they had descended into the boat, they paddled hard; each one paddled as hard as he could, and some used their hands to paddle. They fled with all possible speed, saying to one another as they came, "O warriors, exert all your strength, paddle hard! Let's not do something [wrong] here, lest something happen to us!" . . .

Then they quickly got on their way and soon reached Mexico. It was night when they got there; they came in by night.

During this time Moteucçoma neither slept nor touched food. Whatever he did, he was abstracted; it seemed as though he was ill at ease, frequently sighing. He tired and felt weak. He no longer found anything tasteful, enjoyable, or amusing.

Therefore he said, "What is to come of us? Who in the world must endure it? Will it not be me [as ruler]? My heart is tormented, as though chile water were poured on it; it greatly burns and smarts. Where in the world [are we to turn], o our lord?"

Then [the messengers] notified those who guarded [Moteucçoma], who kept watch at the head of his bed, saying to them, "Even if he is asleep, tell him, 'Those whom you sent out on the sea have come back.'"

But when they went to tell him, he replied, "I will not hear it here. I will hear it at the Coacalco; let them go there." And he gave orders, saying, "Let some captives be covered with chalk [for sacrifice]."

Then the messengers went to the Coacalco, and so did Moteucçoma. Thereupon the captives died in their presence; they cut open their chests and sprinkled their blood on the messengers. (The reason they did it was that they had gone to very dangerous places and had seen, gazed on the countenances of, and spoken to the gods.)

Seventh Chapter, Where Is Told the Account
That the Messengers Who Went to See the Boat
Gave to Moteucçoma

When this was done, they talked to Moteucçoma, telling him what they had beheld, and they showed him what [the Spaniards'] food was like.

And when he heard what the messengers reported, he was greatly afraid and taken aback, and he was amazed at their food. It especially made him faint when he heard how the guns went off at [the Spaniards'] command, sounding like thunder, causing people actually to swoon, blocking the ears. And when it went off, something like a ball came out from inside, and fire went showering and spitting out. And the smoke that came from it had a very foul stench, striking one in the face. And if they shot at a hill, it seemed to crumble and come apart. And it turned a tree to dust; it seemed to make it vanish, as though someone had conjured it away. Their war gear was all iron. They clothed their bodies in iron, they put iron on their heads, their swords were iron, their bows were iron, and their shields and lances were iron.

And their deer that carried them were as tall as the roof. And they wrapped their bodies all over; only their faces could be seen, very white. Their faces were the color of limestone and their hair yellow-reddish, though some had black hair. They had long beards, also yellow-reddish. [The hair of some] was tightly curled. And their food was like fasting food, very large, white, not heavy, like chaff, like dried maize stalks, as tasty as maize stalk flour, a bit sweet or honeyed, honeyed and sweet to eat.

And their dogs were huge creatures, with their ears folded over and their jowls dragging. They had burning eyes, eyes like coals, yellow and fiery. They had thin, gaunt flanks with the rib lines showing; they were very tall. They did not keep quiet, they went about panting, with their tongues hanging down. They had spots like a jaguar's, they were varicolored.

When Moteucçoma heard it, he was greatly afraid; he seemed to faint away, he grew concerned and disturbed.

Eighth Chapter, Where It Is Said How Moteucçoma
Sent Witches, Wizards, and Sorcerers to Do Something
to the Spaniards

Then at that time Moteucçoma sent out emissaries. Those whom he sent were all bad people, soothsayers and witches. He also sent elders, strong warriors, to see to all [the Spaniards] needed as to food: turkey hens, eggs, white tortillas, and whatever they might request, and to look after them well so that they would be satisfied in every way. He sent captives in case [the Spaniards] should drink their blood. And the emissaries did as indicated.

But when [the Spaniards] saw it, they were made sick to their stomachs, spitting, rubbing their eyelids, blinking, shaking their heads. And [the emissaries] sprinkled blood in the food, they bloodied it, which made their stomachs turn and disgusted them, because of the great stench of the blood.

Moteucçoma did this because he took them for gods, considered them gods, worshiped them as gods. They were called and given the name of gods who have come from heaven, and the blacks were called soiled gods. . . .

7. QUESTIONING CONQUEST

In 1542, Bartolome de Las Casas wrote A Short Account of the Destruction of the Indies. *This book, a searing attack on the motives and practices of Spanish conquistadors, was intended to warn the new king of Spain, Philip II, of the horrors being committed in his name. De Las Casas, a settler who had arrived with Columbus's great fleet in 1502, lived in Hispaniola (present-day Haiti and the Dominican Republic) and became a priest in 1510. By 1515, he had witnessed so much brutality toward Indians on the islands of Hispaniola and Cuba that he began a relentless demand for change. Because his books were read worldwide, their horrific descriptions established an image of Spanish conquest, called the Black Legend, that persisted for three hundred years. His preaching and writing convinced Spanish and Portuguese governments to pass laws curbing the violence. This selection describes Spanish settlement practices and the destruction of the people of Hispaniola through disease and military conquest. What kinds of words did Las Casas use to describe Europeans and Indians? How were his descriptions different from those of other Europeans? Where do you see evidence of his ideas about the importance of Christianity? What was Las Casas's plan for the Indians?*

Bartolomé de Las Casas
From *A Short Account of the Destruction of the Indies*
1542[1]

The Americas were discovered in 1492, and the first Christian settlements established by the Spanish the following year. It is accordingly forty-nine years now since Spaniards began arriving in numbers in this part of the world. They first settled the large and fertile island of Hispaniola, which boasts six hundred leagues of coastline and is surrounded by a great many other large islands, all of them, as I saw for myself, with as high a native population as anywhere on earth. . . .

God made all the peoples of this area, many and varied as they are, as open and as innocent as can be imagined. The simplest people in the world—unassuming, long-suffering, unassertive, and submissive—they are without malice or guile, and are utterly faithful and obedient both to their own native lords

---

1. Bartolomé de Las Casas, *A Short Account of the Destruction of the Indies,* trans. Nigel Griffen (New York: Penguin, 1992), 9–17.

and to the Spaniards in whose service they now find themselves. Never quarrelsome or belligerent or boisterous, they harbour no grudges and do not seek to settle old scores; indeed, the notions of revenge, rancour, and hatred are quite foreign to them. At the same time, they are among the least robust of human beings: their delicate constitutions make them unable to withstand hard work or suffering and render them liable to succumb to almost any illness, no matter how mild. . . . They are also among the poorest people on the face of the earth; they own next to nothing and have no urge to acquire material possessions. As a result they are neither ambitious nor greedy, and are totally uninterested in worldly power. Their diet is every bit as poor and as monotonous, in quantity and in kind, as that enjoyed by the Desert Fathers. . . . They are innocent and pure in mind and have a lively intelligence, all of which makes them particularly receptive to learning and understanding the truths of our Catholic faith and to being instructed in virtue; indeed, God has invested them with fewer impediments in this regard than any other people on earth. Once they begin to learn of the Christian faith they become so keen to know more, to receive the Sacraments, and to worship God, that the missionaries who instruct them do truly have to be men of exceptional patience and forbearance; and over the years I have time and again met Spanish laymen who have been so struck by the natural goodness that shines through these people that they frequently can be heard to exclaim: "These would be the most blessed people on earth if only they were given the chance to convert to Christianity."

It was upon these gentle lambs, imbued by the Creator with all the qualities we have mentioned, that from the very first day they clapped eyes on them the Spanish fell like ravening wolves upon the fold, or like tigers and savage lions who have not eaten meat for days. The pattern established at the outset has remained unchanged to this day, and the Spaniards still do nothing save tear the natives to shreds, murder them and inflict upon them untold misery, suffering and distress, tormenting, harrying and persecuting them mercilessly. . . . When the Spanish first journeyed there, the indigenous population of the island of Hispaniola stood at some three million; today only two hundred survive. The island of Cuba . . . is now to all intents and purposes uninhabited; and two other large, beautiful and fertile islands, Puerto Rico and Jamaica, have been similarly devastated. Not a living soul remains today on any of the islands of the Bahamas, which lie to the north of Hispaniola and Cuba, even though every single one of the sixty or so islands in the group, as well as those known as the Isles of Giants and others in the area, both large and small, is more fertile and more beautiful than the Royal Gardens in Seville and the climate is as healthy as anywhere on earth. The native population, which once numbered some five hundred thousand, was wiped out by forcible expatriation to the island of Hispaniola, a policy adopted by the Spaniards in an endeavour to make up losses among the indigenous population of that island. . . .

On the mainland, we know for sure that our fellow-countrymen have, through their cruelty and wickedness, depopulated and laid waste an area which once boasted more than ten kingdoms, each of them larger in area than the whole of the Iberian Peninsula. The whole region, once teeming with human beings, is now deserted over a distance of more than two thousand leagues: a distance, that is, greater than the journey from Seville to Jerusalem and back again.

At a conservative estimate, the despotic, and diabolical behaviour of the Christians has, over the last forty years, led to the unjust and totally unwarranted deaths of more than twelve million souls, women and children among them, and there are grounds for believing my own estimate of more than fifteen million to be nearer the mark.

There are two main ways in which those who have travelled to this part of the world pretending to be Christians have uprooted these pitiful peoples and wiped them from the face of the earth. First, they have waged war on them: unjust, cruel, bloody and tyrannical war. Second, they have murdered anyone and everyone who has shown the slightest sign of resistance, or even of wishing to escape the torment to which they have subjected him. This latter policy has been instrumental in suppressing the native leaders, and, indeed, given that the Spaniards normally spare only women and children, it has led to the annihilation of all adult males, whom they habitually subject to the harshest and most iniquitous and brutal slavery that man has ever devised for his fellow-men, treating them, in fact, worse than animals. All the many and infinitely varied ways that have been devised for oppressing these peoples can be seen to flow from one or other of these two diabolical and tyrannical policies.

The reason the Christians have murdered on such a vast scale and killed anyone and everyone in their way is purely and simply greed. They have set out to line their pockets with gold and to amass private fortunes as quickly as possible so that they can then assume a status quite at odds with that into which they were born. Their insatiable greed and overweening ambition know no bounds; the land is fertile and rich, the inhabitants simple, forbearing and submissive. . . .

Hispaniola

As we have said, the island of Hispaniola was the first to witness the arrival of Europeans and the first to suffer the wholesale slaughter of its people and the devastation and depopulation of the land. It all began with the Europeans taking native women and children both as servants and to satisfy their own base appetites; then, not content with what the local people offered them of their own free will (and all offered as much as they could spare), they started taking for themselves the food the natives contrived to produce by the sweat of their brows, which was in all honesty little enough. Since what a European will consume in a single day normally supports three native households of ten persons each for a whole month, and since the newcomers began to subject the locals to other vexations, assaults, and iniquities, the people began to realize that these men could not, in truth, have descended from the heavens. Some of them started to conceal what food they had, others decided to send their women and children into hiding, and yet others took to the hills to get away from the brutal and ruthless cruelty that was being inflicted on them. The Christians punched them, boxed their ears and flogged them in order to track down the local leaders, and the whole shameful process came to a head when one of the European commanders raped the wife of the paramount chief of the entire island. It was then that the locals began to think up ways of driving the Europeans out of their lands and to take up arms against them. Their weapons, however, were flimsy and ineffective both in attack and in defence (and, indeed, war in the Americas is no more deadly than our jousting, or than many European children's games) and, with their horses and swords and lances, the Spaniards easily fended them off, killing them and committing all kind of atrocities against them.

They forced their way into native settlements, slaughtering everyone they found there, including small children, old men, pregnant women, and even women who had just given birth. They hacked them to pieces, slicing open their bellies with their swords as though they were so many sheep herded into a pen. They even laid wagers on whether they could manage to slice a man in two at a stroke, or cut an individual's head from his body, or disembowel him with a single blow of their axes. They grabbed suckling infants by the feet and, ripping them from their mothers' breasts, dashed them headlong against the rocks. Others, laughing and joking all the while, threw them over their shoulders into a river, shouting: "Wriggle, you little perisher." They slaughtered anyone and everyone in their path, on occasion running through a mother and her baby with a single thrust of their swords. They spared no one, erecting especially wide gibbets on which they could string their victims up with their feet just off the ground and then burn them alive thirteen at a time, in honour of our Saviour and the twelve Apostles, or tie dry straw to their bodies and set fire to it. Some they chose to keep alive and simply cut their wrists, leaving their hands dangling, saying to them: "Take this letter"—meaning that their sorry condition would act as a warning to those hiding in the hills. The way they normally dealt with the native leaders and nobles was to tie them to a kind of griddle consisting of sticks resting on pitchforks driven into the ground and then grill them over a slow fire, with the result that they howled in agony and despair as they died a lingering death.

It once happened that I myself witnessed their grilling of four or five local leaders in this fashion (and I believe they had set up two or three other pairs of grills alongside so that they might process other victims at the same time) when the poor creatures' howls came between the Spanish commander and his sleep. He gave orders that the prisoners were to be throttled, but the man in charge of the execution detail, who was more bloodthirsty than the average common hangman (I know his identity and even met some relatives of his in Seville), was loath to cut short his private entertainment by throttling them and so he personally went round ramming wooden bungs into their mouths to stop them making such a racket and deliberately stoked the fire so that they would take just as long to die as he himself chose. I saw all these things for myself and many others besides. And, since all those who could do so took to the hills and mountains in order to escape the clutches of these merciless and inhuman butchers, these mortal enemies of human kind trained hunting dogs to track them down—wild dogs who would savage a native to death as soon as look, at him, tearing him to shreds and devouring his flesh as though he were a pig. These dogs wrought havoc among the natives and were responsible for much carnage. And when, as happened on the odd occasion, the locals did kill a European, as, given the enormity of the crimes committed against them, they were in all justice fully entitled to, the Spanish came to an unofficial agreement among themselves that for every European killed one hundred natives would be executed.

8. MYTHICAL WEALTH

Fray Marcos de Niza gained instant fame when he reported the existence of the fabulous Seven Cities of Cíbola, which had long been rumored to exist some-where in what is now the American Southwest. De Niza, sent by the ruler of New Spain to investigate the region and the Indians living within it, moved through-out the area in 1538 until he saw a city "bigger than the city of Mexico" on the horizon. Mysteriously, he did not investigate further but hurried back to report his findings. Because of his report, the Spanish government mounted a huge expedition, led by Francisco Vasquez de Coronado, into the interior Southwest in 1540. In this excerpt from his account, de Niza describes his search for Cíbola and the Indians who lived in the region. How was de Niza received by the Indi-ans? How did his expectations about Cíbola affect his decisions? Why would de Niza have been so eager to come back with a report verifying the existence of these golden cities?

Marcos de Niza
Account of the Legend of Cíbola
1538

. . . Here they had as much information of Cíbola, as in New Spain they have of Mexico and in Peru of Cuzco. They described in detail the houses, streets and squares of the town, like people who had been there many times, and they were wearing various objects brought from there, which they had obtained by their services, like the Indians I had previously met. I said to them that it was not possible that the houses should be in the manner which they described to me, so to make me understand they took earth and ashes and mixed them with water, and showed how the stone is placed and the edifice reared, placing stone and mortar till the required height is reached. I asked them if the men of that country had wings to climb those storeys; they laughed and explained to me a ladder, as well as I could do, and they took a stick and placed it over their heads and said it was that height from storey to storey. Here I was also given an account of the woolen cloth of Totonteac, where they say the houses are like those at Cíbola but better and bigger, and that it is a very great place and has no limit. . . .

So I turned to follow my route and was in that valley five days. It is so thickly populated with fine people and so provided with food that there would be enough to supply more than three hundred horsemen. It is all watered and is like a garden. There are villages at every half or quarter league or so. In each of them I had a very long account of Cíbola and they spoke to me in detail about it, as people would who went there each year to earn their living. Here I found a man who was a native of Cíbola. He told me he had fled from the governor whom the lord had placed there in Cíbola—for the lord of these seven cities lives and has his residence in one of them, which is called Ahacus, and in the others he has placed persons who command for him. This citizen of Cíbola is a man of good disposition, somewhat old and much more intelligent than the natives of the valley and those I had formerly met; he told me that he wished to go with me so that I might procure his pardon. I interrogated him carefully and he told me that Cíbola is a big city, that it has a large population and many streets and squares, and that in some parts of the city there are very great houses, ten storeys high, in which the chiefs meet on certain days of the year. He corroborated what I had already been told, that the houses are constructed out of stone and lime, and he said that the doors and fronts of the principal houses are of turquoise; he added that the others of the seven cities are similar, though some are bigger, and that the most important is Ahacus. . . .

He likewise told me that to the south-east there is a kingdom named Totonteac, which he said was the biggest, most populous, and the richest in the world, and that there they wore clothes made of the same stuff as mine, and others of a more delicate material obtained from the animals of which I had already had a description; the people were highly cultured and different from those I had hitherto seen. He further informed me that there is another province and very great kingdom, which is called Acus—for there are Ahacus and Acus; Ahacus, with the aspiration, is one of the seven cities, the most important one, and Acus, without the aspiration, is a kingdom and province by itself.

He corroborated what I had been told concerning the clothes worn in Cíbola and added that all the people of that city sleep in beds raised above the floor, with fabrics and with tilts above to cover the beds. He said that he would go with me to Cíbola and beyond, if I desired to take him along. I was given the same account in this town by many other persons, though not in such great detail.

I travelled in this valley three days and the natives made for me all the feasts and rejoicings that they could. Here in this valley I saw more than two thousand oxhides, extremely well cured; I saw a very large quantity of turquoises and necklaces thereof, as in the places I had left behind, and all said that they came from the city of Cíbola. They know this place as well as I would know what I hold in my hands, and they are similarly acquainted with the kingdoms of Marata, Acus and Totonteac. Here in this valley they brought to me a skin, half as big again as that of a large cow, and told me that it was from an animal which has only one horn on its forehead and that this horn is curved towards its chest and then there sticks out a straight point, in which they said there was so much strength, that no object, no matter how hard, could fail to break when struck with it. They averred that there were many of these animals in that country. The color of the skin is like that of the goat and the hair is as long as one's finger. . . .

At this juncture I met an Indian, the son of one of the chiefs who were journeying with me, who had gone in company with the negro Stephen. [Esteban Dorantes, a black slave who had accompanied an earlier expedition through the Southwest and now worked as a guide for de Niza.] This man showed fatigue in his countenance, had his body covered with sweat, and manifested the deepest sadness in his whole person. He told me that, at a days march before coming to Cíbola, Stephen according to his custom sent ahead messengers with his calabash, that they might know he was coming. . . . He continued his journey till he arrived at the city of Cíbola, where he found people who would not consent to let him enter, who put him in a big house which was outside the city, and who at once took away from him all that he carried, his articles of barter and the turquoises and other things which he had received on the road from the Indians. They left him that night without giving anything to eat or drink either to him or to those that were with him. The following morning my informant was thirsty and went out of the house to drink from a nearby stream. When he had been there a few moments he saw Stephen fleeing away pursued by the people of the city and they killed some of those who were with him. When this Indian saw this he concealed himself and made his way up the stream, then crossed over and regained the road of the desert.

At these tidings, some of the Indians who were with me commenced to weep. As for myself, the wretched news made me fear I should be lost. I feared not so much to lose my life as not to be able to return to give a report of the greatness of the country, where God Our Lord might be so well served and his holy faith exalted and the royal domains of H. M. extended. In these circumstances I consoled them as best I could and told them that one ought not to give entire credence to that Indian, but they said to me with many tears that the Indian only related what he had seen. So I drew apart from the Indians to commend myself to Our Lord and to pray Him to guide this matter as He might best be served and to enlighten my mind. This done, I returned to the Indians and with a knife cut the cords of the packages of dry goods and articles of barter which I was carrying with me and which till then I had not touched nor given away any of the contents. I divided up the goods among all those chiefs and told them not to fear and to go along with me, which they did. . . .

[Two wounded Indians arrive and corroborate the story of the attack on Stephens's party.]

In view of what the Indians had related and the bad outlook for continuing my journey as I desired, I could not help but feel their loss and mine. God is witness of how much I desired to have someone of whom I could take counsel, for I confess I was at a loss what to do. I told them that Our Lord would chastize Cíbola and that when the Emperor knew what had happened he would send many Christians to punish its people. They did not believe me, because they say that no one can withstand the power of Cíbola. I begged them to be comforted and not to weep and consoled them with the best words I could muster, which would be too long to set down here. With this I left them and withdrew a stone's throw or two apart, to commend myself to God, and remained thus an hour and a half. . . . With these and many other words I pacified them somewhat, although there was still high feeling on account of the people killed. I asked that some of them should go to Cíbola, to see if any other Indian had escaped. . . .

9. THE MISSIONARY EFFORT IN NEW FRANCE

Between 1611 and 1764, more than three hundred Jesuits came to North America from France to work with the Indians. Instead of setting up permanent missions as the Spanish did, however, these priests lived among the Indians and learned their languages, habits, and ideas as a way of teaching them Christianity. Each year, the priests sent back elaborate reports about the tribes they had visited and their efforts at conversion. These reports, collectively called the "Jesuit Relations," are one of the most important sources for Indian and European history during this early period. This selection is by Jean de Brébeuf, a priest who had spent several years among the Huron Indians. He wrote these instructions to provide useful advice to other Jesuits about how to begin work in the New World. According to Brébeuf's report, what were the biggest challenges for the Jesuits? What kinds of success did Brébeuf hope to achieve? What were his assumptions about Indians? How do Brébeuf's views compare with De Las Casas's?

Jean de Brébeuf
"Instructions for the Fathers of Our Society Who Shall
Be Sent to the Hurons"
1637

The Fathers and Brethren whom God shall call to the holy Mission of the Hurons ought to exercise careful foresight in regard to all the hardships, annoyances, and perils that must be encountered in making this journey, in order to be prepared betimes for all emergencies that may arise.

You must have sincere affection for the Savages,—looking upon them as ransomed by the blood of the son of God, and as our Brethren with whom we are to pass the rest of our lives.

To conciliate the Savages, you must be careful never to make them wait for you in embarking.

You must provide yourself with a tinder box or with a burning mirror, or with both, to furnish them fire in the daytime to light their pipes, and in the evening when they have to encamp; these little services win their hearts.

You should try to eat their sagamité or salmagundi in the way they prepare it, although it may be dirty, half-cooked, and very tasteless. As to the other numerous things which may be unpleasant, they must be endured for the love of God, without saying anything or appearing to notice them.

It is well at first to take everything they offer, although you may not be able to eat it all; for, when one becomes somewhat accustomed to it, there is not too much.

You must try and eat at daybreak unless you can take your meal with you in the canoe; for the day is very long, if you have to pass it without eating. The Barbarians eat only at Sunrise and Sunset, when they are on their journeys.

You must be prompt in embarking and disembarking; and tuck up your gowns so that they will not get wet, and so that you will not carry either water or sand into the canoe. To be properly dressed, you must have your feet and legs bare; while crossing the rapids, you can wear your shoes, and, in the long portages, even your leggings.

You must so conduct yourself as not to be at all troublesome to even one of these Barbarians.

It is not well to ask many questions, nor should you yield to your desire to learn the language and to make observations on the way; this may be carried too far. You must relieve those in your canoe of this annoyance, especially as you cannot profit much by it during the work. Silence is a good equipment at such a time.

You must bear with their imperfections without saying a word, yes, even without seeming to notice them. Even if it be necessary to criticise anything, it must be done modestly, and with words and signs which evince love and not aversion. In short, you must try to be, and to appear, always cheerful.

Each one should be provided with half a gross of awls, two or three dozen little knives called jambettes (pocketknives), a hundred fish-hooks, with some beads of plain and colored glass, with which to buy fish or other articles when the tribes meet each other, so as to feast the Savages; and it would be well to say to them in the beginning, "Here is something with which to buy fish." Each one will try, at the portages, to carry some little thing, according to his strength; however little one carries, it greatly pleases the savages, if it be only a kettle.

You must not be ceremonious with the Savages, but accept the comforts they offer you, such as a good place in the cabin. The greatest conveniences are attended with very great inconvenience, and these ceremonies offend them.

Be careful not to annoy anyone in the canoe with your hat; it would be better to take your nightcap. There is no impropriety among the Savages.

Do not undertake anything unless you desire to continue it; for example, do not begin to paddle unless you are inclined to continue paddling. Take from the start the place in the canoe that you wish to keep; do not lend them your garments, unless you are willing to surrender them during the whole journey. It is easier to refuse at first than to ask them back, to change, or to desist afterwards.

Finally, understand that the Savages will retain the same opinion of you in their own country that they will have formed on the way; and one who has passed for an irritable and troublesome person will have considerable difficulty afterwards in removing this opinion. You have to do not only with those of your own canoe, but also (if it must be so stated) with all those of the country; you meet some today and others tomorrow, who do not fail to inquire, from those who brought you, what sort of man you are. It is almost incredible, how they observe and remember even the slightest fault. When you meet Savages on the way, as you cannot yet greet them with kind words, at least show them a cheerful face, and thus prove that you endure gayly the fatigues of the voyage. You will thus have put to good use the hardships on the way, and have already advanced considerably in gaining the affection of the Savages.

This is a lesson which is easy enough to learn, but very difficult to put into practice; for, leaving a highly civilized community, you fall into the hands of barbarous people who care but little for your Philosophy or your Theology. All the fine qualities which might make you loved and respected in France are like pearls trampled under the feet of swine, or rather mules, which utterly despise you when they see that you are not as good pack animals as they are. If you could go naked, and carry the load of a horse upon your back, as they do, then you would be wise according to their doctrine, and would be recognized as a great man, otherwise not. Jesus Christ is our true greatness; it is He alone and His cross that should be sought in running after these people, for, if you strive for anything else, you will find naught but bodily and spiritual affliction. But having found Jesus Christ in His cross, you have found the roses in the thorns, sweetness in bitterness, all in nothing.

10. A MICMAC INDIAN QUESTIONS FRENCH HABITS

As a fishing and hunting tribe crucial to both the fur trade and the fishing indus-try, the Micmac Indians of eastern Canada and northern New England had fre-quent contact with French settlers and traders. The French expected people like the Micmac, whom they regarded as savages and pitiable for their primitive liv-ing conditions, to adopt French ways. The Indians, however, found the wonders of French civilization less than impressive: French clothing was uncomfortable, French food tasted bad, French houses were hot, and French people seemed una-ble to function in forests. In this document, recorded and translated by a French missionary, a Micmac elder chastises French settlers for their weakness and wastefulness. What aspects of French life did the Micmacs find most surprising? Did any French things appeal to the Indians? How does this account compare to Aztec descriptions of the Spanish?

Micmac Elder
Speech to French Settlers
c. 1677

I am greatly astonished that the French have so little cleverness, as they seem to exhibit in the matter of which thou hast just told me on their behalf, in the effort to persuade us to convert our poles, our barks, and our wigwams into those houses of stone and of wood which are tall and lofty, according to their account, as these trees. Very well! But why now do men of five to six feet in height need houses which are sixty to eighty? For, in fact, as thou knowest very well thyself, Patriarch—do we not find in our own all the conveniences and the advantages that you have with yours, such as reposing, drinking, sleeping, eat-ing, and amusing ourselves with our friends when we wish? This is not all, my brother, hast thou as much ingenuity and cleverness as the Indians, who carry their houses and their wigwams with them so that they may lodge wheresoever they please, independently of any seignior whatsoever? Thou art not as bold nor as stout as we, because when thou goest on a voyage thou canst not carry upon thy shoulders thy buildings and thy edifices. Therefore it is necessary that thou preparest as many lodgings as thou makest changes of residence, or else thou lodgest in a hired house which does not belong to thee. As for us, we find our-selves secure from all these inconveniences, and we can always say, more truly than thou, that we are at home everywhere, because we set up our wigwams with ease wheresoever we go, and without asking permission of anybody. Thou reproachest us, very inappropriately, that our country is a little hell in contrast with France, which thou comparest to a terrestrial paradise, inasmuch as it yields thee, so thou sayest, every kind of provision in abundance. Thou sayest of us also that we are the most miserable and most unhappy of all men, living without religion, without manners, without honour, without social order, and, in a word, without any rules, like the beasts in our woods and our forests, lacking bread, wine, and a thousand other comforts which thou hast in superfluity in Europe. Well, my brother, if thou dost not yet know the real feelings which our Indians have towards thy country and towards all thy nation, it is proper that I inform thee at once. I beg thee now to believe that, all miserable as we seem in thine eyes, we consider ourselves nevertheless much happier than thou in this, that we are very content with the little that we have; and believe also once for all, I pray, that thou deceivest thyself greatly if thou thinkest to persuade us that thy country is better than ours. For if France, as thou sayest, is a little terrestrial paradise, art thou sensible to leave it? And why abandon wives, children, relatives, and friends? Why risk thy life and thy property every year, and why venture thyself with such risk, in any season whatsoever, to the storms and tempests of the sea in order to come to a strange and barbarous country which thou considerest the poorest and least fortunate of the world? Besides, since we are wholly convinced of the contrary, we scarcely take the trouble to go to France, because we fear, with good reason, lest we find little satisfaction there, seeing, in our own experience, that those who are natives thereof leave it every year in order to enrich themselves on our shores. We believe, further, that you are also incomparably poorer than we, and that you are only simple journeymen, valets, servants, and slaves, all masters and grand captains though you may appear, seeing that you glory in our old rags and in our miserable suits of beaver which can no longer be of use to us, and that you find among us, in the fishery for cod which you make in these parts, the wherewithal to comfort your misery and the poverty which oppresses you. As to us, we find all our riches and all our conveniences among ourselves, without trouble and without exposing our lives to the dangers in which you find yourselves constantly through your long voyages. And, whilst feeling compassion for you in the sweetness of our repose, we wonder at the anxieties and cares which you give yourselves night and day in order to load your ship. We see also that all your people live, as a rule, only upon cod which you catch among us. It is everlastingly nothing but cod—cod in the morning, cod at midday, cod at evening, and always cod, until things come to such a pass that if you wish some good morsels, it is at our expense; and you are obliged to have recourse to the Indians, whom you despise so much, and to beg them to go a-hunting that you may be regaled. Now tell me this one little thing, if thou hast any sense: Which of these two is the wisest and happiest—he who labours without ceasing and only obtains, and that with great trouble, enough to live on, or he who rests in comfort and finds all that he needs in the pleasure of hunting and fishing? It is true that we have not always had the use of bread and of wine which your France produces; but, in fact, before the arrival of the French in these parts, did not the Gaspesians live much longer than now? And if we have not any longer among us any of those old men of a hundred and thirty to forty years, it is only because we are gradually adopting your manner of living, for experience is making it very plain that those of us live longest who, despising your bread, your wine, and your brandy, are content with their natural food of beaver, of moose, of waterfowl, and fish, in accord with the custom of our ancestors and of all the Gaspesian nation. Learn now, my brother, once for all, because I must open to thee my heart: there is no Indian who does not consider himself infinitely more happy and more powerful than the French.

FURTHER READING

Clendinnen, Inga. *Aztecs: An Interpretation.* New York: Cambridge University Press, 1995.
Crosby, Alfred W. *The Columbian Exchange: Biological and Cultural Consequences of 1492.* Westport, CT: Greenwood Press, 1974.
Dickason, Olive Patricia. *A Concise History of Canada's First Nations.* New York: Oxford University Press, 2006.
Dunbar-Ortiz, Roxanne. *An Indigenous Peoples' History of the United States.* Boston: Beacon Books, 2014.
Greer, Allan. *The Jesuit Relations: Natives and Missionaries in Seventeenth-Century North America.* Boston: Bedford/St. Martin's, 2000.
Mann, Charles C. *1493: Uncovering the New World Columbus Created.* New York: Vintage Books, 2011.
Resendez, Andres. *A Land So Strange: The Epic Journey of Cabeza de Vaca* New York: Basic Books, 2007.
Sauer, Carl 0. *Sixteenth Century North America.* Berkeley: University of California Press, 1971.
Stannard, David E. *American Holocaust: The Conquest of the New World.* New York: Oxford University Press, 1992.
Weber, David J. *The Spanish Frontier in North America.* New Haven, CT: Yale University Press, 1992.

A European view of Quebec, 1699. This image, drawn by a French mapmaker, illustrates the mixing of Indian and European peoples that had occurred in North America at the start of the eighteenth century. Quebec appears as a briskly developing commercial city, with large buildings spreading up the hillside and a port filled with ships. It is apparent, however, that this is not a European city, since canoes paddle in the water next to European sailing vessels and Indians cook over a fire in the foreground. What conclusions might eighteenth-century Europeans have drawn about the New World from looking at this image?

From a map by J. B. L. Franquelin. Public Archives of Canada, Canadian Council of Archives.

Conquest and Revolt

3

Seventeenth-Century Wars on Two Frontiers

As European travelers realized that North America did not offer instant riches they could simply transport back home, they began to look to colonization and settlement. North America could provide raw materials for the mother country but only if European colonizers found a way to coerce indigenous Americans to provide the needed labor to grow, mine, and harvest raw materials. Forced labor, slavery, and captivity became a central part of early colonial efforts, as did converting Native peoples to Christianity. These twin goals, profit and conversion, both required military force and personal contact.

In the 1600s and 1700s, the major European players in North American colonization—the English, the Dutch, the French, and the Spanish—all built institutions that combined profit with conversion to Christianity. These ideas and ways of making a profit often clashed with Indian conceptions of how life should be organized and valued. In this early period, the English and the Dutch tended to operate on the edges of the continent, partly because their ventures were funded with private capital and partly because they had less interest in converting the Indians. The Spanish and the English, the focus of this chapter, had very different ways of making a living in North America. They developed relationships, both good and bad, with Native people. However, even though New

England towns and Spanish missions presented different challenges to both natives and newcomers, they both needed Indian knowledge and labor to make their "new worlds" work, and they put Christianity at the center of their plans.

Spreading Christianity, however, involved more than preaching and persuasion; it often involved forced conversion and slavery. Accepting Christianity meant that Indian peoples had to accept the Spanish or English king as their ruler and give up their lands to work for the new colonizers. When Indians resisted these demands, officials and soldiers often killed or enslaved them. Native people fought back fiercely and successfully. The mission system, which spread from Florida to California along the Spanish frontier in North America, reflected Spain's interwoven imperial and religious aims. The Spanish intended to create institutions that would transform the New World into New Spain and native peoples into tax-paying Christians. The missions would serve as a primary defense against other European powers and provide a way to control the Indians. In the sixteenth and seventeenth centuries, Spain concentrated its building efforts in Florida, where the first missions were built in 1566, and in New Mexico, where they were established in 1598.

The mission complex consisted of a central church and clusters of houses, often surrounded by lands settled on by the church and worked by Native peoples who lived nearby. To ensure both spiritual and economic success, the Spanish required that Natives live in the missions. The ideas was to convert them to Christianity and to have them learn Spanish habits, such as working in the fields, going to confession, attending Mass, and producing food and trade goods for the mission. Spanish soldiers, with guns and horses, policed the missions. The Indians in the missions may have taken on the outward signs of Catholicism, but few could be counted as real converts. Some absorbed pieces of Catholic ritual and language into their own religious traditions; others practiced Christianity in public and their own religions in private. In spite of their failure to win converts, the missions served as significant footholds for Spanish settlement in what would become Texas, New Mexico, Arizona, and California.

Native people paid a high price. The greatest cost exacted by the mission system was the massive death toll from epidemic disease. Germs carried by the Spanish spread quickly in the close living quarters of the missions; Indians died in huge numbers, and some tribes disappeared altogether. In the last decades of the 1600s, fighting intensified on the frontiers of both New England and New Spain and became outright rebellions. Though the timing of these outbreaks was coincidental, their causes were not. When European colonizers first arrived to remake North America into New England or New France or New Spain, the land's original inhabitants watched warily. But once they realized that the Europeans intended to stay, they resisted. In many cases, their resistance was so effective that it seriously threatened the future of European efforts to colonize North America. Amid epidemic disease and cultural assault, Indian people refused to give up their homes and their way of life. Powerful Indian nations allied with each other—and with other European nations—to wage war against European settlers, threatening settlers in frontier areas. Two clashes in particular exemplify the period's frontier turmoil: King Philip's War in New England (1675–76) and the Pueblo Revolt in New Mexico (1680).

In the English colonies, especially New England, Europeans and Indians came to blows because the colonists took land that Indians had always lived on. Finally, in New England in the early 1670s, tensions over land, hunting, and the fur trade provoked a devastating war. Much of the violence occurred between Indian nations, particularly as the expanding Iroquois Confederacy struggled to maintain its military control over New France and New England. In the summer of 1675, King Philip (or Metacom), the leader of the Wampanoag tribe and enemy of the Iroquois Confederacy, watched in frustration as his people lost land, legal status, and religious influence to English settlers. After several Wampanoags were arrested and hanged for burglary, King Philip united many of the New England tribes and initiated a series of lightning attacks against the settlers. In a matter of weeks, the Indians had burned towns and taken captives all over New England. Thousands of Indians and English were killed over the course of a year. Although King Philip's War ended when the powerful New York Iroquois allied themselves with the English, it marked the beginning of nearly a hundred years of bloody frontier fighting.

Similar tensions characterized life in frontier New Mexico. Like the New England tribes, the Pueblo peoples of the Rio Grande Valley were not immediately concerned when, in 1598, a small band of Spanish colonists and Franciscan priests, led by Juan de Oñate, arrived in northern New Mexico. The group came hoping to mine precious metals and establish Spanish towns. Although Oñate failed to find treasure or to build lasting settlements, the Franciscan priests were more successful. They moved into Pueblo communities, constructed churches, and became part of Indian life. Building on this foothold, they turned New Mexico into a center of missionary and settlement activity. The Pueblo Indians supplied the labor for both enterprises.

Because the Spanish offered the Pueblos, in their widely spread towns, protection from their traditional enemies, the Apaches and Navajos, the Pueblo peoples adapted to the Spanish and Franciscan presence. Eventually, however, Indian resentment over being used as slave labor, over the destruction of their religion and culture, and over the loss of their land ignited a powerful uprising. In the late summer of 1680, the Pueblos coordinated their efforts in a surprise attack against the Spanish, headquartered in Santa Fe. The rebels burned Spanish towns, destroyed churches, and killed more than four hundred settlers, including most of the region's priests. Surprised and outnumbered, the Spanish abandoned New Mexico, fleeing to what is now Texas. It took them more than fifteen years to regain control.

The selections in this chapter focus on how Native people responded to the pressures of European colonists, who arrived with the dual goals of making profits and converting Indians to Christianity. Native nations responded powerfully to these pressures. These documents, written by colonial officials, priests, and Native people, illustrate the tensions that arose along these new frontiers.

AS YOU READ: Think about the role of religion in settling the New World. How did religious concerns affect economic decisions? Why did the Spanish and the English think conversion was so important? Did Indians respond in different ways to Spanish and English pressures to convert or to trade? Did living together under frontier conditions change the ways in which Indians and Europeans viewed each other?

11. WAMPUM DIPLOMACY AND THE SIX IROQUOIS NATIONS

Iroquois and Dutch Treaty, 1613—The Two-Row Wampum Belt Controversy (see p. 45)

The William Penn and Lenape Agreement, Pennsylvania, 1682 (see p. 45)

Tradition credits the formation of the Iroquois confederacy, between 1570 and 1600, to Dekanawidah, a member of a Huron tribe. He had a vision about using rituals, to advance "peace, civil authority, righteousness, and the great law," and using wampum belts as appeals for unity. These wampum belts, made from strings of seashells from the Great Lakes, the Gulf of Mexico, and the Atlantic Ocean, were used to run meetings. Wearing and exchanging wampum enabled enemies to "hear" each other, whether they were from Europe or from North American. One of these is a two-row wampum belt from 1613 crafted from marine shells in white and purple. Its two parallel purple rows against a field of white beads represent the parallel paths and equal power of Dutch and Iroquoian development. The Iroquois translated the belt to say, "We will not be like Father and Son, but like Brothers. This wampum belt confirms our words. . . . Neither of us will try to steer the other's vessel." The other wampum belt was given to William Penn when he made his treaty of peace with the Lenape Indians and was intended to remind English settlers of their "brotherly love" and "perpetual friendship" with local Indians. How might other people "read" such a document? Why did Iroquois leaders value these shells? Can you imagine how these were used as visual signals? How might European observers have interpreted or misinterpreted what a wampum belt signified?

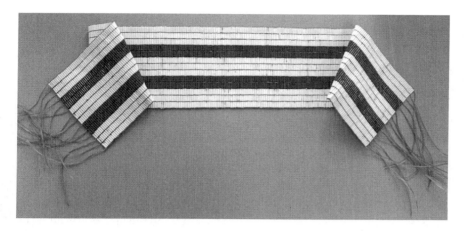

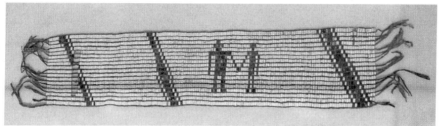

Wampum belts. *Top,* two-row wampum belt, 1613. Rochester New York Museum and Science Center; *bottom,* William Penn wampum belt, 1683. Penn Treaty Museum, Philadelphia, Pennsylvania.

12. A WHITE WOMAN'S TALE OF CAPTIVITY

In February 1676, a band of southern New England Wampanoag and Nipmucs attacked the town of Lancaster, Massachusetts, capturing Mary Rowlandson and her three children. Rowlandson spent three months with them as they battled their way through all of Massachusetts. This kind of captivity was long a part of Native life—captives replaced women and children lost in war and in epidemics, who were often treated well by their captors. Rowlandson, from an entirely different world, did not see anything but violence. Though she lost her children, she survived because she adapted to Indian ways. As King Philip's War ground to an end, the Indians released her and other captives in exchange for ransom payments. Rowlandson attributed her survival to her Puritan faith and published a narrative of her experience as evidence of God's support of the New England colonists' cause. First published in 1682, it became an instant best seller. This excerpt illustrates Rowlandson's horror at her situation, but it also reveals the deep cultural differences between the English and the Indians. What did Rowlandson consider the most difficult aspects of her captivity? How did her faith help her understand her circumstances? What details of Indian life do we learn of from her account? Compare her attitude toward the Indians with that of Spanish missionaries and officials.

Mary Rowlandson

From *The Sovereignty and Goodness of God*
1682[1]

On the tenth of February 1675, Came the *Indians* with great numbers upon *Lancaster:* Their first coming was about Sun-rising; hearing the noise of some Guns, we looked out; several Houses were burning, and the Smoke ascending to Heaven. There were five persons taken in one house, the Father, and the Mother and a sucking Child, they knockt on the head; the other two they took and carried away alive. There were two others, who being out of their Garison upon some occasion were set upon; one was knockt on the head, the other escaped: Another there was who running along was shot and wounded, and fell down; he begged of them his life, promising them Money (as they told me) but they would not hearken to him but knockt him in head, and stript him naked, and split open his Bowels. Another seeing many of the *Indians* about his Barn, ventured and went out, but was quickly shot down. There were three others belonging to the same Garison who were killed; the *Indians* getting up upon the roof of the Barn, had advantage to shoot down upon them over their Fortification. Thus these murtherous wretches went on, burning, and destroying before them.

At length they came and beset our own house, and quickly it was the dolefullest day that ever mine eyes saw. The House stood upon the edge of a hill; some of the *Indians* got behind the hill, others into the Barn, and others behind any thing that could shelter them; from all which places they shot against the House, so that the Bullets seemed to fly like hail; and quickly they wounded one man among us, then another, and then a third. About two hours (according to my observation, in that amazing time) they had been about the house before they prevailed to fire it . . . . they fired it once and one ventured out and quenched it, but they quickly fired again, and that took. Now is that dreadfull hour come, that I have often heard of (in time of War, as it was the case of others) but now mine eyes see it. Some in our house were fighting for their lives, others wallowing in their blood, the House on fire over our heads, and the bloody Heathen ready to knock us on the head, if we stirred out. Now might we hear Mothers & Children crying out for themselves, and one another, *Lord,*

---

1. Mary Rowlandson, *The Sovereignty and Goodness of God,* ed. Neal Salisbury (1682; Boston: Bedford Books, 1997), 68–71, 87–91, 101–2, 104–7.

What shall we do? Then I took my Children (and one of my sisters, hers) to go forth and leave the house: but as soon as we came to the door and appeared, the *Indians* shot so thick that the bullets rattled against the House, as if one had taken an handfull of stones and threw them, so that we were fain to give back. We had six stout Dogs belonging to our Garrison, but none of them wou'd stir, though another time, if any *Indian* had come to the door, they were ready to fly upon him and tear him down. The Lord hereby would make us the more to acknowledge his hand, and to see that our help is always in him. But out we must go, the fire increasing, and coming along behind us, roaring, and the Indians gaping before us with their Guns, Spears and Hatchets to devour us. No sooner were we out of the House, but my Brother in Law (being before wounded, in defending the house, in or near the throat) fell down dead, whereat the *Indians* scornfully shouted, and hallowed, and were presently upon him, stripping off his cloaths, the bulletts flying thick, one went through my side, and the same (as would seem) through the bowels and hand of my dear Child in my arms. One of my elder Sisters Children, named *William,* had then his Leg broken, which the *Indians* perceiving, they knockt him on head. Thus were we butchered by those merciless Heathen, standing amazed, with the blood running down to our heels. My eldest Sister being yet in the House, and seeing those wofull sights, the Infidels haling Mothers one way, and Children another, and some wallowing in their blood: and her elder Son telling her that her Son *William* was dead, and my self was wounded, she said, And, *Lord, let me dy with them;* which was no sooner said, but she was struck with a Bullet, and fell down dead over the threshold. I hope she is reaping the fruit of her good labours, being faithfull to the service of God in her place. . . .

I had often before this said, that if the *Indians* should come, I should chuse rather to be killed by them than be taken alive, but when it came to the tryal my mind changed; their glittering weapons so daunted my spirit, that I chose rather to go along with those (as I may say) ravenous Beasts, than that moment to end my dayes; and that I may the better declare what happened to me during that grievous Captivity, I shall particularly speak of the severall Removes we had up and down the Wilderness.

The First Remove

Now away we must go with those Barbarous Creatures, with our bodies wounded and bleeding, and our hearts no less than our bodies. About a mile we went that night, up upon a hill within sight of the Town, where they intended to lodge. There was hard by a vacant house (deserted by the English before, for fear of the *Indians*). I asked them whither I might not lodge in the house that night to which they answered, what will you love *English men* still? This was the dolefullest night that ever my eyes saw. Oh the roaring, and singing and danceing, and yelling of those black creatures in the night, which made the place a lively resemblance of hell. And as miserable was the waste that was there made, of Horses, Cattle, Sheep, Swine, Calves, Lambs, Roasting Pigs, and Fowls (which they had plundered in the Town) some roasting, some lying and burning, and some boyling to feed our merciless Enemies; who were joyfull enough though we were disconsolate. To add to the dolefulness of the former day, and the dismalness of the present night: my thoughts ran upon my losses and sad bereaved condition. All was gone, my Husband gone (at least separated from me, he being in the Bay; and to add to my grief, the *Indians* told me they would kill him as he came homeward) my Children gone, my Relations and Friends gone, our House and home and all our comforts within door, and without, all was gone, (except my life) and I knew not but the next moment that might go too. There remained nothing to me but one poor wounded Babe, and it seemed at present worse than death that it was in such a pitiful condition, bespeaking Compassion, and I had no refreshing for it, nor suitable things to revive it. . . .

The Thirteenth Remove

Instead of going toward the Bay, which was that I desired, I must go with them five or six miles down the River into a mighty Thicket of Brush: where we abode almost a fortnight. Here one asked me to make a shirt for her *Papoos* for which she gave me a mess of Broth, which was thickened with meal made of the Bark of a Tree, and to make it the better, she had put into it about a handfull of Pease, and a few roasted Ground-nuts. . . . In this place, on a cold night, as I lay by the fire, I removed a stick that kept the heat from me, a *Squaw* moved it down again, at which I lookt up, and she threw a handfull of ashes in mine eyes: I thought I should have been quite blinded, and have never seen more: but lying down, the water run out of my eyes, and carried the dirt with it, that by the morning, I recovered my sight again. Yet upon this, and the like occasions, I hope it is not too much to say with Job, *Have pitty upon me, have pitty upon me, O ye my friends, for the Hand of the Lord has touched me.* And here I cannot but remember how many times sitting in their *Wigwams,* and musing on things past, I should suddenly leap up and run out, as if I had been at home, forgetting where I was, and what my condition was: But when I was without, and saw nothing but *Wilderness,* and *Woods,* and a company of barbarous heathens: my mind quickly returned to me, which made me think of that, spoken concerning *Sampson,* who said, *I will go out and shake myself as at other times, but he wist not that the Lord was departed from him.* . . . About this time they came yelping from *Hadly,* where they had killed three *English men,* and brought one Captive with them, *viz. Thomas Read.* They all gathered about the poor Man, asking him many Questions. I desired also to go and see him; and when I came, he was crying bitterly, supposing they would quickly kill him. Whereupon I asked one of them, whether they intended to kill him; he answered me, they would not:

to guard and protect the religious ministers and the temples—the cunning and cleverness of the rebels were such, and so great, that my efforts were of little avail. . . .

On the eve of the day of the glorious San Lorenzo, having received notice of the said rebellion from the governors of Pecos and Tanos who said that two Indians had left the Teguas, and particularly the pueblos of Tesuque, to which they belonged, to notify them to come and join the revolt, and that they [the governors] came to tell me of it and of how they were unwilling to participate in such wickedness and treason, saying that they now regarded the Spaniards as their brothers, I thanked them for their kindness in giving the notice and told them to go to their pueblos and remain quiet. . . . He told me also that the said Indians had retreated to the sierra with all the cattle and horses belonging to the convent, and with their own.

The receipt of this news left us all in the state that may be imagined. I immediately and instantly sent the maese de campo, Francisco Gómez, with a squadron of soldiers sufficient to investigate this case and also to attempt to extinguish the flame of the ruin already begun. He returned here on the same day, telling me that the report of the death of the said Fray Juan Pío was true. He said also that there had been killed that same morning Father Fray Tomás de Torres, guardián of Nambé, and his brother, with the latter's wife and a child, and another resident of Taos, and also Father Fray Luis de Morales, guardián of San Ildefonso, and the family of Francisco de Anaya; and in Poxuaque Don Joseph de Goitia, Francisco Ximénez, his wife and family, and Doña Petronila de Salas with ten sons and daughters; and that they had robbed and profaned the convents and had robbed all the haciendas of those murdered and also all the horses and cattle of that jurisdiction and La Cañada.

Upon receiving this news I immediately notified the alcalde mayor of that district to assemble all the people in his house in a body, and told him to advise at once the alcalde mayor of Los Taos to do the same. On this same day I received notice that two members of a convoy had been killed in the pueblo of Santa Clara, six others having escaped by flight. Also at the same time the sargento mayor, Bernabé Márquez, sent to ask me for assistance, saying that he was surrounded and hard pressed by the Indians of the Queres and Tanos nations. . . .

Seeing myself with notices of so many and such untimely deaths, and that not having received any word from the lieutenant general was probably due to the fact that he was in the same exigency and confusion, or that the Indians had killed most of those on the lower river, and considering also that in the pueblo of Los Taos the father guardianes of that place and of the pueblo of Pecuríes might be in danger, as well as the alcalde mayor and the residents of that valley, and that at all events it was the only place from which I could obtain any horses and cattle—for all these reasons I endeavored to send a relief of soldiers. Marching out for that purpose, they learned that in La Cañada, as in Los Taos and Pecuríes, the Indians had risen in rebellion, joining the Apaches of the Achos nation. . . . It was necessarily supposed that they would join all their forces to take our lives, as was seen later by experience.

On Tuesday, the 13th of the said month, at about nine o'clock in the morning, there came in sight of us in the suburb of Analco, in the cultivated field of the hermitage of San Miguel, and on the other side of the river from the villa, all the Indians of the Tanos and Pecos nations and the Queres of San Marcos, armed and giving war whoops. As I learned that one of the Indians who was leading them was from the villa and had gone to join them shortly before, I sent some soldiers to summon him and tell him on my behalf that he could come to see me in entire safety, so that I might ascertain from him the purpose for which they were coming. Upon receiving this message he came to where I was, and, since he was known, as I say, I asked him how it was that he had gone crazy too—being an Indian who spoke our language, was so intelligent, and had lived all his life in the villa among the Spaniards, where I had placed such confidence in him—and was now coming as a leader of the Indian rebels. He replied to me that they had elected him as their captain, and that they were carrying two banners, one white and the other red, and that the white one signified peace and the red one war. Thus if we wished to choose the white it must be upon our agreeing to leave the country, and if we chose the red, we must perish, because the rebels were numerous and we were very few; there was no alternative, inasmuch as they had killed so many religious and Spaniards.

On hearing this reply, I spoke to him very persuasively, to the effect that he and the rest of his followers were Catholic Christians, asking how they expected to live without the religious; and said that even though they had committed so many atrocities, still there was a remedy, for if they would return to obedience to his Majesty they would be pardoned; and that thus he should go back to his people and tell them in my name all that had been said to him, and persuade them to agree to it and to withdraw from where they were; and that he was to advise me of what they might reply. He came back from there after a short time, saying that his people asked that all classes of Indians who were in our power be given up to them, both those in the service of the Spaniards and those of the Mexican nation of that suburb of Analco. He demanded also that his wife and children be given up to him, and likewise that all the Apachemen and women whom the Spaniards had captured in war be turned over to them, inasmuch as some Apaches who were among them were asking for them. If these things were not done they would declare war immediately, and they were unwilling to leave the place where they were because they were awaiting the Taos, Pecuríes, and Teguas nations, with whose aid they would destroy us.

. . . I told him (having given him all the preceding admonitions as a Christian and a Catholic) to return to his people and say to them that unless they immediately desisted from sacking the houses and dispersed, I would send to drive them away from there. Whereupon he went back, and his people received him with peals of bells and trumpets, giving loud shouts in sign of war.

With this, seeing after a short time that they not only did not cease the pillage but were advancing toward the villa with shamelessness and mockery, I ordered all the soldiers to go out and attack them until they succeeded in dislodging them from that place. Advancing for this purpose, they joined battle, killing some at the first encounter. Finding themselves repulsed, they took shelter and fortified themselves in the said hermitage and the houses of the Mexicans, from which they defended themselves a part of the day with the firearms that they had and with arrows. . . . Many of the rebels remained dead and wounded, and our men retired to the casas reales with one soldier killed and the maese de campo, Francisco Gómez, and some fourteen or fifteen soldiers wounded, to attend them and intrench and fortify ourselves as best we could.

On the morning of the following day, Wednesday, I saw the enemy come down all together from the sierra where they had slept, toward the villa. Mounting my horse, I went out with the few forces that I had to meet them, above the convent. . . .

I paused thus for a short time, in battle formation, and the enemy turned aside from the eminence. . . .

On . . . Friday, the nations of the Taos, Pecuríes, Jemez, and Queres having assembled during the past night, when dawn came more than 2,500 Indians fell upon us in the villa, fortifying and intrenching themselves in all its houses and at the entrances of all the streets, and cutting off our water, which comes through the arroyo and the irrigation canal in front of the casas reales. They burned the holy temple and many houses in the villa. We had several skirmishes over possession of the water, but, seeing that it was impossible to hold even this against them, and almost all the soldiers of the post being already wounded, I endeavored to fortify myself in the casas reales and to make a defense without leaving their walls. The Indians were so dexterous and so bold that they came to set fire to the doors of the fortified tower of Nuestra Señora de las Casas Reales, and, seeing such audacity and the manifest risk that we ran of having the casas reales set on fire, I resolved to make a sally into the plaza of the said casas reales with all my available force of soldiers, without any protection, to attempt to prevent the fire which the enemy was trying to set. With this endeavor we fought the whole afternoon, and, since the enemy, as I said above, had fortified themselves and made embrasures in all the houses, and had plenty of harquebuses, powder, and balls, they did us much damage. Night overtook us and God was pleased that they should desist somewhat from shooting us with harquebuses and arrows. We passed this night, like the rest, with much care and watchfulness, and suffered greatly from thirst because of the scarcity of water.

On the next day, Saturday, they began at dawn to press us harder and more closely with gunshots, arrows, and stones, saying to us that now we should not escape them, and that, besides their own numbers, they were expecting help from the Apaches whom they had already summoned. They fatigued us greatly on this day, because all was fighting, and above all we suffered from thirst, as we were already oppressed by it. At nightfall, because of the evident peril in which we found ourselves by their gaining the two stations where the cannon were mounted, which we had at the doors of the casas reales, aimed at the entrances of the streets, in order to bring them inside it was necessary to assemble all the forces that I had with me. . . . Instantly all the said Indian rebels began a chant of victory and raised war whoops, burning all the houses of the villa, and they kept us in this position the entire night, which I assure your reverence was the most horrible that could be thought of or imagined, because the whole villa was a torch and everywhere were war chants and shouts. What grieved us most were the dreadful flames from the church and the scoffing and ridicule which the wretched and miserable Indian rebels made of the sacred things, intoning the alabado and the other prayers of the church with jeers.

Finding myself in this state, with the church and the villa burned, and with the few horses, sheep, goats, and cattle which we had without feed or water for so long that many had already died, and the rest were about to do so, . . . I determined to take the resolution of going out in the morning to fight with the enemy until dying or conquering. Considering that the best strength and armor were prayers to appease the divine wrath, though on the preceding days the poor women had made them with such fervor, that night I charged them to do so increasingly, and told the father guardián and the other two religious to say mass for us at dawn, and exhort all alike to repentance for their sins and to conformance with the divine will, and to absolve us from guilt and punishment. These things being done, all of us who could mounted our horses, and the rest went on foot with their harquebuses. . . . On coming out of the entrance to the street it was seen that there was a great number of Indians. They were attacked in force, and though they resisted the first charge bravely, finally they were put to flight, many of them being overtaken and killed. Then turning at once upon those who were in the streets leading to the convent, they also were put to flight with little resistance. . . . The deaths of both parties in this and the other encounters exceeded three hundred Indians.

14. AN INDIAN VIEW OF THE PUEBLO REVOLT

After the revolt ended, and more than two thousand Spanish had been driven from their homes, stunned officials tried to figure out what had happened. Special interviewers sent by the Catholic Church and the Spanish government questioned as many people as possible, hoping to assess blame. When they fled New Mexico, the Spanish had captured and imprisoned a number of Pueblo Indians, both those who had been part of the plot and those who had not. Josephe, a Spanish-speaking Indian who had been a servant in one of the missions, was

said coyote Catití would come down with all the men of the Queres and Jemez nations, only the said Catití attempting to speak with the said Spaniards, and at a shout from him they would all rush down to kill the said Spaniards; and he gave orders that all the rest who were in the other junta where the said Don Luis and El Ollita were present, should at the same time attack the horse drove, so as to finish that too. This declarant being present during all these proceedings, and feeling compassion because of the treason they were plotting, he determined to come to warn the Spaniards, as he did, whereupon they put themselves under arms and the said Indians again went up to the heights of the sierra, and the Spaniards withdrew. Thus he replies to the question.

Having been asked repeated questions touching on the matter, he said that he has already told all he knows; that what he might say further is that they should be constantly on the alert, because the traitors have all planned to join together and follow the Spaniards as far as the pueblo of La Isleta, so as to fall upon them by night and take away the horses, for on being left afoot they could do nothing and they would kill them. He said that what he has stated in his declaration is the truth and what he knows, under charge of his oath, which he affirms and ratifies, this, his said declaration, being read to him. He did not sign because of not knowing how, nor does he know his age. Apparently he is about twenty years old. His lordship signed it with the interpreters and assisting witnesses, before me, the present secretary. . . .

Francisco Xavier, secretary of government and war.

FURTHER READING

Bailyn, Bernard. *The Barbarous Years: The Peopling of North America and the Conflict of Civilizations, 1600–1675*. New York: Vintage, 2013.

Barr, Juliana. *Peace Came in the Form of a Woman: Indians and Spaniards in the Texas Borderlands*. Chapel Hill: University of North Carolina Press, 2007.

Gutierrez, Ramon A. *When Jesus Came, the Corn Mothers Went Away: Marriage, Sexuality, and Power in New Mexico, 1500–1846*. Stanford, CA: Stanford University Press, 1991.

Hackel, Steven. *Children of Coyote, Missionaries of Saint Francis: Indian-Spanish Relations in Colonial California, 1769–1850*. Chapel Hill: University of North Carolina Press, 2005.

Knaut, Andrew L. *The Pueblo Revolt of 1680: Conquest and Resistance in Seventeenth-Century New Mexico*. Norman: University of Oklahoma Press, 1996.

Lepore, Jill. *The Name of War: King Philip's War and the Origins of American Identity*. New York: Alfred A. Knopf, 1998.

Monroy, Douglas. *Thrown among Strangers: The Making of Mexican Culture in Frontier California*. Berkeley: University of California Press, 1990.

Richter, Daniel. *Trade, Land, and Power: The Struggle for Eastern North America*. Philadelphia: University of Pennsylvania Press, 2014.

Weber, David J. *The Spanish Frontier in North America*. New Haven, CT: Yale University Press, 1992.

Karl Ferdinand Wimar, *The Abduction of Boone's Daughter by the Indians,* 1855. This painting re-creates a famous moment in frontier Kentucky that occurred in 1776. Shawnee and Cherokee warriors, angry at legendary frontiersman Daniel Boone for not living up to his promises, kidnapped his daughter and two of her young cousins. Capturing young women was a common tactic for Native peoples and a retaliation that terrified backcountry migrants. Finding themselves in Indian Territory and unable to protect their women and children pushed every cultural button. Boone became a hero when he rescued the girls, but the story frightened generations of fathers. Wimar's painting plays on these fears and ideas about the weakness of women and the savagery of Indians.

Amon Carter Museum, Fort Worth, Texas.

New Worlds for All

Conquest and Accommodation in the Eighteenth Century

4

The story of eighteenth-century North America turns on two issues: the development of immigrant communities and the perpetual challenge to old ideas about authority that took place when these communities ran up against Native nations. Both generated tension as well as opportunity. Europeans and Indians alike adapted to new conditions and, in many cases, prospered in ways previously impossible. The concept of the frontier operated without regard to geography. Philadelphia, where Anglo-American seamen, Native American traders, French seamstresses, and English servants intermingled, was as much a frontier as St. Louis or Santa Fe. In all these places, people from different cultures encountered new ways of doing things, from women who controlled property to the words they used to describe their lives. Yet they continued to cling to recognizable parts of their own cultures. As a result, Spanish communities looked different from English ones, and Indian towns would never have been mistaken for French settlements.

Immigration from Europe changed the face of North America. Francophone communities were scattered over the hinterlands of the St. Lawrence River, the Great Lakes, and the Mississippi River Valley. Colonists, soldiers, and priests spread out across the Spanish borderlands of what is now Texas, New Mexico, Arizona, and California. In the

English colonies, the European population doubled every twenty years, shifting the demographic profile of the region east of the Appalachian Mountains. Though the populations of Native nations slowly declined, while their lands and wealth decreased because of warfare and the ravages of European disease, they continued to be powerful players in the imperial and cultural negotiations of the period. Turned into migrants, the Indians were engaged in remaking their world in the face of these cataclysmic changes. Whether European or Indian, these new communities did not replicate the societies from which these people had come. They were in fact original hybrids.

Perhaps the most significant characteristics of these New World communities were their ethnic complexity and class flexibility. By midcentury, for example, the French had built a trading empire that reached from the mouth of the St. Lawrence River through the river systems of the Great Lakes and down the Mississippi River to New Orleans. Founded in 1718, New Orleans became a significant trading center for slaves and sugar, which were crucial to the plantations being built along the Mississippi. New Orleans developed into a center of French power in North America, but with its complicated mixture of Africans, Europeans, and Indians, of slaves and slaveholders, it bore little resemblance to the cities of France.

Similarly, Spanish communities in North America encompassed a variety of peoples, who both mixed blood and heritage and enjoyed social mobility unimaginable in Spain. San Antonio de Bexar, for example, founded in 1716, is representative of the cosmopolitan societies that emerged on the Texas frontier. The Spanish colonists who settled in Texas were in fact mestizos of combined Spanish, Mexican, and indigenous heritage. Their complex social and racial hierarchies were based on blood, marriage, and economic status. Intermarriage, encouraged by the Catholic church, meant that social and racial categories remained fluid. Slavery, captivity, and adoption, common among all of the people living in the region, made cultural mixing the norm. This flexibility, coupled with the fact that people from many classes were able to own land, propelled Spanish colonies to economic prosperity and forged community bonds in isolated San Antonio or Santa Barbara that were different from those in Spain, or even Mexico, where social and racial stratification limited access to opportunity.

In the English colonies, recruiters brought immigrants from all over Europe, and slavers brought people from Africa. By midcentury, Germans, Scots-Irish, and especially African slaves made up nearly half the population of the colonies. Some lived and worked in urban centers like Boston, New York, Philadelphia, and Charleston, but most farmed in rural areas. They had come to North America because of the promise of land, a scarce resource in Europe. The availability of land turned social classifications upside down: former servants could become landowners, and widows powerful property owners. Concerns over authority and who should rule households became central to North American legal codes and debates over property ownership. For European men, and for some women (Native and newcomer), the New World offered significant opportunity, but it required hard work and adaptation.

Of course, these Europeans worked land that Indians had long considered their own. As population pressures along the Atlantic seaboard increased, European immigrants and their Indian neighbors pushed into interior areas beyond the Appalachians, what the English colonists called the backcountry. Here, English, Dutch, and German settlers became neighbors to Native nations. They borrowed Indian farming techniques and hunting tactics, and even wore Indian clothes, but retained their language, religion, and many other aspects of their original cultures.

The backcountry, however, was often a violent place. White newcomers taking Indian land resulted in waves of warfare that ravaged the backcountry for a century. Though both cultures exchanged ideas and practices, the Indians usually lost more than they gained. Because of the terrible costs of epidemic disease and the steady loss of agricultural and hunting land, many Indians became dependent on trade with Europeans and adapted their living and hunting patterns to these new realities. Native communities also took all kinds of people captive to rebuild their populations and to get revenge for the assaults on their villages.

Language, housing styles, warfare, family patterns, clothing, racial and ethnic mixing all show the cultural complexities of the period. The documents in this chapter illustrate the great variety of communities that emerged in eighteenth-century North America and how people adapted to new situations. The drawings of town plans reveal European newcomer's hopes about how they might order new places and the realities of the long-settled world they found. Daniel Boone's account of his trek to Kentucky evokes the rhythms of life in the backcountry, while a set of legal documents about marriage and property illuminates changing social conditions in more settled areas. Finally, a Cree Indian describes the changed lives of his people.

AS YOU READ: As you examine these documents, think about cultural complexity. How did people decide how their societies should work? What happened when poor people got property or women controlled inheritance? In what contexts did people from different cultures meet? How would trade, captivity, slavery, and war have affected people's expectations about life?

15. EXPANDING COMMUNITIES

Europeans established settlements and towns in North America that served a variety of economic and social groups. English farmers, Spanish soldiers, and French fur traders each had their own ideas about how to organize a community drawn from their European past. Native people moved their communities to take advantage of trade. In most communities, available building materials and new climates required adaptation and adopting Native ways of doing things. Europeans designing colonial settlements often drew up plans of these new communities to attract potential migrants or to secure funding from the government or religious groups, and such town plans reveal a great deal about European hopes and ideals. Military and government officials also drew up town plans to use for strategic planning, and these convey more about the reality of the situation. The following selection includes both kinds: the ideal and the real. Can you tell the difference between Spanish, French, and English town plans? How is the Arikara map different from the others? What are the most important characteristics of the "ideal" plans? How do the "real" plans reflect particular conditions in North America?

French, Spanish, and English Colonial Town Plans
1760–78

Plan of the Fort at Detroit, 1760 *(see p. 65)*

Detroit was built as a military installation and fur-trading establishment, part of the overall French plan to control the river systems of the Great Lakes region. This drawing shows the interior of the fort and the plans for farming the land around it. The key on the right reads, "A. Fort commander's quarters; B. Guardhouse; C. Church; D. Powder magazine; E. Chaplain's quarters." What do the names of streets tell you? How would a military community differ from a farming community? How is this "ideal" plan different from the one of San Fernando (see p. 68), drawn by a Spanish cleric?

Plan of Santa Fe, New Mexico, c. 1766 *(see p. 66)*

Drawn by a Spanish explorer, this plan was intended to provide information to military leaders in case of an attack. By 1766, Santa Fe had become the government center of New Mexico and a successful agricultural community. The drawing shows a broad view of the town, including the river and major irrigation ditches (acequias) and important roads (caminos). The key in the lower left corner reads, "A. Church and Convent of St. Francis; B. Governor's house; C. Chapel of Our Lady of Light; D. Church of San Miguel; E. Pueblo and community of Indians who were here when the first Spaniard arrived to conquer this region for the King." Do you see a central square? What does it mean that some buildings are bigger than others? How is this community different from San Fernando de Bexar on page 68?

A Plan of the Town and Port of Edenton, North Carolina, 1769 (see p. *67*)

Edenton never existed except in the minds of its creators. Throughout the eighteenth century, English investors hoping to make huge profits bought up large chunks of land in unsettled areas and then tried to divide it up and

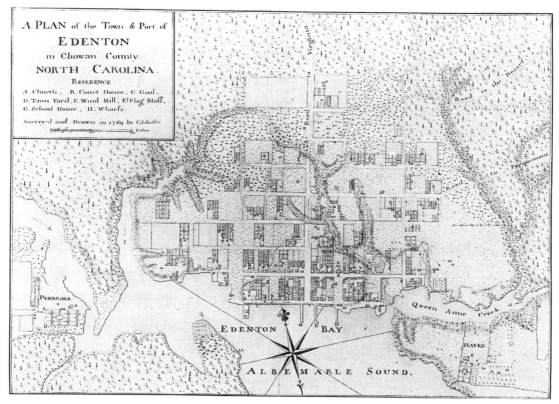

A plan of the town and port of Edenton, North Carolina, 1769. Drawn by C. J. Sauthier, 1769. William L. Clements Library, University of Michigan, Ann Arbor.

Richard Henderson, one of the people who invested heavily in Kentucky land. It shows a primitive fort rather than the agricultural community people like Henderson hoped to build. Which of the other town plans does this resemble the most? Can you tell whether wealth or social status affected living conditions in this setting? Would an image like this have attracted potential settlers?

16. THE WORLD OF THE BACKCOUNTRY

Daniel Boone, the quintessential American frontiersman, never wrote a book. Much of his fame came from a biography written by John Filson, which popularized Boone's life and the lands west of the Appalachians. Though Filson's account made his subject into an impossibly heroic figure, Boone's life accurately

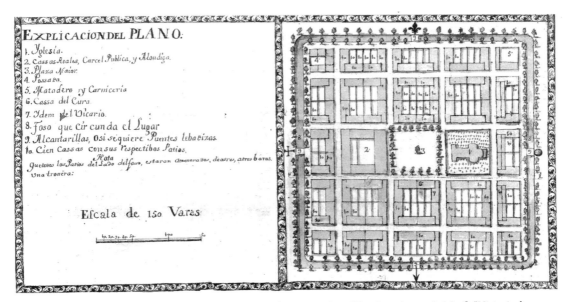

EXPLICACION DEL PLANO:
1. Iglesia.
2. Cassas Reales, Carcel Publica, y Alondiga.
3. Plaza Maior.
4. Possada.
5. Matadero y Carniceria.
6. Cassa del Cura.
7. Idem del Vicario.
8. Foso que circunda el Lugar.
9. Alcantarillas, O si siquiere Puentes lebadizas.
10. Cien Cassas con sus respectibos Patios.

Nota
Quetodos los Patios del Lado del Foso, estaran amenosas, deotro, atres baras.
Una tronera:

Escala de 150 Varas

Plan of the pueblo of San Fernando de Bexar, c. 1777. From the manuscript of Fray Juan Augustín Morfi, "Historia de Texas." Manuscripts Division, Library of Congress.

View of Boonesborough, Kentucky, 1778. Drawn by George Ranck after a plan by Judge Richard Henderson, Boonesborough, Louisville, 1901. Olin Library, Cornell University, Ithaca, New York.

reflected a growing backcountry ethic. Boone and his neighbors lived by hunting (and by speculating in land) and survived by adapting to Indian ways and by fighting when necessary. Boone pioneered a trail over the Appalachian Mountains from North Carolina into Kentucky in 1769, violating the Proclamation of 1763, which made settlement west of the Appalachians illegal. Like Boone, thousands of other white squatters ignored the law and took their chances with the British government and with the Indians. Land hunger, movement, and cultural conflict characterized the backcountry experience of common white people in the eighteenth century. This account, which Filson claimed came directly from Boone himself, describes the process of finding new land and its dangers and pleasures. It also demonstrates the significance of land and the fluid qualities of culture in eighteenth-century North America. Why did Boone want to move his family, given the dangers he had faced? Why did Filson want to make a man like Boone into a hero?

John Filson

From The Adventures of Col. Daniel Boon
1784

It was on the first of May, in the year 1769, that I resigned my domestic happiness for a time, and left my family and peaceable habitation on the Yadkin River, in North-Carolina, to wander through the wilderness of America, in quest of the country of Kentucke, in company with John Finley, John Stewart, Joseph Holden, James Monay, and William Cool. We proceeded successfully, and after a long and fatiguing journey through a mountainous wilderness, in a westward direction, on the seventh day of June following, we found ourselves on Red-River, where John Finley had formerly been trading with the Indians, and, from the top of an eminence, saw with pleasure the beautiful level of Kentucke. . . . In this forest, the habitation of beasts of every kind natural to America, we practised hunting with great success until the twenty-second day of December following.

This day John Stewart and I had a pleasing ramble, but fortune changed the scene in the close of it . . . . In the decline of the day, near Kentucke river, as we ascended the brow of a small hill, a number of Indians rushed out of a thick cane-brake upon us, and made us prisoners. The time of our sorrow was now arrived, and the scene fully opened. The Indians plundered us of what we had, and kept us in confinement seven days, treating us with common savage usage. During this time we discovered no uneasiness or desire to escape, which made them less suspicious of us; but in the dead of night, as we lay in a thick cane-brake by a large fire, when sleep had locked up their senses, my situation not disposing me for rest, I touched my companion and gently awoke him. We improved this favourable opportunity, and departed, leaving them to take their rest, and speedily directed our course towards our old camp, but found it plundered, and the company dispersed and gone home. About this time my brother, Squire Boon, with another adventurer, who came to explore the country shortly after us, was wandering through the forest, determined to find me, if possible, and accidentally found our camp. . . .

. . . We were then in a dangerous, helpless situation, exposed daily to perils and death amongst savages and wild beasts, not a white man in the country but ourselves . . . .

We continued not in a state of indolence, but hunted every day, and prepared a little cottage to defend us from the Winter storms. We remained there undisturbed during the Winter; and on the first day of May, 1770, my brother returned home to the settlement by himself, for a new recruit of horses and ammunition, leaving me by myself, without bread, salt or sugar, without company of my fellow creatures, or even a horse or dog. I confess I never before was under greater necessity of exercising philosophy and fortitude. . . .

Thus, through an uninterrupted scene of sylvan pleasures, I spent the time until the 27th day of July following, when my brother, to my great felicity, met me according to appointment, at our old camp. Shortly after, we left this place, not thinking it safe to stay there longer, and proceeded to Cumberland river, reconnoitring that part of the country until March, 1771, and giving names to the different waters.

Soon after, I returned home to my family with a determination to bring them as soon as possible to live in Kentucke, which I esteemed a second paradise, at the risk of my life and fortune.

I returned safe to my old habitation, and found my family in happy circumstances. I sold my farm on the Yadkin, and what goods we could not carry with us; and on the twenty-fifth day of September, 1773, bade a farewel to our friends, and proceeded on our journey to Kentucke, in company with five families more, and forty men that joined us in Powel's Valley, which is one hundred and fifty miles from the now settled parts of Kentucke. This promising beginning was soon overcast with a cloud of adversity; for upon the tenth day of October, the rear of our company was attacked by a number of Indians, who killed six, and wounded one man. Of these my eldest son was one that fell in the action. Though we defended ourselves, and repulsed the enemy, yet this unhappy affair scattered our cattle, brought us into extreme difficulty, and so discouraged the whole company, that we retreated forty miles, to the settlement on Clench river. . . .

I remained with my family on Clench until the sixth of June, 1774, when I and one Michael Stoner were solicited by Governor Dunmore, of Virginia, to go to the Falls of the Ohio, to conduct into the settlement a number of surveyors that had been sent thither by him some months before; this country having about this time drawn the attention of many adventurers. We immediately complied with the Governor's request, and conducted in the surveyors, compleating a tour of eight hundred miles, through many difficulties, in sixty-two days.

Soon after I returned home, I . . . was solicited by a number of North-Carolina gentlemen, that were about purchasing the lands lying on the S. side of Kentucke River, from the Cherokee Indians, to attend their treaty at Wataga, in March, 1775, to negotiate with them, and, mention the boundaries of the purchase. This I accepted, and at the request of the same gentlemen, undertook to mark out a road in the best passage from the settlement through the wilderness to Kentucke. . . .

I soon began this work, having collected a number of enterprising men, well armed. We proceeded with all possible expedition until we came within fifteen miles of where Boonsborough now stands, and where we were fired upon by a party of Indians that killed two, and wounded two of our number; yet, although surprised and taken at a disadvantage, we stood our ground. This was on the twentieth of March, 1775. Three days after, we were fired upon again, and had two men killed, and three wounded. Afterwards we proceeded on to Kentucke river without opposition; and on the first day of April began to erect the fort of Boons borough, at a salt lick, about sixty yards from the river, on the S. side.

On the fourth day, the Indians killed one of our men. . . . We were busily employed in building this fort, until the fourteenth day of June following, without any farther opposition from the Indians; and having finished the works, I returned to my family, on Clench.

In a short time, I proceeded to remove my family from Clench to this garrison; where we arrived safe without any other difficulties than such as are common to this passage, my wife and daughter being the first white women that ever stood on the banks of Kentucke river.

17. FAMILY DYNAMICS IN THE COLONIAL WORLD

The availability of land, which created wealth and social mobility in eighteenth-century North America, also challenged traditional ideals about gender and marriage. In both well-settled and frontier areas, men often went off (like Daniel Boone) to conduct business, to hunt, and to captain ships, leaving women to handle family and household matters. In wealthy families, women managed slaves and Indian servants and directed the operation of plantations or ranchos; in poor families, women worked in shops, plowed land, and hunted. Traditional English marriage laws, in which women lost all economic and social power when they married, clashed with the reality of day-to-day life. These rules were very different from Spanish practices, which allowed women to retain more property. The legal system began to adjust to such social realities in the middle of the eighteenth century. Marriage contracts and court-mandated property settlements reveal the changing view of marriage from a male-dominated economic institution to an economic partnership. Divorce became more common though still very difficult for female petitioners to achieve. These documents, a postmarital contract from Virginia, a Spanish Californian woman's description of her escape from an arranged marriage to a Yankee, and a divorce decree from Pennsylvania, illustrate concerns over property and how it created tensions in colonial marriages. What do these documents tell you about women's property rights? What do they tell you about women's obligations? What kinds of behavior are grounds for divorce?

Marriage Documents from California, Pennsylvania, and Virginia, 1714, 1782, 1826

Articles of Agreement Between Mr. John Custis and His Wife, 1714[1]

Whereas some differences and quarrels have arisen between Mr. John Custis of York County and Frances his wife concerning some money, plate and other things taken from him by the said Frances and a more plentiful maintenance for her. Now to the end and so all animosities and unkindness may cease and a perfect love and friendship may be renewed between them they have mutually agreed upon the following articles this—day of June anno Domi 1714:

1st. First it is agreed that the said Frances shall return to the said John all the money, plate and other things whatsoever that she had taken from him or removed out of the house upon oath and be obliged never to take away by herself or any other, anything of value from him again or run him in debt without his consent, nor sell, give away or dispose of anything of value out of the family without his consent, upon the condition that the plate and damask linen shall not be given or disposed of by the aforesaid John from the said during her life and the said John doth covenant said plate and linen to be delivered by the said Frances to the said John shall be given to the children of the said John by the said Frances immediately after her decease.

2d. That Frances shall henceforth forbear to call him the said John any vile names or give any ill language, neither shall he give her any but to live lovingly together and to behave themselves to each other as a good husband and good wife ought to do. And that she shall not intermeddle with his affairs but that all business belonging to the husband's management shall be solely transacted by him, neither shall he intermeddle in her domestic affairs but that all business properly belonging to the management of the wife shall be solely transacted by her.

3d. That the said John shall pay all the debts he has already contracted out of the debts now due to the estate and the money he has received if there will be sufficient to pay them; and that he shall enter into bond to Philip Ludwell in the sum of one thousand pounds that from hence forward he shall keep true and

---

1. *Virginia Magazine of History and Biography* 4 (1879): 64–66. Reprinted in *New World, New Roles: A Documentary History of Women in Pre-Industrial America*, ed. Sylvia R. Frey and Marian J. Morton (New York: Greenwood Press, 1986), 217–18.

Doña Josefa Fitch, "Wedding Story," 1826[3]

I asked her how her marriage to Captain Enrique Fitch had come about. She said that she met Captain Fitch in 1826 when he came to California as commander of the brig *María Ester* to engage in trade for Don Enrique Virmond. Virmond was a gentleman who had a huge fortune and was regularly engaged in large business enterprises with the Mexican government. Since she found the refined manners and handsome presence of the young man from Massachusetts to her liking, when he asked for her hand in marriage, she accepted. In March 1829, Señor Fitch returned to the port of San Diego as commander of the *Buitre*. At that time, San Diego was a port equipped for foreign trade. After Señor Fitch discussed the marriage proposal with my parents, they arranged for an altar to be prepared at home, and they had Reverend Father Fray Antonio Menéndez of the Dominican order come to our home. Dressed with the paraphernalia that ministers of the altar normally wore on such occasions, he proceeded to celebrate my marriage. He had barely begun the ritual when, by order of His Excellency General Echeandía, Señor Don Domingo Carrillo appeared in the *sala*. Carrillo was the assistant to His Excellency. In the name of the "citizen governor," he ordered Father Menéndez to immediately halt the tying of the nuptial knot, under penalty of incurring the wrath of the civil, military, and ecclesiastical authorities. That peremptory command was announced in the presence of a large gathering of people who, by character and upbringing, were used to blindly obeying all governmental orders. The announcement weighed so heavily on the spirit of the poor friar, who had just arrived in San Diego, that he decided to stop my marriage ceremony. He removed his ceremonial robes and left my parents' home as quickly as possible. Shortly after Fray Menéndez left, so too did Captain Fitch. He knew that his friend Don Pío Pico was a man whom you did not have to ask twice if it came to helping a woman, especially if that woman was his relative. So Fitch told Pico everything he wanted Pico to do to help him carry out his just intentions and thwart the selfish designs of Governor Echeandía.

Echeandía was a man with liberal ideas, but in this instance he allowed his desires to lead him off the path of good sense and thus gave the order to stop the celebration of a function that was sanctioned by civil and ecclesiastical laws. During that time, I, as well as my female friends and relatives, harbored deep resentment toward Governor Echeandía. But a few years later, I forgave him with all my heart, since he was the one who liberated my country from the yoke of the tyrant Victoria. I concluded that his persecution of me and my husband was no more than an act motivated by the despair that had taken hold of his soul. He was convinced that I had shown preference for a rival whom he

3. Rose Marie Beebe and Robert Senkewicz, eds, *Testimonios: Early California through the Eyes of Women, 1815–1848* (Berkeley, CA: Heyday Books, 2006), 76–81.

detested. Pío Pico advised Captain Fitch to board the ship he commanded and prepare to weigh anchor. As soon as it got very dark, Fitch was to send out a small boat for Doña Josefa. Pico would take care of getting her out of the house. Don Enrique Fitch followed his friend's advice. At the appointed hour a fine boat was ready and waiting at the place they had agreed upon ahead of time. In the meantime, Pío Pico came to my home. Using the types of arguments that have great impact on the soul of a young woman in love, especially coming from a person my parents considered worthy of their trust, Pico did not have any trouble convincing me to accompany him. Together we rode on a fine horse to the place where Don Enrique Fitch was waiting for us with a sail-boat manned by six sailors specifically chosen for that occasion.

Since it was already late, she only took from her home a small trunk containing a few petticoats and other items for daily use. She left her home and went to the place where Pío Pico was waiting for her. He helped her get on the horse first, then he got on and they rode as quickly as possible to the place where the boat sent by Captain Fitch was waiting for them. Once in the presence of her future husband, Don Pío Pico said, "Good-bye, cousin. May God bless you. And you, cousin Enrique, take care not to give Josefa reason to regret having joined her lot with yours." Captain Fitch answered that he promised, before God and man, that as long as he was alive, his wife would be happy. Doña Josefa Fitch says that he faithfully kept his promise. During the twenty years he lived by her side, he never caused her a moment's grief. Captain Fitch died on January 14, 1849. He was forty-nine years old, give or take a few months; Fitch was born on May 7, 1798. His wife was born in San Diego on December 29, 1810. The fruits of this marriage were: Enrique Eduardo, born June 23, 1830; Federico, born June 28, 1832; Guillermo, born November 7, 1834; José, born March 19, 1836; Josefa, born November 2, 1837; Juan, born April 6, 1839; Isabela, born August 24, 1840; Carlos, born September 1, 1842; Miguel, born March 13, 1844; María Antonia Natalia, born September 19, 1845; and Anita, born April 13, 1848.

Captain Fitch had barely arrived on board the *Buitre* when the main-sails were unfurled and the ship set sail. After seventy-four days at sea, the ship arrived safely at the port of Valparaíso, where Captain Fitch immediately ordered that preparations be made for the wedding. The marriage ceremony was celebrated by the parish priest of Valparaíso. The load of hides and tallow carried on the *Buitre* was sold in Valparaíso. Someone also offered to buy the *Buitre,* and the ship was sold in Valparaíso. Shortly afterward, Captain Fitch purchased the frigate *Leonora.* Loaded with bundles of food and other goods intended for the market in Alta California, the ship set sail for San Diego with a stop at the port of Callao. There, they loaded on board a large quantity of sugar and large jugs of *pisco de aguardiente de Ica.* When the *Leonora* left the port of Valparaíso, the ship was flying the flag of North America, but Captain Fitch was planning to engage in coastal trading. He knew that at the ports in California every ship captain did what suited him best. He also knew that in the ports of the other states of the Union, only ships flying the Mexican flag could engage in coastal trading. He therefore decided to enter the port of Acapulco to register his ship. He did so with little difficulty. From Acapulco he headed for San Diego. At that time, Don Juan Bandini was the customs administrator in San Diego. Bandini appraised part of the cargo and then sent the ship off to sail to ports along the coast.

While the cargo was being appraised, the *Leonora* remained anchored in the port of San Diego. Señora Fitch says that all the women who lived in the area came to pay her a visit and welcome her, including her mother and sisters. After exchanging greetings, Señora Fitch's mother told her that her father was very angry with her. He had vowed to kill her the moment he laid eyes on her again. When she heard this, she decided to go ashore without delay, because she preferred to risk death rather than live in anger with the man who had given her life. Once the decision had been made, she went ashore, accompanied by her female relatives and friends. She placed the young son she was carrying in her sister's arms and headed to her family home by herself. When she arrived at the threshold of her father's home, she pushed the half-open door. The first person she caught sight of was her father, who was seated near a small desk. He had a shotgun by his side. As soon as she saw him, she said, "Father, I have returned to San Diego to ask you to forgive me for leaving your home." Whether her father heard what she said or not, he kept silent. Seeing that a veritable storm was stirring within her father's soul, she threw herself down on her knees at the door of the room. In a humble tone, she again asked her father for forgiveness. She told him that if she had disobeyed him, she did it for the sole purpose of getting away from an odious tyranny that laws and customs condemned. She says that she spoke for a long time, but her father remained motionless and did not respond. Noticing that her father was no longer looking at the weapon, she crawled on her knees to the middle of the room. While she was moving, she continued to plead with her father. Finally, he was touched by her words. When she was but six *varas* away from where her father was seated, he got up, moved toward her, and took her in his arms.

18. NEW WORLDS ON THE GREAT PLAINS

As Native people negotiated the changes driven by European colonization, their cultures also changed. One of the most dramatic examples was the emergence of the nomadic buffalo-hunting culture of the Great Plains. In the late seventeenth and early eighteenth centuries, as European settlement pushed agricultural tribes westward, the Plains peoples first encountered horses, which had escaped from the Spanish in the Southwest. Riding horses allowed them to hunt buffalo much more efficiently, and large groups moved onto the plains over the course of the century. For many of these tribes, particularly in the areas east of the Rocky Mountains, horses, guns, and buffalo brought a cultural revolution. Horses and guns determined a tribe's status; guns made intertribal warfare a much deadlier affair. Saukamappee, a Cree Indian living among the Blackfeet in what is now Montana, told fur trapper David Thompson the following story. It describes the period, probably in the 1730s, when horses, guns, and disease transformed the lives of the Blackfeet. What were the most significant changes in the lives of the Blackfeet? Why was war so important? How did weapons and war strategies change over time? Did Saukamappee connect the presence of white people with either horses or smallpox?

Saukamappee

An Account of the Arrival of Horses, Guns, and Smallpox
1787[1]

The Peeagans were always the frontier Tribe, and upon whom the Snake Indians made their attacks, these latter were very numerous, even without their allies; and the Peeagans had to send messengers among us to procure help. . . .

By this time the affairs of both parties had much changed; we had more guns and iron headed arrows than before; but our enemies the Snake Indians and their allies had Misstutim (Big Dogs, that is Horses) on which they rode, swift as the Deer, on which they dashed at the Peeagans, and with their stone Pukamoggan knocked them on the head, and they had thus lost several of their best men. This news we did not well comprehend and it alarmed us, for we had no idea of Horses and could not make out what they were. . . . After a few days march our scouts brought us word that the enemy was near in a large war party, but had no Horses with them, for at that time they had very few of them. When we came to meet each other, as usual, each displayed their numbers, weapons and shiel[d]s, in all which they were superior to us, except our guns which were not shown, but kept in (their leathern cases), and if we had shown [them], they would have taken them for long clubs. For a long time they held us in suspense; a tall Chief was forming a strong party to make an attack on our centre, and the others to enter into combat with those opposite to them; We prepared for the battle the best we could. Those of us who had guns stood in the front line, and each of us [had] two balls in his mouth, and a load of powder in his left hand to reload. . . .

. . . The War Chief was close to us, anxious to see the effect of our guns. The lines were too far asunder for us to make a sure shot, and we requested him to

---

1. (J. B. Tyrrell, ed., *David Thompson's Narrative of His Explorations in Western America, 1784–1812* (Toronto: The Champlain Society, 1916), 328–38.

close the line to about sixty yards, which was gradually done, and lying flat on the ground behind the shields, we watched our opportunity when they drew their bows to shoot at us, their bodies were then exposed and each of us, as opportunity offered, fired with deadly aim, and either killed, or severely wounded, every one we aimed at.

The War Chief was highly pleased, and the Snake Indians finding so many killed and wounded kept themselves behind their shields; the War Chief then desired we would spread ourselves by two's throughout the line, which we did, and our shots caused consternation and dismay along their whole line. The battle had begun about Noon, and the Sun was not yet half down, when we perceived some of them had crawled away from their shields, and were taking to flight. The War Chief seeing this went along the line and spoke to every Chief to keep his Men ready for a charge of the whole line of the enemy, of which he would give the signal; this was done by himself stepping in front with his Spear, and calling on them to follow him as he rushed on their line, and in an instant the whole of us followed him, the greater part of the enemy took to flight, but some fought bravely and we lost more than ten killed and many wounded; Part of us pursued, and killed a few, but the chase had soon to be given over, for at the body of every Snake Indian killed, there were five or six of us trying to get his scalp, or part of his clothing, his weapons, or something as a trophy of the battle. . . .

. . . We pitched away in large camps with the women and children on the frontier of the Snake Indian country, hunting the Bison and Red Deer which were numerous, and we were anxious to see a horse of which we had heard so much. At last, as the leaves were falling we heard that one was killed by an arrow shot into his belly, but the Snake Indian that rode him, got away; numbers of us went to see him, and we all admired him, he put us in mind of a Stag that had lost his horns; and we did not know what name to give him. But as he was a slave to Man, like the dog, which carried our things; he was named the Big Dog.

We set off for our people, and on the fourth day came to a camp of Stone Indians, the relations of our companions, who received us well and we staid a few day[s]. The Scalps were placed on poles, and the Men and Women danced round them, singing to the sound of Rattles, Tambours and flutes. When night came, one of our party, in a low voice, repeated to the Chief the narrative of the battle, which he in a loud voice walking about the tents, repeated to the whole camp. After which, the Chiefs called those who followed them to a feast, and the battle was always the subject of the conversation and driving the Snake Indians to a great distance. . . .

The terror of that battle and of our guns has prevented any more general battles, and our wars have since been carried by ambuscade and surprize, of small camps, in which we have greatly the advantage, from the Guns, arrow shards of iron, long knives, flat bayonets and axes from the Traders. While we have these weapons, the Snake Indians have none, but what few they sometimes take from one of our small camps which they have destroyed, and they have no Traders among them. We thus continued to advance through the fine plains to the Stag River when death came over us all, and swept away more than half of us by the Small pox, of which we knew nothing until it brought death among us. We caught it from the Snake Indians. Our Scouts were out for our security, when some returned and informed us of a considerable camp which was too large to attack and something very suspicious about it; from a high knowl they had a good view of the camp, but saw none of the men hunting, or going about; there were a few Horses, but no one came to them, and a herd of Bisons [were] feeding close to the camp with other herds near. This somewhat alarmed us as a stratagem of War; and our Warriors thought this camp had a larger not far off; so that if this camp was attacked which was strong enough to offer a desperate resistance, the other would come to their assistance and overpower us as had been once done by them, and in which we lost many of our men.

. . . Next morning at the dawn of day, we attacked the Tents, and with our sharp flat daggers and knives, cut through the tents and entered for the fight; but our war whoop instantly stopt, our eyes were appalled with terror; there was no one to fight with but the dead and the dying, each a mass of corruption. We did not touch them, but left the tents, and held a council on what was to be done. We all thought the Bad Spirit had made himself master of the camp and destroyed them. It was agreed to take some of the best of the tents, and any other plunder that was clean and good, which we did, and also took away the few Horses they had, and returned to our camp.

The second day after this dreadful disease broke out in our camp, and spread from one tent to another as if the Bad Spirit carried it. We had no belief that one Man could give it to another, any more than a wounded Man could give his wound to another. We did not suffer so much as those that were near the river into which they rushed and died. We had only a little brook, and about one third of us died, but in some of the other camps there were tents in which every one died. When at length it left us, and we moved about to find our people, it was no longer with the song and the dance; but with tears, shrieks, and howlings of despair for those who would never return to us. War was no longer thought of, and we had enough to do to hunt and make provision for our families, for in our sickness we had consumed all our dried provisions; but the Bisons and Red Deer were also gone, we did not see one half of what was before, whither they had gone we could not tell, we believed the Good Spirit had forsaken us, and allowed the Bad Spirit to become our Master. What little we could spare we offered to the Bad Spirit to let us alone and go to our enemies. To the Good Spirit we offered feathers, branches of trees, and sweet smelling grass. Our hearts were low and dejected, and we shall never be again the same people. To hunt for our families was our sole occupation and kill Beavers,

Wolves and Foxes to trade our necessaries; and we thought of War no more, and perhaps would have made peace with them for they had suffered dreadfully as well as us and had left all this fine country of the Bow River to us.

FURTHER READING

Aron, Stephen. *How the West Was Lost: The Transformation of Kentucky from Daniel Boone to Henry Clay.* Baltimore: Johns Hopkins University Press, 1996.

Blyth, Lance R. *Chiricahua and Janos: Communities of Violence in the Southwestern Borderlands, 1680–1880.* Lincoln: University of Nebraska Press, 2011.

Calloway, Colin G. *New Worlds for All: Indians, Europeans, and the Remaking of Early America.* Baltimore: Johns Hopkins University Press, 1997.

Countryman, Edward. *Americans: A Collision of Histories.* New York: Hill and Wang, 1997.

Duval, Kathleen. *Native Ground: Indians and Colonists in the Heart of the Continent.* Philadelphia: University of Pennsylvania Press, 2007.

Faragher, John Mack. *Daniel Boone: The Life and Legend of an American Pioneer.* New York: Henry Holt, 1992.

Furstenberg, Francois. *When the United States Spoke French: Five Refugees Who Shaped a Nation.* New York: Penguin Books, 2015.

Rushforth, Brett. *Bonds of Alliance: Indigenous and Atlantic Slaveries in New France.* Chapel Hill: University of North Carolina Press, 2014.

Silver, Peter. *Our Savage Neighbors: How Indian War Transformed Early America.* New York: Norton, 2007.

Snyder, Christina. *Slavery in Indian County: The Changing Face of Captivity in Early America.* Chapel Hill: University of North Carolina Press, 2007.

THE AMERICAN MAGAZINE,

PRÆVALEBIT ÆQUIOR.

AND

MONTHLY CHRONICLE for the BRITISH Colonies.

Vol. I. N°. VI. FOR MARCH 1758.

Praevalebit Aequior, 1758. This woodcut from the cover of a popular magazine published in Philadelphia shows two traders vying for an Indian's furs. The English trader holds a Bible and a bolt of cloth, while the French trader offers a gun and a tomahawk. In fact, the French were much more successful in maintaining trade relationships with a wide range of tribes, which annoyed the British mightily. The Latin inscription reads "justice will prevail." What did the artist mean? Which deal, French or British, did he think was just? American Antiquarian Society, Worcester, Massachusetts.

From Middle Ground to Settler Frontier

Trade, Warfare, and Diplomacy

E xpensive hats and fashionable furs generated vast wealth and international war on the North American continent. From the beginning, Europeans sought ways to fund colonization, so trade in valuable fur drove territorial expansion and economic development. Many North American places, such as Albany, Charleston, Detroit, Los Angeles, Montreal, Santa Fe, and St. Louis, became fur- and hide-trading centers. However, because the fur trade required Europeans to do business with Native nations on Native terms, it changed the world Europeans expected to build. Diplomacy, marriage, and close personal contact became part of doing business. Native nations that had long controlled trade in North America saw Europeans as potential diplomatic allies and European women and children as potential family members. They also wanted to acquire the trade goods that Europeans offered in return for furs. However, the trade also carried devastating consequences. Not only did European diseases spread through interior tribes and decimate native populations, but Indians grew dependent on European manufactured goods, such as traps, pots, guns, and alcohol. These last two items made intertribal warfare a much deadlier affair.

As this trade occurred over a vast continent, it developed a cultural zone, which historians have labeled "the middle ground." Here Native and European nations and citizens met and devised new customs, sometimes through bloody warfare and other times through friendly accommodation, in order to make the fur trade work. Many Native and European peoples and empires met on this middle ground, but until the French and Indian War in 1763, no one group controlled the destiny of the interior of North America. Because European traders and hunters traveled among the Indians, lived among them, were captured by them, and sometimes married into their tribes, the fur trade operated as one of the most powerful vehicles of cultural integration. The backcountry, which included the entire region between the Appalachian mountains, had all kinds of communities, where people of different races and heritages made lives together. In French fur-trading towns along the St. Lawrence and the Great Lakes and in the maroon communities of the southern interior, where white and Indian traders and escaped African and Native slaves resided, all kinds of people prospered in surprising ways.

Competition created tension among European and Native nations eager to monopolize the lucrative trade in animal pelts. Sometimes this strategy backfired, when powerful tribes demanded preferential treatment or battled each other for supremacy in the trade. In the Beaver Wars of the mid-1600s, the Iroquois attacked the Hurons and their neighbors in the Great Lakes region and raided as far south as the Carolinas in an effort to protect their trade monopolies with the English and Dutch.

In the eighteenth century, the fur trade aggravated existing hostilities between the English and the French. Between 1700 and 1750, England and France were constantly at war with each other. In North America, most of the struggle concerned alliances with the Indians and control over river systems and forts. Colonists and Native peoples who lived anywhere near the uncertain borders of New England and New France felt the effects of this conflict as territory, alliances, and policies shifted with the treaties of 1697, 1713, and 1748.

During the period of relative calm in Europe after 1748, the French and their Native allies spread a network of trading posts and forts south from Canada and east from the Mississippi into the Ohio River valley. There, they intended to build forts and form alliances with the Ohio Indians, effectively cutting the British off from participation in the rich fur trade. At the same time, colonial speculators from Virginia and British government officials formed a land company to sell off lands in Ohio to eager colonial farmers. Both Britain and France claimed the land as theirs, and in 1753 both nations sent troops to claim the spot where the Ohio River began, present-day Pittsburgh. A number of Native nations, including the Huron and Shawnee and parts of the powerful Iroquois Confederacy, had claims in the region as well. Most Native people supported neither the British nor the French; instead they gambled that their future lay in pitting these two empires against each other.

Thus a world war began. Called the French and Indian War (1754–63) in North America, it eventually spread to Europe as the Seven Years' War. The

Brother

Out of regard to you and the Friendship that formerly subsisted between [our] Grandfathers and the English, which has been lately renewed by us, we come to inform you of the news we have heared which you may depend upon is true Brother

All the English that were at Detroit were killed ten days ago, not one left alive. At Sandusky all the white People there was killed 5 days ago, Nineteen in number except the Officer who is a Prisoner and one Boy who made his escape who we have not heard off. At the Mouth of the Twightwee River (about 80 Miles from Sandusky by Water) Hugh Crawford with one Boy was taken Prisoner and Six Men killed. At the Salt Licks five days ago 5 White Men were killed we received the Account this day: we have seen a number of Tracks on the Road between this and Sandusky not far off, which we are sure is a Party coming to cut you and your People off, but as we have sent a Man to watch their motions, [we] request [that] you may think of nothing you have here, but make the best of your way to some place of safety, as we would not desire to see you killed in our Town be carefull to avoid the Road and every part where Indians resort.

What Goods and other Effects you have here, you need not be uneasie about them, we assure you that we will take care to keep them safe for Six Months, perhaps by that time, we may see you or send you word what you may expect from us further. We know there is one White Man at Gichauga that [. . .] don't be concerned for him we will take care to send him [safely back]. Brother

We desire you to tell George Croghan and all your great Men [that they] must not ask us anything about this News, or what has happen[ed] as we are not at all concerned in it: the Nations that have taken up the Hatchett against you are the Ottawas and Chepewas and when you first went to speak with these People you did not consult us upon it, therefore desire you may not expect that we are to Account for any mischief they do, and what you would know further about this News you must learn it by the same Road you first went, but if you will speak with us you must send one or two Men only, and we will hear them. Brother

We thought your King had made Peace with us and all the Western Nations of Indians, for our parts we joined it heartily and desired to hold it allways good, and you may depend upon it we will take care not to be readily cheated or drawn into a war again, but as we are settled between you and these Nations who have taken up the Hatchet against you we desire you will send no Warriors this way till we are removed from this, which we will do as soon as we conveniently can; when we shall permitt you to pass without taking notice; till then we desire they may go by the first Road you went

Gave a String

6th Nothing Extraordinary . . .

9th By a large smoke which rose up the River, we suppose the Enemy has burnt Mr Croghans House, the smoke rising where we imagine his House stood. Nine o'Clock two more Expresses were sent to Venango.

10th This Morning the two Expresses returned having lost themselves in the Night. A[b]out 10 o'Clock in the Morning as some of the Militia were puting up some Fences about 1000 yards from the Fort the Enemy fired on them, they retreated safe to the Fort.

June the 11th At break of day some Indians were discovered amo[ng the houses of the] upper Town, About 10 o'Clock at Night they set fire to [ ] House, on which a Shell was thrown among them, some time [afterwards some] were seen in the lower Town and some hollowing heard at a [ ] from the Fort.

12th An Indian was discovered from the Garden, about 11 o'Clock a Party out cutting Spelts saw two Indians and fired on them, on which a number more appeared and fired on our People, who returned it an[d] some more shot being fired from the Cannon in the Fort the Indians ran off.

13th and 14th Nothing worth Notice . . . .

29th This morning numbers of Mockeson tracks were see in the Ditch where the Enemy were last night.

30th Nothing Extraordinary, a few Indians seen who called to a man that went to drive some Cattle in.

July 1st Six or seven Indians showed themselves this morning at the upper end of the Garden.

2d About 7 o'Clock this Morning some Indians appeared on Grant's Hill, at 12 o'Clock they came into the Cornfield, drove off a number of Cows and shott at several this Night several Indians were seen near Glacies.

3d At 10 o'Clock this morning as a party [went to the] Garden for greens etc. they were fired upon by [Indians] who had hid within 60 yards of the Fort, our [ ] forward and fired upon them and it was thought that [ ] Terrence either killed or wounded one badly as the others were seen helping or Carrying him away, our people pursued íem till they were ordered back, they found his Tomhawk pipe and a Handkerchef which he drop'd. At 1 o'Clock 2 Guns were heard on the opposite side of the Allegany and immediatly four Indians appeared naked and their Bodies painted with different Colours singing as they came along according to their Custom when appearing as friends, they had two small setts of British Colours; Mr McKee went down and asked who they were and what their business was; they answered him they were Ottawas and came from D'Troit 10 days ago where they said everything was settled between them and us in peace and that they had brought Letters from the Commanding Officer there, therefore desired to be brought over. Notwithstanding the fair appearance they came under Mr McKee directed them to go up the River and Cross to a place where the Indians were frequently seen crossing and while they were away, a Cannoe was sent and left for them on the other side; When they came over Mr McKee went and met them a small distance from the Fort. One of them (Commonly called Chatter-box) [ ] large Belts of wampum tied on a stick [delivered the] following Speech to Mr McKee

Brother

Shewing the Belts one of which he called the Friendship Belt; the other for clearing the Path between them and us, this is what we called the Writing we had for you and we are sent (by our Chiefs who will be here to morrow) to acquaint you that they are coming to renew their Friendship by these Belts and to assure you that they are coming with a got intent and hope to be received as friends, this is all we have to say, we propose to go and meet our Chiefs this Afternoon and will return tomorrow. Then asked for some Bread and Tobacco. During this time on Grants Hill a number of Indians appeared very uneasy and came running down towards us, five more appeared over the Ohio or Allegahny, upon this the Ottawas went to their Cannoe where they met those Indians that came from Grants Hill, they talked some time together, during this our People fired several shot at them that came from the Hill which they returned....

8th Nothing Extraordinary. *9th and 10th* None of the Enemy appeared. The People grown careless and stragle about the Fields in as much security as if n Enemy ever had appeared about us. I doubt we shall pay dear for it.

11th All quiet. *12th* Ditto. *13th* Ditto the first Night I have striped since the begining of the allarm.

14th One of the Militia fired on and wounded in three places by some Indians within Two Hundred Yards of the Fort as they were taking care of some Cattle we sent out a Party and brought him in, but fear he will dye being shot through the Arm, Body and thigh and the Bone broke.

15th 16 and 17th nothing more than a number of Indians appearing and the Man wounded the 14th dying....

30th The Enemy last Night gathered under the Bank and we imagined they intended to make an Attack, they fired at the Fort random Shotts all day and Night, the whole under Arms all Night, But few Shot fired from us.

31st The Enemy continued firing random shott. Two shells thrown at some Reaping in Hulings field. In the Evening they called to the Fort and told us they had Letters from Col. Bouquet and George Croghan and desired me to goe for the Letters and they would give them to me. Continued firing at the Fort all Night threw some Hand Grenadoes into the Ditch were we imagined some of the Enemy were.

August 1st The Enemy continued firing Random Shotts from under the bank of Ohio till about three o'Clock when they withdrew and soon [ ] numbers crossing from this to the opposite side of the [ ] luggage. About 6 o'Clock they put up a paper fired [ ] from under the Bank.

August 2d All quiet till about 11 o'Clock when two Indians with a White Man came down on the opposite side of the Ohio and called over that they were expresses from Col. Boquet and G. Croghan at Bedford. . . . after they had read the Letters and heard the Message he delivered them from Mr. Croghan some set of home and some few to War against the Settlements and some Wayondotts to reconnoiter our Army. The Wayondotts in a Council they had declared that they would carry on the war against us while there was a man of them living and told the Delawares and Shawnese that they might do as they pleased. In the Evening he set of with Letters down the Country. . . .

4th Everything quiet—Some Indians lying yet on the opposite side of the Ohio. This Afternoon heard three Death hollows on the opposite side of the River.

5 Three Expresses came in from Col. Boquet who they left with the Troops at Ligonier. These Expresses report they heard at Small's Plantation at Turtle Creek about 18 Miles from here a great deal of Choping Shooting and Bells and see some Indians. We imagine they are gathering there t[o] attack the Col. and 9 o'Clock 2 Expresses were dispatched to meet the Col.

6, 7. 8th Nothing Extraordinary, but the Troops not arriving according to Expectation makes us fear they have been Attacked on their March.

9th Everything quiet, no word of the Troops.

10th at Break of day in the Morning Miller who was sent Express the 5th with two others came in from Col. Boquet, who he left at the Nine Mile Run, he brings an Account that the Indians engaged our Troops for two days, that our People beat them off. . . .

Benjamin West, *The Indians Delivering Up the English Captives to Colonel Bouquet*, 1764.
William Smith, *An Historical Account of the Expedition of the Ohio Indians in the Year 1764*
(Hanover, NH: Dartmouth College, 1766).

Benjamin West's The Indians Delivering Up the
English Captives to Colonel Bouquet, *1764*
(see above)

*When the French and Indian War came to an end in 1764, an aspect of the
peace negotiation involved the thousands of captives taken by Indians during
the course of the war. Many of the captives, especially those who had been taken
as children, did not want to return to their British families. In this engraving,
tearful Shawnees are giving up European children they had adopted into their
families.*

John Vanderlyn, *The Death of Jane McCrea*, 1804. Wadsworth Atheneum, Hartford, Connecticut.

John Vanderlyn's The Death of Jane McCrea, *1804*

This painting, one of the most famous and often copied American images of the nineteenth century, offers another view of captivity, demonstrating that by 1804, the world of the middle ground had disappeared. Here, Indians are clearly savages threatening the life of Jane McCrea, a white woman taken captive in an Indian raid.

FURTHER READING

Anderson, Fred. *The War That Made America: A Short History of the French and Indian War.* New York: Penguin Books, 2007.

Diouf, Sylviane. *Slavery's Exiles: The Story of the American Maroons.* New York: New York University Press, 2014.

Dowd, Gregory. *War under Heaven: Pontiac, the Indian Nations, and the British Empire.* Baltimore: Johns Hopkins University Press, 2004.

Richter, Daniel K. *Before the Revolution: America's Ancient Pasts.* Cambridge, MA: Belknap Press of Harvard University Press, 2011.

Taylor, Alan. *American Colonies: The Settling of North America,* New York: Penguin Books, 2002.

Van Kirk, Sylvia. *Many Tender Ties: Women in Fur Trade Society in Western Canada, 1670–1870.* Norman: University of Oklahoma Press, 1983.

White, Richard. *The Middle Ground: Indians, Empires, and Republics in the Upper Great Lakes, 1650–1815.* Cambridge: Cambridge University Press, 1991.

Witgen, Michael. *An Infinity of Nations: How the Native New World Shaped Early America.* Philadelphia: University of Pennsylvania Press, 2013.

A New Map of The World, with Captain Cook's Tracks, His Discoveries and Those of the Other Circumnavigators. British mapmakers drew this map after Captain James Cook (1776) and other British explorers had explored the Pacific and the northwest coast of North America. It reflects an enormous explosion in knowledge, but one that changed global relationships. Looking carefully at this map, what remains unknown? What does it mean to rename places that indigenous Americans had long used and named? Why divide the world into Eastern and Western Hemispheres?

Robert Laurie and James Whittle, eds., 1812, 3rd ed. Boston Public Library, Boston, Massachusetts.

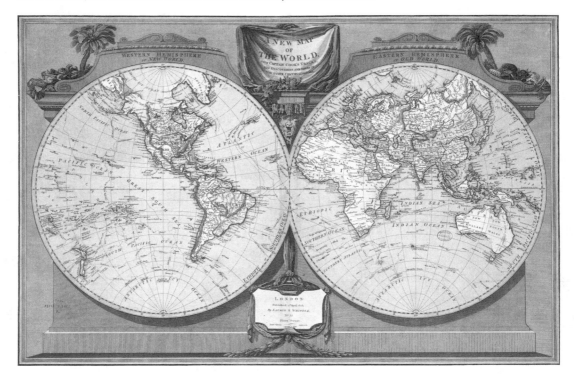

This news I received the day before yesterday, at about nine o'clock at night, when the Captain Commandant, Don Fernando, came bringing it and the mail.

Yesterday, with the best part of the morning taken up with the Office for the Dead, the high Mass, and low Masses for the repose of the deceased Father's soul, and the afternoon, with Don Fernando's second visit and his departure, all I could do was to finish reading the letters. He told us that he was leaving in the afternoon, and I proposed to him that a religious go with him. But he answered that he would travel very fast, and nothing would hold him back; that probably he would not even get off his horse at the various missions en route. I then asked him if later, they could provide an escort for a religious to go down there. His answer was no, because of the few soldiers that were left behind.

On this account, I gave up, as out of the question, my plans to go down there, and help in the re-establishment of the two missions that have been lost at a single blow—namely, San Diego Mission and San Juan Capistrano. Seeing that it is equally impossible for me to write to the three Fathers, who are there, any instructions, and that I have no way of knowing what attention they would pay to my advice to them, since they are busily engaged with setting up a judicial inquiry into the affair, I leave the whole matter in the hands of God. In the field of human help, I have no other recourse than Your Excellency's authority and protection. And so I beseech you earnestly to order most emphatically that the two aforesaid missions be re-established, with all possible speed, on the same sites where they were before, when the outbreak at San Diego took place—if it had not already been done when Your Excellency's orders arrive.

The reason for losing San Capistrano Mission was this. After spending many days in carefully looking over the surrounding country—and I have a long diary of it covering seven sheets from the missionary in charge of the said new mission—the mission was founded with the usual ceremonies on October 30, the octave day of the Saint's feast, in the place that seemed the best suited for it. The site was blessed, the first high Mass was sung, the sacred standard of the cross was raised, etc. Thus a new pueblo of Christians was considered as having been started, with the name of the said patron saint, and situated twenty-three leagues from San Diego, and nineteen from San Gabriel de los Temblores, close by the Camino Real and forming an important link in the chain of missions on that highway.

Since that day, the Fathers, with the help of a few California Indians and other servants, and with some help from the soldiers, began and carried forward such poor buildings as are possible at the start of things, until the day of November 7, in the afternoon, when a letter from San Diego arrived for the Lieutenant of that presidio who was present at the new foundation in order to foster it. The letter brought news of what had happened on the fifth, and the sad news of the Father's death, etc. Accordingly the said

Officer decided that all the soldiers should go to the presidio at San Diego, and that the said foundation should be abandoned. And that is what took place, to the great sorrow of the two Fathers who founded it—Fathers whom the gentiles of that country had received and feasted with many demonstrations of affection.

And that is how the two missions were lost at one blow. They both had given promise of a very prosperous future.

May God's Holy Will be done. Your Excellency, for the love of God, come to their assistance, I beseech you once more.

On the subject of the loss of San Diego Mission, various thoughts have come to my mind. But since complaining about the past remedies nothing, I will change the subject. But, while I think of it, I might suggest again to Your Excellency what I proposed in one of my earlier letters: that in conquests of this kind the place where soldiers are most important is in the missions. The presidios, in many places, may be most suitable and very necessary; but for the situation here, I describe only what is before my eyes.

The San Diego Mission is about two leagues from the presidio, but it is in such a position that, throughout the day, they can see the mission from the presidio; and the gunshot that is fired each morning at dawn in the presidio, to change the watchword of the night guard, can generally be heard in the Mission. Yet while the mission was all on fire, the flames leaping up to a great height from one or two o'clock in the morning until dawn, and during all that time shooting was going on, they saw and heard nothing at the presidio; and the wind, they say, was favorable.

Although there were only two men who fired shots during all that time, many lives were saved which would have been lost without the said defense. And now, after the Father has been killed, the Mission burned, its many and valuable furnishings destroyed, together with the sacred vessels, its paintings, its baptismal, marriage and funeral records, and all the furnishings for the sacristy, the house, and the farm implements—now, the forces of both presidios come together to set things right. . . .

What happened was that before they set about re-establishing the Mission, they wanted to join the various presidios together, and lay hands on the guilty ones who were responsible for the burning of the Mission, and the death of the Fathers, and chastise them. The harassed Indians rebelled anew and became more enraged. I had to stay home and not set out for the Mission and I do not know whether, up to the present time, the Mission has been re-established or not.

And so the soldiers there are gathered together in their presidios, and the Indians in their state of heathenism.

Most Excellent Lord, one [of] the most important requests I made of the Most Illustrious Inspector General, at the beginning of these conquests was: if ever the Indians, whether they be gentile or Christian, killed me, they should be forgiven. The same request I make of Your Excellency. It has been my own fault I did not make this request before. To see a formal statement drawn up by Your Excellency to that effect, in so far as it concerns me, and the other religious who at present are subject to me or will be in the future, would be for me a special consolation during the time Our Lord God will be pleased to add to my advancing years.

While the missionary is alive, let the soldiers guard him, and watch over him, like the pupils of God's very eyes. That is as it should be. Nor do I disdain such a favor for myself. But after the missionary has been killed, what can be gained by campaigns?

Some will say to frighten them and prevent them from killing others.

What I say is that, in order to prevent them from killing others, keep better guard over them than they did over the one who has been killed; and, as to the murderer, let him live, in order that he should be saved—which is the very purpose of our coming here, and the reason which justifies it. Give him to understand, after a moderate amount of punishment, that he is being pardoned in accordance with our law, which commands us to forgive injuries; and let us prepare him, not for death, but for eternal life.

Most Excellent Lord, may Your Excellency pardon me for my interference, who knows for what result. . . .

From this Mission, totally dependent on Your Excellency, of San Carlos de Monterey, December 15, 1775. . . .

Fray Junípero Serra

25. THE GREAT PEACE IN NEW MEXICO

Ecueracapa (Leather Cape) was the name the New Mexican Spaniards gave to the principal chief of the Kotsoteka Comanches. Decades of bitter and brutal warfare between the Spanish, Mexican, and Native nations of the southern plains plagued the region throughout much of the 1700s. Tired of the expense, of the disruption of trade and hunting, as well as of the constant fear of raids, everyone sought peace. In 1785, the Comanches held a huge peace gathering and trade fair along the Arkansas River and agreed to allow Ecueracapa to represent them in negotiations with the Spanish. After months of careful diplomacy, Governor Juan Bautista de Anza, military and political leader of New Mexico, welcomed Ecueracapa and six thousand Comanches to Santa Fe. They hammered out a lasting agreement that improved life and business for everyone. Is the power relationship here one between two sovereign powers or two very unequal groups? What concerns each side the most? How will they guarantee that each side sticks to its promises? Which issues seem most difficult to negotiate from these two very different worldviews?

Ecueracapa

Spanish-Comanche Peace Treaty, New Mexico

1786[1]

Articles of Peace agreed upon and arranged in the Villa of Santa Fe and the Pueblo of Pecos between Colonel Don Juan Bautista de Anza, Governor of the province of New Mexico, and the Comanche captain, Ecueracapa, Commissioner-General of this nation on the days, 25th and 28th of February of 1786.

Articles proposed by Ecueracapa	Replies of the Governor	Resolutions of the Commander-General
1. That in the name of all his nation, he was soliciting a new and better established peace with the Spaniards, understanding that it would not be infringed on their part by any word nor at any time, particularly with the advice of the captains and principal men.	Conceded under the particular nature which this article sets forth.	Approved. The cessation of hostilities being understood on the part of the Comanches of New Mexico, Texas, Colony of Santander and in other parts of the Dominions of his Majesty and with all his vassals wherever they might find them.
2. That the nation is admitted under the protection of the king, and allowed to establish itself not far distant from the settlements.	Conceded with the conditions which the Commander General may take or prescribe admitting them, meanwhile, to live in our territory.	Concerning the first, I extend to the Comanche nation under the name of his Majesty the protection which it solicits while that nation subsists under our guardianship. In virtue of the above the governor will take care that the Utes maintain the peace celebrate by his mediation, always provided that the Comanches do not break it, promising them similar good offices by means of the chiefs of Louisiana with the Pawnees and the rest of the groups of our alliance with whom they have war, now and in the future. The Comanches in return must keep peace with all the Indians who may be the friends of the Spaniards. With regard to the second, it is approved, under the condition that they must establish themselves in the regions and in the number which the governor may assign to them and must obtain his permission every time they might wish to move their establishment closer to the province.
.[???] That for the cultivation of [???] of both [???] free and passage be [???] to the [???] himself [???] Pecos to capital to re-[???] his trips, [???] provided [???]: it is convenient; and to the community of the nation, the establishment of fairs and free trade with the cited pueblo.	Conceded to the Commissioner-General, proposing entrance to Santa Fe for the ends which he seeks, and also to the fairs in Pecos for all his nation under equitable rules which must be established during consultation with the Señor Commander-General.	Approved. A regulation of trade will be drawn up in consultation with the plenipotentiary, Ecueracapa, and other captains of the nations who represent their rights in arrangement with the particular measures which I am proposing to the governor.

---

1. In A.B. Thomas, *Forgotten Frontiers:* A Study of the Spanish Indian policy of Don Juan Bautista de Anza, Governor of New Mexico, 1777–1787 (Norman, University of Oklahoma Press, 1932), 329–331

4. That desirous of returning the favors he has received and hoping to enjoy the friendship of the Spaniards, he binds himself to declare more offensively than ever against the common Apache enemies, offering at the same time to join expeditions of troops provided they take a direction and range which they [the Comanches] can follow.

This offer is accepted. With regard to carrying it out whatever is convenient will be agreed upon separately.

Agreed to in such a manner that the Comanches may proceed in this article in agreement with the orders and instructions of the governor of New Mexico with respect to that province and to that of Texas concerning the war against the eastern Apaches, provided always that for this purpose the rancherías next to the Taguayaces and the rest of the allies in that region be called upon.

5. That the reply to the points referred to be reserved to be placed before the other captains and ones authorized who were following and would arrive at Pecos; that he be given a token or credential so that with those as additional witnesses he could give evidence to the scattered rancherías that the entire nation was at peace so that none of the captains with the pretext of ignorance could avoid fulfilling what was delegated to them.

Agreed, delivering to him, as I do deliver my staff to exhibit it to the absent rancherías as a token of admission to peace with the obligation of returning the staff afterwards.

Approved. I await the union, harmony, and observation of these articles by all the branches and rancherías of the Comanche nation under whatever denomination they may exist, as it will be maintained and fulfilled on our part.

Pueblo of Pecos, February 28, 1786.
Juan Bautista de Anza.

Chihuahua, October 5, 1786.

Jacob Ugarte y Loyola

These articles of peace were proposed in this Villa of Santa Fe by Captain Ecueracapa, Plenipotentiary of the Comanche nation, on February 25 of this year, and conceded in Pecos on the 28th of the same, in the terms which appear opposite each one, by me, Colonel Don Juan Bautista de Anza, Governor of New Mexico, authorized for this purpose by the Señor Commander-General. The captain of the nation itself, Tosacondata, Tosapoy, Hichapat, Paraginanchi, Cuentaninaveni, Quihuanteantime, Sohucat, Canaguaipe, Pasimampat, Toyamancare, Tichinalla, and thirty-one other distinguished individuals were present and empowered by guarantees for its fulfillment, having come before me after having ratified the articles on their part Captains Huanecoruco, and Oxamaquea, of the same branch; Chama, Hisaquebera, Tuchubara, and Encantime of that of the Yupes; with El Querenilla or Priest of their religion, and Tosaporua, Pasahuoques, Paxabipo, Cunabunit, and Quahuahacante of that of the Yamparicas, with many individuals dependent upon the above-mentioned chiefs. Of this I certify. Santa Fe, July 14, 1786. Juan Bautista de Anza.

It is a copy of which I certify, Chihuahua. December 21, 1786.

Pedro Garrido y Duran

26. A BIG NEW WORLD IN THE PACIFIC

Captain James Cook, a fine naval commander, writer, and mapmaker, was an exceptional fundraiser and explorer in an age crowded with ambition and talent. Cook led three lengthy circumnavigations that included the discovery of New Zealand and Australia, New Guinea, Tahiti, and the Hawa'iian islands. His extensive voyages between 1768 and 1779 were sponsored by the Royal Society and made him a hero of scientific exploration. On his third voyage, he mapped the Western Pacific, but his principal goal was to explore the West Coast of North America north of the Spanish settlements in California. Cook's ships landed on the Oregon coast at a place he called Cape Foulweather, and he then headed north to Nootka Sound in what is now British Columbia. This selection from Cook's journals describes his landing at a Native village called Yuquot. Cook would be killed several months later by native Hawa'iians. What surprises Cook and his men about the situation in Nootka? How does Cook describe the landscape? Can you see anything in their interactions with Native people that could have led to his death later?

Captain James Cook
"Nootka Sound and the Northwest Coast Native Nations"
1776[1]

KING George's Sound was the appellation given by the Commodore to this inlet, on our first arrival; but he was afterwards informed that the natives called it Nootka. The entrance is in the east corner of Hope Bay; its latitude is 49 d. 33 m. N. and its longitude 233 d. 12 m. E. The east coast of that bay is covered by a chain of sunken rocks; and, near the Sound, are some islands and rocks above water. We enter the Sound between two rocky points, lying E. S. E. and W. N. W. from each other, distant about four miles. The Sound widens within these points, and extends in to the northward at least four leagues.

A number of islands, of various sizes, appear in the middle of the Sound. The depth of water, not only in the middle of the Sound, but also close to some parts of its shore, is from forty-seven to ninety fathoms, or more. Within its circuit, the harbours and anchoring places are numerous. The cove, where our ships anchored, is on the east side of the Sound, and also on the east of the largest island. It is, indeed, covered from the sea, which is its principal recommendation, for it is exposed to the S. E. winds, which sometimes blow with great violence, and make 'great devastation,' as was but too apparent in many places.

Upon the sea coast the land is tolerably high and level; but, within the Sound, it rises into steep hills, which have an uniform appearance, ending in roundish tops, with sharp ridges on their sides. Many of these hills are high, and others are of a moderate height; but all of them are covered to their tops with the thickest woods. Some bare spots are to be seen on the sides of some of the hills, but they are not numerous, though they sufficiently shew the general rocky disposition of these hills. They have, indeed, no soil upon them, except what has been produced from rotten mosses and trees, of the depth of about two feet. Their foundations are, indeed, nothing more than stupendous rocks; which are of a

---

1. James Cook. *Captain Cook's Voyages Round the World: . . . Including Captain Furneaux's Journal . . .* Glasgow: Printed for Niven, Napier & Khull, for W.D. & A. Brownlie . . ., 1807–1809 Vol 3, 149, 162–166. (Hathitrust Digital)

grey or whitish cast when exposed to the weather; but, when broken, are of a blueish grey colour. The rocky shores consist entirely of this; and the beaches of the little coves in the Sound are composed of fragments of it.

During our stay the weather nearly corresponded with that which we had experienced when we were off the coast. We had fine clear weather, if the wind was between N. and W. but if more to the southward, hazy, accompanied with rain. The climate appears to be infinitely milder than that on the east coast of America, under the same parallel of latitude. We perceived no frost in any of the low ground; but, on the contrary, vegetation proceeded very briskly, for we saw grass, at this time, upwards of a foot long.

. . . The ornamental figures in these garments are disposed with great taste, and are generally of a different colour, being usually dyed either of a deep brown or yellow; the latter of which when new, equals, in brightness, the best in our carpets.

Their fondness for carving on all their wooden articles, corresponds with their taste in working figures upon their garments. Nothing is to be seen without a freeze-work, or a representation of some animal upon it; but the most general figure is that of the human face, which is frequently cut out upon birds, and the other monstrous things already mentioned; and even upon their weapons of bone and stone.

The general design of these figures conveys a sufficient knowledge of the objects they are intended to represent; though, in the carving, very little dexterity is displayed. But, in the execution of many of the masks and heads, they have shewn themselves ingenuous sculptors. They preserve, with the greatest exactness, the general character of their own faces, and finish the most minute parts with great accuracy and neatness. That these people have a strong propensity to works of this sort, is observable in a variety of particulars. Representations of human figures; birds; beasts; fish; models of their canoes, and household utensils, were found among them in very great abundance.

Having mentioned their skill in some of the imitative arts, such as working figures in their garments and engraving, or carving them in wood; we may also add their drawing them in colours. The whole process of their whale fishery has been represented, in this manner, on the caps they wear. This, indeed, was rudely executed, but served, at least, to convince us, that, though they have not the knowledge of letters amongst them, they have a notion of representing actions, in a lasting way, exclusive of recording them in their songs and 'traditions.' They have also other painted figures, which, perhaps, have no established significations, and are only the creation of fancy or caprice.

Though the structure of their canoes is simple, they appear well calculated for every useful purpose. The largest, which contain upwards of twenty people, are formed of a single tree. The length of many of them is forty feet, the breadth seven, and the depth three. They become gradually narrower from the middle towards each end, the stern ending perpendicularly, with a knob at the top. The fore part stretches forwards and upwards, and ends in a point or prow, much higher than the sides of the canoe, which are nearly straight. The greatest part of them are without any ornament; some have a little carving and are studded with seals' teeth on the surface. Some have also in additional prow, usually painted with a figure of some animal. They have neither seats nor any other supporters, on the inside, except some small round sticks, about the size of a walking cane placed across, about half the depth of the canoe. They are very light, and, on account of their breadth and flatness, swim firmly, without an outrigger, of which they are all destitute. Their paddles, which are small and light, resemble a large leaf in shape, being pointed at the bottom, broad in the middle, and gradually becoming narrower in the shaft; the whole length being about five feet. By constant use, they have acquired great dexterity in the management of these paddles; but they never make use of any sails.

For fishing and hunting, their instruments are ingeniously contrived, and completely made. They consist of nets, hooks, and lines, harpoons, gigs, and an instrument resembling an oar. The latter is about twenty feet in length, four or five inches in breadth, and of the thickness of half an inch. The edges, for about two thirds of its length, are set with sharp bone teeth, about two inches in length; the other third serving for a handle. With this instrument they attack herrings and sardines, and such other fish as come in shoals. It is struck into the shoal, and the fish are taken either upon, or between the teeth. Their hooks, which are made of bone and wood, display no great ingenuity, but the harpoon, which is used in striking whales, and other sea animals, manifests a great extent of contrivance. It consists of a piece of bone, formed into two barbs, in which the oval blade of a muscle shell, and the point of the instrument is fixed. Two or three fathoms of rope is fastened to this harpoon, and, in throwing it, they use a shaft of about fifteen feet long, to which the rope is fastened; to one end of which the harpoon is fixed so as to leave the shaft floating, as a buoy upon the water, when the animal is struck: with the harpoon.

We are strangers to the manner of their catching or killing land animals, but, it is probable, that they shoot the smaller sort with their arrows; and encounter bears, wolves, and foxes, with their spears. They have several sorts of nets, which are perhaps applied to that purpose; it being customary for them to throw them over their heads, to signify their use, when they offered them for sale. Sometimes they decoy animals, by disguising themselves with a skin, and running upon all fours, in which they are remarkably nimble; making, at the same time, a kind of noise, or neighing. The masks, or carved heads, as well as the dried heads of different animals, are used upon these occasions.

Every thing of the rope kind, which they use in making their various articles, is formed either from thongs of skins, and sinews of animals, or from the flaxen substance, of which they manufacture their mantles. The sinews were sometimes to remarkably long, that it was hardly possible they could have belonged

Excerpt from the journal of Father Thomas de la Peña, a member of the Spanish 1774 Perez Expedition. On August 8, they met a group of Native Americans who were probably the Nootka.

On the 8th [of August, 1774]…About four o'clock three canoes came out to us…They remained at some distance from the ship, crying out and making gestures that we should go away. After some time, we having made signs to them that they should draw near without fear, they did so, and we gave them to understand that we were in search of water; but they could not have been very satisfied with our signs, and went back to land. In going back they met with two other canoes which were coming out to the ship; but, after communication had between them, they turned back towards the land…About eight o'clock at night three canoes, with fifteen pagans in them came to us; but they remained at a distance from the ship, their occupants crying out in a mournful tone of voice. We called to them, and they drew near. Shortly afterward they said goodbye, but, until after eleven o'clock, they remained at a distance of about a musket-shot from the ship, talking among themselves and sometimes crying out. The canoes of these pagans are not so large as those we saw at Point Santa Margarita in latitude 55° [where they met the Haida Indians of the Queen Charlotte Islands]…The paddles are very handsome and are shaped like a shovel with a point…very well made.

The 9th dawned calm and clear towards the northwest…there arrived fifteen canoes with about a hundred men and women. We gave them to understand that they might draw near without fear, and presently they came to us and began to trade with our people what they brought in their canoes, which consisted only of skins of otters and other animals, hats of rushes, painted and with the crown pointed, and cloths woven of a kind of hemp, having fringes of the same, with which they clothe themselves, most of them wearing a cape of this material. Our people bought several of these articles, in exchange for old clothes, shells which we had brought from Monterey and some knives; for these and the shells they manifested greater liking.

to any other animal than the whale. The same conjecture may be hazarded with regard to the bones, of which they make their instruments and weapons.

The assistance they receive from iron tools, contributes to their dexterity in wooden performances. Their implements are almost wholly made of iron; at least, we saw but one chissel that was not made of that metal, and that was only of bone. The knife and the chissel are the principal forms that iron assumes amongst them. The chissel consists of a flat long piece, fastened into a wooden handle. A stone is their mallet, and a bit of fish skin their polisher. Some of these chissels were nine or ten inches in length, and three or four in breadth; but they were, in general, considerably smaller.

Some of their knives were very large, and their blades are crooked; the edge being on the back or convex part. What we have seen among them, were about the breadth and thickness of an iron hoop; and their singular form sufficiently proves that they are not of European make. These iron tools are sharpened upon a coarse slate whetstone, and the whole instrument is kept continually bright.

Iron is called by the natives *seekemaile,* a name which they also gave to tin, and other white metals. It being so common among these people, we were anxious to discover how it could be conveyed to them. As soon as we arrived in the Sound, we perceived that they had a knowledge, of traffic, and an inclination to pursue it; and we were afterwards convinced that they had not acquired this knowlege from a cursory interview with any strangers, but it seemed habitual to them, and was a practice in which they were well skilled.

With whom they carry on this traffic, we cannot ascertain; for, though we saw several articles of European manufacture, or such, at least, as had been derived from some civilized nation, such as brass and iron, it does not certainly follow that they were received immediately from these nations. For we never could obtain the least information of their having seen ships, like ours, before, nor of their having been engaged in commerce with such people. Many circumstances corroborate to prove this beyond a doubt. On our arrival, they were earnest in their enquiries, whether we meant to settle amongst them, and whether we were friendly visitors; informing us, at the same time, that they freely gave us wood and water from motives of friendship.

27. SUPPRESSING THE WHISKEY REBELLION

Nearly 80 percent of the federal budget was spent battling Indians and protecting white settlers in the backcountry between New England and the Ohio Country. To recover some of these costs, Congress passed a tax on whiskey stills. Common on backcountry farms, stills made whiskey from grain, providing one of the few sources of cash for farmers. Furious cash-poor farmers refused to pay the tax, and in western Pennsylvania they started a little war. After a confrontation with a tax collector in 1794, protesters marched to Pittsburgh, where they threatened to kill wealthy landowners. President Washington, fearing a widespread revolt, sent out thirteen thousand troops to quell the rebellion and occupy western Pennsylvania. Charged with delivering President Washington's specific orders, outlined in the following letter, Secretary of the Treasury Alexander Hamilton accompanied the army as it moved through rebellious counties. What were Washington's objectives in sending out so many troops? Was Hamilton concerned about issues of civil liberty? How did he suggest that the militia go about determining which citizens should be imprisoned and which let go?

Alexander Hamilton
Orders to Governor Lee of Pennsylvania
1794[1]

Bedford, 20th October, 1794

Sir:—I have it in special instruction from the President of the United States, now at this place, to convey to you, on his behalf, the following instructions, for the general direction of your conduct, in command of the militia army, with which you are charged.

The objects for which the Militia have been called forth, are,

1. To suppress the combinations which exist in some of the western counties of Pennsylvania, in opposition to the laws laying duties upon spirits distilled within the United States, and upon stills.
2. To cause the laws to be executed.

These objects are to be effected in two ways:

1. By military force.
2. By judiciary process, and other civil proceedings.

The objects of the military force are two-fold:

1. To overcome any armed opposition which may exist.
2. To countenance and support the civil officers in the means of executing the laws.

With a view to the first of these two objects, you may proceed as speedily as may be with the army under your command, into the insurgent counties, to attack, and as far as shall be in your power, subdue all persons whom you may find in arms, in opposition to the laws above mentioned. You will march your army in two columns, from the places where they are now assembled, by the most convenient routes, having regard to the nature of the roads, the convenience of supply, and the facility of coöperation and union, and bearing in mind that you ought to act until the contrary shall be fully developed, on the general principle of having to contend with the whole force of the counties of Fayette, Westmoreland, Wash-

1. H.M. Brackenbridge, *History of the Western Insurrection in Western Pennsylvania Commonly Called the Whiskey Insurrection* (Pittsburgh: W.S. Haven, 1859), 283–285.

ington and Allegheny, and of that part of Bedford which lies westward of the town of Bedford; and that you are to put as little as possible to hazard. The approximation, therefore, of your columns, is to be sought; and the subdivision of them, so as to place the parts out of mutual supporting distance, to be avoided, as far as local circumstances will permit. Parkinsons Ferry appears to be a proper point toward which to direct the march of the columns for the purpose of ulterior measures.

When arrived within the insurgent country, if an armed opposition appear, it may be proper to publish a proclamation inviting all good citizens, friends to the constitution and laws, to join the standard of the United States. If no armed opposition exist, it may still be proper to publish a proclamation, exhorting to a peaceful and dutiful demeanor, and giving assurances of performing, with good faith and liberality, whatsoever may have been promised by the commissioners, to those who have complied with the conditions prescribed by them, and who have not forfeited their title by subsequent misdemeanor.

Of these persons in arms, if any, whom you may make prisoners; leaders, including all persons in command, are to be delivered to the civil magistrates; the rest to be disarmed, admonished, and sent home, (except such as may have been particularly violent, and also influential,) causing their own recognizances for their good behavior to be taken, in the cases which it may be deemed expedient.

With a view to the second point, namely, the countenance and support of the civil officers in the means of executing their laws: you will make such dispensations as shall appear proper, to countenance and protect, and if necessary, and required by them, to support and aid the civil officers in the execution of their respective duties; for bringing offenders and delinquents to justice; for seizing the still of delinquent distillers, as far as the same shall be deemed eligible by the supervisor of the revenue, or chief officer of inspection; and also for conveying to places of safe custody such persons as may be apprehended and not admitted to bail.

The objects of judiciary process and other civil proceedings shall be:

1. To bring offenders to justice.
2. To enforce penalties on delinquent distillers by suit.
3. To enforce the penalties of forfeiture on the same persons by the seizure of their stills and spirits.

The better to effect these purposes, the Judge of the district, Richard Peters, Esq., and the Attorney of the district, William Rawl, Esq., accompany the army.

You are aware that the Judge cannot be controlled in his functions. But I count on his disposition to coöperate in such a general plan, as shall appear to you consistent with the policy of the case. But your method of giving direction to proceedings, according to your general plan, will be by instructions to the district attorney.

He ought particularly to be instructed (with due regard to time and circumstances,) 1st, To procure to be arrested all influential actors in riots and unlawful assemblies, relating to the insurrection and combination to resist the laws; or having for object to abet that insurrection and these combinations; and who shall not have complied with the terms offered by the commissioners, or manifested their repentance in some other way, which you may deem satisfactory. 2d. To cause process to issue, for enforcing penalties on delinquent distillers. 3d. To cause offenders who may be arrested, to be conveyed to jails where there will be no danger of rescue—those for misdemeanors to the jails of York and Lancaster—those for capital offenses to the jail of Philadelphia, as more secure than the others. 4th. Prosecute indictable offenses in the court of the United States; those for penalties, or delinquents, under the laws before mentioned, in the courts of Pennsylvania. . . .

The seizure of stills is of the province of the supervisor, and other officers of inspection. It is difficult to chalk out a precise line concerning it. There are opposite considerations which will require to be nicely balanced, and which must be judged of by those officers on the spot. It may be useful to confine the seizure of stills to the most leading and refractory distillers. It may be advisable to extend them far into the most refractory county.

When the insurrection is subdued, and the requisite means have been put in execution to secure obedience to the laws, so as to render it proper for the army to retire, (an event which you will accelerate as much as shall be consistent with the object,) you will endeavor to make an arrangement for attaching such a force as you may deem adequate, to be stationed within the disaffected counties, in such a manner as best to afford protection to well disposed citizens, and the officers of the revenue; and to suppress by their presence the spirit of riot and opposition to the laws.

But, before you withdraw the army, you shall promise, on be half of the President, a general pardon to all such as shall not have been arrested, with such exceptions as you shall deem proper. The promise must be so guarded, as not to affect pecuniary claims under the revenue law. In this measure it is advisable there should be a coöperation with the Governor of Pennsylvania.

On the return of the army, you will adopt some convenient and certain arrangements for restoring to the public magazines, the arms, accoutrements, military stores, tents, and other articles of camp equipage and entrenching tools which have been furnished, and shall not have been consumed or lost.

You are to exert yourself by all possible means to preserve discipline amongst the troops, particularly a scrupulous regard to the rights of persons and property, and a respect for the authority of the civil magistrates; taking especial care to inculcate, and cause to be observed this principle—that the duties of the army are confined to attacking and subduing of armed opponents of the laws, and to the supporting and aiding of the civil officers in the execution of their functions. . . .

With great respect, I have the honor to be, Sir,

Your obedient servant,
ALEXANDER HAMILTON.

28. MISSIONS, FAMILY AUTHORITY, AND NATIVE REBELLION

Franciscan priests and Spanish soldiers established the Santa Clara Mission along San Francisco Bay in 1777. The mission became the center of a successful agricultural and trade community. Like all missions, Santa Clara used local Native people as laborers to build the mission, to work the fields, and to serve in the households of priests and soldiers. Their labor, however, was not voluntary. Spanish priests believed that the gift of hearing the Christian word was payment for any sacrifices Native Californians made. Spanish soldiers did marry local Indian women, but violence stood at the center of these relationships as well, as most women were captured from Native villages. By 1812, when several hundred missions sprinkled what is now the Southwest, it is apparent how challenging mission life was. In this document, a questionnaire sent by Catholic authorities about conditions in the mission, we can see that the missions succeeded in one sense. They did become productive agricultural and trade centers, and they transported the ideas of Spanish Catholicism to New Spain. However, the missions failed miserably at their central task. Fifty years after the California missions had been established, what issues were most challenging at Santa Clara? What kind of community had developed there? How did mission fathers measure success? How was Native people's refusal to adapt Spanish ways of thinking and living made apparent?

Father Jose SeDan

Replies of the Sta. Clara of Alta California to the Government's Questionnaire Communicated by the Illustrious Bishop of Sonora, 1812.[1]

[Father SeDan's answers to the questions are in bold.]

To which will reply those individuals consulted by the civil and ecclesiastical authorities of the Americas and its Islands concerning the various articles included. Expecting that through their zeal, instruction and knowledge they will fulfill this assignment employing all possible critical observations, so that by this means the government may have the information to guide it impartially in the direction of all that is useful and beneficial for those vassals.

1. Let them state the number of casta found in the population, that is Americans, Europeans, Indians, Mestizos, Blacks, etc., without any omissions.

---

1. Santa Clara University Mission Collection, http://content.scu.edu/cdm/ref/collection/msc/id/88.

Long live Jesus, Mary and Joseph
To the 1st question . . . That this mission consists of 2 European missionaries of the Colegio Apostolico de San Fernando in Mexico, and of 1,347 Christian Indians. There is besides the guard or escort, which consists of a corporal and 5 soldiers all of them married and with family or children, and these as well as the inhabitants of the adjacent town of San Jose of Guadalupe, which consists of 277 souls total, and because they have no parish priest, the missionary fathers of this mission take charge of them spiritually, we consider them all Spaniards or people of reason, although there might be some among them from other classes.

2. What is the origin of these castas, with the exception of the first two. Because, concerning Blacks, they do not all share the same origin, for although the majority that migrated to America are Africans, there are Blacks in the Philippines who are native to that territory, who hide in the hills since the Malays dominated those Islands.

That the Indians were all born in this Mission and its surroundings. That there are no more to conquer, except to the east, 20 leagues away, neither the Christians nor the pagans know anything about their origin (of the people 20 leagues away). That Spanish and Indians have married but no blacks.

4. If they love their wives and their children, what type of education do they give to their children, and if they are trained in agriculture or the mechanical arts.

To the 4th . . . That generally the Indians, Christians as well as pagans, love their wives and children. That they do not educate their children at all. That they do not know, or need agriculture, because they are satisfied with the wild seeds, hunting and fishing of which there is plenty in mountains, fields, ocean, rivers and lakes. That they do not have or know any skills other than making bows and arrows, which they make with perfection and shoot with dexterity. That the Christians here in the Mission receive daily instruction, and they are taught agriculture and other mechanical skills.

5. If they have the Europeans and Americans in good esteem, or if they have any reasons for complain or hatred against them, and what are they.
6. Considering the causes that contribute to this problem, what would be the means necessary to reconcile them.

To the 5th and 6th . . . Since the Indians feel affection and respect toward the people of reason, there is no need of any means to attract them. Holy

matrimony between soldiers and Native women and their children creates affections, but hatred when men return to Mexico.

7. If they have an inclination to read and write in their own languages. If they use our paper or the leaves or barks from trees, or plants. Identify them by name.

To the 7th . . . The Indians have no inclination towards reading or writing. It is true that the boys learn to read easily, especially some of them, but since we the missionaries have no other interest than to teach the doctrine, and have singers and musicians for the functions of the church, we are satisfied with this, being aware of their lack of interest and our heavy work.

That the Christian Indians already understand and speak Spanish, with the sole stimulation of the missionary fathers and with frequent communication with the people of reason, and also with the school for the young ones; we know no easier and simpler ways, and if these Indians do not speak, and understand more Spanish, it is because of their coarseness and extreme unwillingness to leave what is theirs.

9. What are their strongest virtues, are they charitable, generous, compassionate. Differentiate between the two genders. . . .

That their dominant virtues without doubt are their love to their relatives and servants, the docility, respect and obedience to the Spaniards or people of reason, and especially to the missionary fathers.

That the Indians are very superstitious. They worship the devils offering them seeds, fasts and dances, for them to be favorable. They believe that they can free themselves from their enemies and illnesses through vain observances and the use of some plants, roots, feathers and other things. They try to harm others, and seek vengeance through spells and with herbs and thorns. And finally they believe everything they dream. We know no other means to destroy such evil than frequent sermons and instruction, time and patience.

14. What type of pacts or conditions do they observe for their matrimonial alliances, what type of service do the suitors provide to the parents of the bride, and for how long?

To the 14th . . . That the Indians as pagans do not engage in formal deals, pacts or conditions. Once the suitor obtains the consent of the bride and her parents, he presents them with a gift, and from then on they consider themselves married. They are married in the mission with the solemnity of the church, with no other pacts or services from the couple than some presents given before the ceremony to the bride, her parents or close relatives.

FURTHER READING

Cook, James R. *The Journals of Captain Cook,* abr. ed. New York: Penguin Books, 2000.

Countryman, Edward. *Americans: A Collision of Histories.* New York: Hill and Wang, 1996.

Hackel, Steven W. *Junípero Serra: California's Founding Father.* New York: Hill and Wang, 2015.

Hämäläinen, Pekka N. *The Comanche Empire.* New Haven, CT: Yale University Press, 2009.

Horsman, Reginald. *Expansion and American Indian Policy, 1783–1812.* Norman: University of Oklahoma Press, 1992.

Igler, David. *The Great Ocean: Pacific Worlds from Captain Cook to the Gold Rush.* New York: Oxford University Press, 2013.

Little, Ann. *The Many Captivities of Esther Wheelwright.* New Haven, CT: Yale University Press, 2016.

Middlekauff, Robert. *The Glorious Cause: The American Revolution, 1763–1789.* New York: Oxford University Press, 1982.

Saunt, Claudio. *West of the Revolution: An Uncommon History of 1776.* New York: W. W. Norton, 2014.

Weber, David J. *The Spanish Frontier in North America.* New Haven, CT: Yale University Press, 1992.

Arikara map, 1804. When Lewis and Clark traveled up the Missouri River on their great exploratory tour in 1804, part of their charge was to learn who lived on the river and what "the borders of their countries" were. Through translators, they asked local Indian nations to describe where they lived and how they organized their villages. An Arikara leader, Inquidanecharo, drew this map of Arikara villages at Clark's request, and it was part of the material he delivered to President Thomas Jefferson in 1806. What does this map tell you about how the Arikara imagined their landscape? How would a map drawn entirely by Jefferson's soldiers be different?

From Carte ethnographique de la vallée du Missouri. Bibliotheque Nationale, Paris.

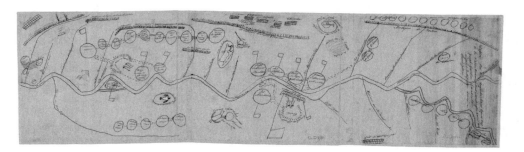

Creating the United States

Incorporating the First West

After the 1783 Treaty of Paris ended the American Revolution, the former colonies faced crucial challenges. They had to build a government; demobilize an army; and transform rebels, loyalists, and the undecided into a nation of citizens. Communities had to decide who could be citizens and who couldn't. What about women, slaves, members of Native nations, or residents of French or Spanish colonies? The new government, an alliance of states held together by the Articles of Confederation, had little power; most Americans wanted a powerful local and a weak national government. That desire was complicated by the situation created by treaty negotiations with Great Britain: thirteen colonies along the Atlantic seaboard and a vast swath of unassigned land between the Appalachian Mountains and the Mississippi River. This was, of course, Indian country.

During the revolution, thousands of white residents had moved onto this land, and migration increased dramatically when the war ended. The new immigrants also took up land claimed by the British, the Spanish, and the Native nation in the Mississippi and Ohio River valleys. From the perspective of Euro-American newcomers, under attack by Indians and unable to use the rivers because of the British and Spanish, the fledgling nation's Congress seemed ineffectual. In Kentucky, new residents threatened to join with the British. President George Washington worried that he would lose the entire region to the British if they saw its real instability. He described the loyalties of backcountry settlers as being so delicate that "the touch of a feather would drive them away."

Congress sought ways to build authority in the West and to incorporate the region physically and culturally into a nation. Congress appointed Thomas Jefferson to draft a policy to manage land in the national domain. Jefferson's attempt to create rules about how Americans could use or acquire land had to ensure that national and local goals were balanced. Together, the Land Ordinance of 1785 and the Northwest Ordinance of 1787 gave Americans a way to survey, claim, and develop land for individual farms and for larger communities. A reflection of Jefferson's practicality and rationality, the ordinances imposed a rigid grid on the landscape. They also represented his vision of individuals and communities farming in the West. The legislation offered new communities a blueprint for forming governments, so that they could become permanent states within the union.

However, this legislation did not solve the most serious obstacle to land settlement: the dozens of powerful Indian nations that occupied and fiercely protected their land west of the Appalachians. After a few treaties had been carefully negotiated and signed by some Iroquois, Huron, and Delaware bands, in 1786 a united Indian confederation led by the Shawnees announced that no more land would be given away without unanimous Indian consent and that the Indians would "prevent your surveyors and other people from coming upon our side of the Ohio River," exactly the land that had just been fought over and divided up as part of the national domain. It would take two decades of violent warfare to wrest the land from Native peoples.

Backcountry warfare cost the government an enormous price in cash and lives, neither of which the new republic could afford to pay. In 1790, confederated Native warriors led by Little Turtle (Miami) and Blue Jacket (Shawnee) defeated fifteen hundred American troops. In 1791, the Western Indian Confederation routed General Arthur St. Clair's army in western Ohio, killing six hundred men and wounding three hundred more. For a time, Indian Territory looked impregnable. However, a new army, led by General Anthony Wayne, won a victory at the Battle of Fallen Timbers in 1794. As a result, a thousand Indian delegates came to the signing of the Treaty of Greenville and ceded most of Ohio and Indiana to the United States. The battle over land shifted farther west.

By 1800, the United States was one of the world's largest nations in terms of geography. Many Americans at the time feared size already divided the nation in significant ways: East versus West, seaboard versus backcountry, commercial economy versus subsistence economy, slave labor versus free labor, Native farmers versus white farmers. Thomas Jefferson, who became president in

1800, imagined a nation of small independent farmers linked east to west by transportation networks, a political vision that pleased neither wealthy merchants nor subsistence farmers. Small farmers, particularly those who didn't own slaves and who lived in the West far from markets, had little interest in paying taxes to improve commerce for wealthy merchants. Wealthy merchants were similarly unhappy because Spain owned New Orleans and thus controlled access to the Mississippi River. Native peoples, who still outnumbered Euro-Americans, felt cheated and pressured by white squatters and were angry at the US Army, which never kept its promises about protection or treaty rights.

Complication became crisis in 1802, when Spain closed the port of New Orleans to American traders and announced that it had ceded the territory of Louisiana (then more than half of the trans-Mississippi West) to Napoleonic France. Napoleon envisioned a great French empire in the New World based on sugar, a serious threat to American development. Jefferson sent negotiators to Paris to buy New Orleans. By early 1803, when negotiations began, the Haitian Revolution had driven the French out of the sugar business, and another war loomed between England and France. Daunted by these crises and the expense of building an American empire, Napoleon offered to sell all of Louisiana to the United States for the bargain price of $15 million. The American negotiators, stunned by the offer, accepted eagerly, even though neither they nor the president had the constitutional authority to do this.

This purchase doubled the landmass of the United States and included much of what was labeled as "Indian country" on maps of the period. Few US citizens understood the massive scope of the acquisition. It included all the land that drained into the Mississippi and Missouri Rivers south to the Arkansas River, a giant swath that few white Americans could even imagine. It had long been occupied by Native nations, as well as mixed communities, in which French, Spanish, Russian, and Native people lived and traded. These people knew the region intimately, but their knowledge was not readily available to the American public, and many mountain and river systems had never been mapped. Jefferson, the most geographically sophisticated politician in the nation, recognized that official knowledge about the Louisiana Purchase was crucial to its becoming part of the nation.

First, however, Jefferson and the nation had to understand more about the vast region they had acquired and more about the millions of people living there. To explore the drainage area of the Missouri River, he sent his personal secretary, Captain Meriwether Lewis, and a military hero, William Clark, as coleaders of an ambitious expedition. They had three big tasks: to find the new national border, to find a practical water route (the infamous Northwest Passage) to connect the Mississippi River with the Pacific, and to determine if this vast landscape could include Indian Country.

The documents in this chapter highlight the challenges of defining a new nation and defining and developing a citizenry. A set of maps shows how borders and geographical understanding evolved in the late eighteenth century because of new explorations and shared knowledge. Thomas Jefferson's Land Ordinance of 1785 lays out how the new nation could use the additional land. Little Turtle, a Miami Indian, comments on the meaning of land to his people. To expand the United States even farther and create new challenges in Indian country, Thomas Jefferson authorizes the Lewis and Clark expedition to the West, and William Clark describes the most difficult part of the trip. Finally, Tecumseh, a great Shawnee warrior, explains how to defeat the US Army a generation later.

29. BOUNDARIES FOR THE NEW NATION

Understanding the boundaries of the new nation challenged a generation of diplomats and surveyors. The 1783 Treaty of Paris, which severed the United States from the British Empire, designated the Mississippi River as the nation's western border and the St. Lawrence and the Great Lakes as the northern border. Spain got control of the entire southern Atlantic and Gulf Coast from Georgia to what is now Texas. Lack of accurate maps and the ignorance of diplomats left details murky, although some maps drawn by Native people demonstrated a depth of knowledge that few politicians had. The following maps, drawn with imagination and hope more than actual knowledge, demonstrate the complexity of borders and land ownership in the early republic. Where is the boundary between backcountry and more settled regions in the 1790s? What do these maps reveal about attitudes toward land ownership. How are Indians' claims designated? How did Indian or European mapmakers deal with regions they knew little about?

English, Native American, and Anglo-American Maps of North America
1771–1811

A General Map of the Middle British Colonies in America, 1771 (see pp. 132–33)

Drawn before the American Revolution, this map by Lewis Evans shows details of the middle colonies. It also lays out Indian claims in the much-disputed Ohio country west of the Appalachian Mountains and identifies deer and beaver-hunting regions.

The United States in 1783 (see pp. 134–35)

This, the first widely distributed map of the new United States, shows the borders as they were understood by the treaty signers in Paris in 1783. Compare this map by John Wallis to the preceding one. What has happened to Indian claims?

The Genesee Country, 1800 (see p. 136)

Published to help resolve the question of competing land claims, this map by Charles Williamson shows the complexity of "the Genesee country" of Upstate New York, so called because of the land claims of the Genesee Company. The map reflects the various ways land was bought up in the early years of the republic. Some individuals owned enormous tracts, while Revolutionary War veterans and small farmers received smaller grants.

The Interior of North America, 1811 (see p. 137)

This map by Aaron Arrowsmith, first published in 1795 and then in this revised form in 1811, shows the rapid growth of the new nation. It also illustrates how poorly official geographic understanding meshed with the reality of rapid migration. What important geographic features are missing from this map?

30. IMAGINING THE ORDERLY REPUBLIC

The Land Ordinance of 1785 represented a congressional attempt to impose order on the nation's western borders, where squatters, speculators, and Indians battled each other over land ownership. One of the federal government's motives was to find ways to sell the land quickly in order to raise revenue for its impoverished treasury. Thomas Jefferson wrote the ordinance specifically for the Ohio River Valley, but he intended it to apply to all further land cessions. Jefferson devised a grid system of squares that could be divided into 640-acre claims for individuals or into larger claims for townships or companies. This system required that land be carefully surveyed before it could be sold and that land offices be established to record sales and issue deeds, measures that solved the problem of squatters and unscrupulous speculators, who sold one piece of land many times over. However, official surveyors moved far more slowly than backcountry settlement took place, and the issue of competing claims and squatters remained contentious for at least another century. What does this piece of legislation demonstrate about American hopes for the future? How did Jefferson (and Congress) envision the ideal community? How did this vision conflict with the goals of individual white settlers or of Native nations in the West?

Next page: A general map of the middle British colonies in America, 1771. Map Division, Library of Congress.

Next spread: The United States in 1783. Map Division, Library of Congress.

THE
UNITED STATES
of
AMERICA
laid down
From the best Authorities,
Agreeable to the Peace of
— 1783. —
Published April 3.d 1783,
by the Proprietor
JOHN WALLIS.

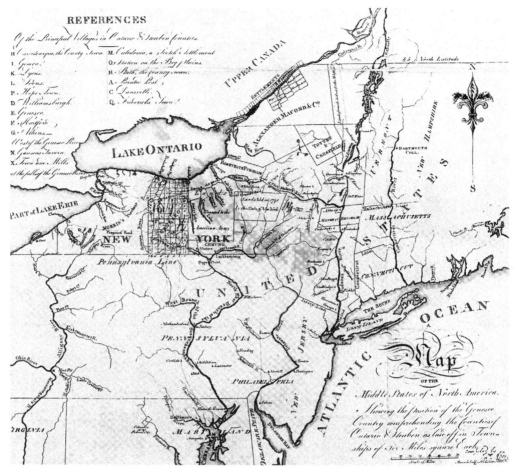

The Genesee country, 1800. Map Division, Library of Congress.

The Land Ordinance of 1785

*An Ordinance for Ascertaining the Mode of
Disposing of Lands in the Western Territory.*

Be it ordained by the United States in Congress assembled, that the territory ceded by individual States to the United States, which has been purchased of the Indian inhabitants, shall be disposed of in the following manner:

A surveyor from each state shall be appointed by Congress, or a committee of the States, who shall take an Oath for the faithful discharge of his duty,

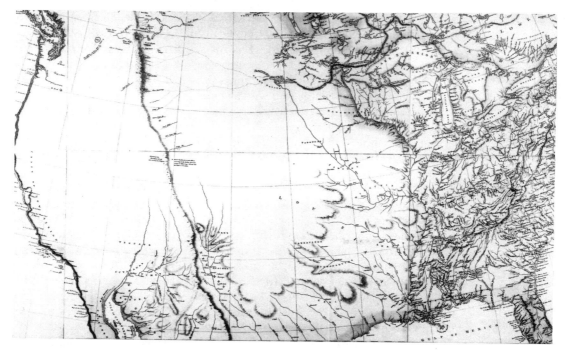

The Interior of North America, 1811. Special Collections, University of Virginia, Charlottesville.

before the Geographer of the United States, who is hereby empowered and directed to administer the same; and the like oath shall be administered to each chain carrier, by the surveyor under whom he acts.

The Geographer, under whose direction the surveyors shall act, shall occasionally form such regulations for their conduct, as he shall deem necessary; and shall have authority to suspend them for misconduct in Office, and shall make report of the same to Congress, or to the Committee of the States; and he shall make report in case of sickness, death, or resignation of any surveyor.

The Surveyors, as they are respectively qualified, shall proceed to divide the said territory into townships of six miles square, by lines running due north and south, and others crossing these at right angles, as near as may be, unless where the boundaries, of the late Indian purchases [refers to lands received at the Treaty of Fort Stanwix in 1784] may render the same impracticable, and then they shall depart from this rule no farther than such particular circumstances may require; and each surveyor shall be allowed and paid at the rate of two dollars for every mile, in length, he shall run, including the wages of chain carriers, markers, and every other expense attending the same.

The first line, running north and south as aforesaid, shall begin on the river Ohio, at a point that shall be found to be due north from the western termination of a line, which has been run as the southern boundary of the state of Pennsylvania; and the first line, running east and west, shall begin at the same point, and shall extend throughout the whole territory. . . .

The lines shall be measured with a chain; shall be plainly marked by chaps on the trees, and exactly described on a plat; whereon shall be noted by the surveyor, at their proper distances, all mines, salt springs, salt licks and mill seats, that shall come to his knowledge, and all water courses, mountains and other remarkable and permanent things, over and near which such lines shall pass, and also the quality of the lands.

The plats of the townships respectively, shall be marked by subdivisions into lots of one mile square, or 640 acres, in the same direction as the external lines, and numbered from 1 to 36; always beginning the succeeding range of the lots with the number next to that with which the preceding one concluded. And where, from the causes before mentioned, only a fractional part of a township shall be surveyed, the lots, protracted thereon, shall bear the same numbers as if the township had been entire. And the surveyors, in running the external lines of the townships, shall, at the interval of every mile, mark corners for the lots which are adjacent, always designating the same in a different manner from those of the townships. . . .

As soon as seven ranges of townships, and fractional parts of townships, in the direction from south to north, shall have been surveyed, the geographer shall transmit plats thereof to the board of treasury, who shall record the same, with the report, in well bound books to be kept for that purpose. . . .

The board of treasury shall transmit a copy of the original plats, previously noting thereon, the townships, and fractional parts of townships, which shall have fallen to the several states, by the distribution aforesaid, to the Commissioners of the loan office of the several states, who, after giving notice of not less than two nor more than six months, by causing advertisements to be posted up at the court houses, or other noted places in every county, and to be inserted in one newspaper, published in the states of their residence respectively, shall proceed to sell the townships, or fractional parts of townships, at public vendue, in the following manner, viz: The township, or fractional part of a township, N 1, in the first range, shall be sold entire; and N 2, in the same range, by lots; and thus in alternate order through the whole of the first range. The township, or fractional part of a township, N 1, in the second range, shall be sold by lots; and N 2, in the same range, entire; and so in alternate order through the whole of the second range; and the third range shall be sold in the same manner as the first, and the fourth in the same manner as the second, and thus alternately throughout all the ranges; provided, that none of the lands, within the said territory, be sold under the price of one dollar the acre, to be paid in specie, or loan office certificates, reduced to specie value, by the scale of depreciation, or certificates of liquidated debts of the United States, including interest, besides the expense of the survey and other charges thereon, which are hereby rated at thirty six dollars the township, in specie, or certificates as aforesaid, and so in the same proportion for a fractional part of a township, or of a lot, to be paid at the time of sales; on failure of which payment, the said lands shall again be offered for sale.

There shall be reserved for the United States out of every township, the four lots, being numbered 8, 11, 26, 29, and out of every fractional part of a township, so many lots of the same numbers as shall be found thereon, for future sale. There shall be reserved the lot N 16, of every township, for the maintenance of public schools, within the said township; also one third part of all gold, silver, lead and copper mines, to be sold, or otherwise disposed of as Congress shall hereafter direct. . . .

And be it further Ordained, That the towns of Gnadenhutten, Schoenbrun and Salem, on the Muskingum, and so much of the lands adjoining to the said towns, with the buildings and improvements thereon, shall be reserved for the sole use of the Christian Indians, who were formerly settled there, or the remains of that society, as may, in the judgment of the Geographer, be sufficient for them to cultivate.

Saving and reserving always, to all officers and soldiers entitled to lands on the northwest side of the Ohio, by donation or bounty from the commonwealth of Virginia, and to all persons claiming under them, all rights to which they are so entitled, under the deed of cession executed by the delegates for the state of Virginia, on the first day of March, 1784, and the act of Congress accepting the same: and to the end, that the said rights may be fully and effectually secured, according to the true intent and meaning of the said deed of cession and act aforesaid, Be it Ordained, that no part of the land included between the rivers called little Miami and Sciota, on the northwest side of the river Ohio, be sold, or in any manner alienated, until there shall first have been laid off and appropriated for the said Officers and Soldiers, and persons claiming under them, the lands they are entitled to, agreeably to the said deed of cession and act of Congress accepting the same.

Done by the United States in Congress assembled, the 20th day of May, in the year of our Lord 1785, and of our sovereignty and independence the ninth.

31. AN INDIAN VIEW OF LAND ISSUES

The expansionistic aims of the United States foundered on the reality that Native nations controlled most of the land the Americans had won from the British. In the years just after the revolution, the young nation struggled to develop a workable Indian policy, the center of which was the treaty. In theory, treaty negotiations with Indian nations were given the same standing as international diplomacy, but in practice the United States often ignored its treaty obligations and took land it had guaranteed to Indians. Determined to answer the question of who controlled Ohio River country, and equally determined to keep his government from looking weak to the British, President Washington instructed his army to force all Indians out of Ohio. After several years of brutal defeats at the hands of Native armies, the United States finally won a significant victory against the Ohio Indians. Now, Washington and his secretary of war, Henry Knox, intended to push all Native peoples into the Mississippi Valley. Little Turtle, a Miami leader, who had witnessed several rounds of treaty-making with the United States and suffered defeat in the battle at Fallen Timbers, understood the reality of his situation in 1795. Referring to the government negotiator as an "elder brother" in the following remarks about the Treaty of Greenville, Little Turtle expresses his hope that the government would respect this final border. How did Little Turtle claim Indian rights to land? Why was the issue of who built forts in the region so important? How did his assumptions about land use differ from those reflected in the Land Ordinance of 1785?

Little Turtle
Comments on the Treaty of Greenville
1795[1]

Elder Brother, and all you present: I am going to say a few words, in the name of the Pottawatamies, Weas and Kickapoos. It is well known to you all, that people are appointed on those occasions, to speak the sentiments of others; therefor am I appointed for those three nations.

Elder Brother: You told your younger brothers, when we first assembled, that peace was your object; you swore your interpreters before us, to the faithful discharge of their duty, and told them the Great Spirit would punish them, did they not perform it. You told us, that it was not you, but the President of the Fifteen Fires of the United States, who spoke to us; that, whatever he should say, should be firm and lasting; that it was impossible he should say what was not true. Rest assured, that your younger brothers, the Miamis, Ottawas, Chippewas, Pottawatamies, Shawnees, Weas, Kickapoos, Piankeshaws, and Kaskaskias, are well pleased with your words, and are persuaded of their sincerity. You have told us to consider of the boundaries you showed us; your younger brothers have done so, and now proceed to give you their answer.

Elder Brother: Your younger brothers do not wish to hide their sentiments from you. I wish to be the same with those of the Wyandottes and Delawares; you have told us that most of the reservations you proposed to us belonged to

1. "Little Turtle Responds to the Treaty of Greenville," in *Indian Oratory: Famous Speeches by Noted Indian Chieftains,* ed. W.C. Vanderwerth (Norman: University of Oklahoma Press, 1971), 55–59.

our fathers, the French and the British. Permit your younger brothers to make a few observations on this subject.

Elder Brother: We wish you to listen with attention to our words. You have told your younger brothers that the British imposed falsehoods on us when they said the United States wished to take our lands from us, and that the United States had no such designs. You pointed out to us the boundary line, which crossed, a little below Loromie's Store and struck Fort Recovery and run from thence to the Ohio, opposite the mouth of the Kentucky river.

Elder Brother: You have told us to speak our minds freely, and we now do it. This line takes in the greater and best part of your brothers' hunting ground. Therefore, your younger brothers are of opinion you take too much of their lands away and confine the hunting of our young men within the limits too contracted. Your brothers, the Miamis, the proprietors of those lands, and all your younger brothers present, wish you to run the lines as you mentioned to Fort Recovery and to continue it along the road; from thence to Fort Hamilton, on the great Miami River. This is what your brothers request you to do, and you may rest assured of the free navigation of that river, from thence to its mouth, forever.

Brother: Here is the road we wish to be the boundary between us. What lies to the east we wish to be yours; that to the west, we would desire to be ours.

Elder Brother: In speaking of the reservations, you say they are designed for the same purpose as those for which our fathers, the French and English, occupied them. Your younger brothers now wish to make some observations on them.

Elder Brother: Listen to me with attention. You told us you discovered on the Great Miami traces of an old fort. It was not a French fort, brother; it was a fort built by me. You perceived another at Loromies. 'Tis true a Frenchman once lived there for a year or two. The Miami villages were occupied as you remarked, but it was unknown to your younger brothers until you told them that we had sold the land there to the French or English. I was much surprised to hear you say that it was my forefathers had set the example to other Indians in selling their lands. I will inform you in what manner the French and English occupied those places.

Elder Brother: These people were seen by our forefathers first at Detroit. Afterwards we saw them at the Miami village—that glorious gate, which your younger brothers had the happiness to own, and through which all the good words of our chiefs had to pass, from the north to the south, and from the east to the west. Brothers, these people never told us they wished to purchase our lands from us. *FR + ENG*

Elder Brother: I now give you the true sentiment of your younger brothers the Miamis, with respect to the reservation at the Miami villages. We thank you for kindly contracting the limits you at first proposed. We wish you to take this six miles square on the side of the river where your fort now stands, as your younger brothers wish to inhabit that beloved spot again. You shall cut hay for your cattle wherever you please, and you shall never require in vain the assistance of your younger brothers at that place.

Elder Brother: The next place you pointed to was the Little River, and said you wanted two miles square at that place. This is a request that our fathers, the French or British, never made us. It was always ours. This carrying place has heretofore proved in a great degree the subsistence of your younger brothers. That place has brought us in the course of one day the amount of one hundred dollars. Let us both own this place and enjoy in common the advantages it affords. You told us at Chicago the French possessed a fort. We have never heard of it. We thank you for the trade you promised to open in our country, and permit us to remark that we wish our former traders may be continued and mixed with yours.

Elder Brother: On the subject of hostages, I have only to observe that I trust all my brothers present are of my opinion with regard to peace and our future happiness. I expect to be with you every day when you settle on your reservations, and it will be impossible for me or my people to withhold from you a single prisoner. Therefore, we don't know why any of us should remain here. These are the sentiments of your younger brothers present, on these particulars.

32. LOUISIANA: ENCOUNTERING ANOTHER NATIVE WEST

Jefferson had planned a scientific investigation of the West long before he even became president, but the Louisiana Purchase enabled him to carry it out. In January of 1803, Jefferson sent Congress a confidential request to fund a trip to learn more about Native nations west of the Mississippi. He directed Lewis and Clark and their retinue of soldiers, called the "Corps of Discovery," along with guides, Indians, slaves, and animals, to head to the Pacific Coast, deep in British territory, a fact he left out of the message to Congress. When Lewis and Clark headed up the Missouri River in the summer of 1804, they knew only a little about what they might find. They set off from St. Louis with forty-four men, including American soldiers, French trappers, guides of mixed European and Indian descent, and William Clark's slave, York. They also hired a Shoshoni woman, Sacajawea, the wife of one of their interpreters, to serve as a guide. Lewis and Clark, the two captains of this "corps of discovery," knew they would have to negotiate two rivers and a huge distance. They did not expect to find the massive Rocky Mountain ranges, hundreds of miles wide and covered in deep snow much of the year. How did Jefferson make the expedition sound like a worthy enterprise? What did Jefferson lead Congress to expect about Indian country west of the Mississippi? For Lewis and Clark, what were the most difficult aspects of travel in the mountains? How did their description change ideas about what was possible in the West?

Thomas Jefferson

Secret Message to Congress
1803[1]

January 18, 1803.

Gentlemen of the Senate and of the House of Representatives:

As the continuance of the act for establishing trading houses with the Indian tribes will be under the consideration of the Legislature at its present session, I think it my duty to communicate the views which have guided me in the execution of that act, in order that you may decide on the policy of continuing it in the present or any other form, or discontinue it altogether if that shall, on the whole, seem most for the public good.

The Indian tribes residing within the limits of the United States have for a considerable time been growing more and more uneasy at the constant diminution of the territory they occupy, although effected by their own voluntary sales, and the policy has long been gaining strength with them of refusing absolutely all further sale on any conditions, insomuch that at this time it hazards their friendship and excites dangerous jealousies and perturbations in their minds to make any overture for the purchase of the smallest portions of their land. A very few tribes only are not yet obstinately in these dispositions. In order peaceably to counteract this policy of theirs and to provide an extension of territory which the rapid increase of our numbers will call for, two measures are deemed expedient. First, To encourage them to abandon hunting, to apply to the raising [of] stock, to agriculture, and domestic manufacture, and thereby prove to themselves that less land and labor will maintain them in this better than in their former mode of living. The extensive forests necessary in the hunting life will then become useless, and they will see advantage in exchanging them for the means of improving their farms and of increasing their domestic comforts. Secondly, To multiply trading houses among them, and place within their reach those things which will contribute more to their domestic comfort than the possession of extensive but uncultivated wilds. Experience and reflection will develop to them the wisdom of exchanging what they can spare and we want for what we can spare and they want. In leading them thus to agriculture, to manufactures, and civilization; in bringing together their and our sentiments, and in preparing them ultimately to participate in the benefits of our Government, I trust and believe we are acting for their greatest good. At these trading houses we have pursued the principles of the act of Congress which directs that the commerce shall be carried on liberally, and requires only that the capital stock shall not be diminished. We consequently undersell private traders, foreign and domestic, drive them from

---

1. "President Thomas Jefferson's Secret Message to Congress" in *A Compilaton of the Messages and Papers of the Presidents*, ed. James D. Richardson, v. 1 (New York: Bureau of National Literature, 1896), 352–54.

the competition, and thus, with the good will of the Indians, rid ourselves of a description of men who are constantly endeavoring to excite in the Indian mind suspicions, fears, and irritations toward us. . . .

While the extension of the public commerce among the Indian tribes may deprive of that source of profit such of our citizens as are engaged in it, it might be worthy the attention of Congress in their care of individual as well as of the general interest to point in another direction the enterprise of these citizens, as profitably for themselves and more usefully for the public. The river Missouri and the Indians inhabiting it are not as well known as is rendered desirable by their connection with the Mississippi, and consequently with us. It is, however, understood that the country on that river is inhabited by numerous tribes, who furnish great supplies of furs and peltry to the trade of another nation, carried on in a high latitude through an infinite number of portages and lakes shut up by ice through a long season. The commerce on that line could bear no competition with that of the Missouri, traversing a moderate climate, offering, according to the best accounts, a continued navigation from its source, and possibly with a single portage from the Western Ocean, and finding to the Atlantic a choice of channels through the Illinois or Wabash, the Lakes and Hudson, through the Ohio and Susquehanna, or Potomac or James rivers, and through the Tennessee and Savannah rivers. An intelligent officer, with ten or twelve chosen men, fit for the enterprise and willing to undertake it, taken from our posts where they may be spared without inconvenience, might explore the whole line, even to the Western Ocean, have conferences with the natives on the subject of commercial intercourse, get admission among them for our traders as others are admitted, agree upon convenient deposits for an interchange of articles, and return with the information acquired in the course of two summers. Their arms and accouterments, some instruments of observation, and light and cheap presents for the Indians would be all the apparatus they could carry, and with an expectation of a soldier's portion of land on their return would constitute the whole expense. Their pay would be going on whether here or there. While other civilized nations have encountered great expense to enlarge the boundaries of knowledge by undertaking voyages of discovery, and for other literary purposes, in various parts and directions, our nation seems to owe to the same object, as well as to its own interests, to explore this the only line of easy communication across the continent, and so directly traversing our own part of it. The interests of commerce place the principal object within the constitutional powers and care of Congress, and that it should incidentally advance the geographical knowledge of our own continent can not but be an additional gratification. The nation claiming the territory, regarding this as a literary pursuit, which it is in the habit of permitting within its dominions, would not be disposed to view it with jealousy, even if the expiring state of its interests there did not render it a matter of indifference. The appropriation of $2,500 "for the purpose of extending the external commerce of the United States," while understood and considered by the Executive as giving the legislative sanction, would cover the undertaking from notice and prevent the obstructions which interested individuals might otherwise previously prepare in its way.

TH: JEFFERSON

Meriwether Lewis and William Clark
Journal Entries
1804–6[1]

Tuesday [September] 10. The morning being fair all the hunters were sent out, and the rest of the party employed in repairing their clothes: two of them were sent to the junction of the river from the east, along which the Indians go to the Missouri. . . . Towards evening one of the hunters returned with three Indians, whom he had met in his excursion up Traveller's-rest creek: as soon as they saw him they prepared to attack him with arrows, but he quieted them by laying down his gun and advancing towards them, and soon persuaded them to come to the camp. Our Shoshonee guide could not speak the language of these people, but by the universal language of signs and gesticulations, which is perfectly intelligible among the Indians, he found that these were three Tushepaw Flatheads in pursuit of two men, supposed to be Shoshonees, who had stolen twenty-three of their horses: we gave them some boiled venison and a few presents; such as a fishhook, a steel to strike fire, and a little powder; but they seemed better pleased with a piece of riband which we tied in the hair of each of them. They were however in such haste, lest their horses should be carried off, that two of them set out after sunset in quest of the robbers: the third however was persuaded to remain with us and conduct us to his relations: these he said were numerous, and resided on the Columbia in the plain below the mountains. From that place he added, the river was navigable to the ocean; that some of his relations had been there last fall and seen an old white man who resided there by himself, and who gave them some handkerchiefs like those we have. The distance from this place is five sleeps or days' journey. When our hunters had all joined us we found our provisions consisted of four deer, a beaver, and three grouse.

The observation of to-day gave 46° 48′ 28″ as the latitude of Travellers-rest creek. . . .

Thursday 12. There was a white frost this morning. We proceeded at seven o'clock and soon passed a stream falling in on the right, near which was an old Indian camp with a bath or sweating-house covered with earth. At two miles distance we ascended a high, and thence continued through a hilly and thickly

1. Meriwether Lewis, *Original Journals of the Lewis and Clark Expedition*, ed. R. Thwaites, v. 7 (New York: Dodd, Mead, 1905), 481–87.

timbered country for nine miles, when we came to the forks of the creek, where the road branches up each fork. We followed the western route, and finding that the creek made a considerable bend at the distance of four miles, crossed a high mountain in order to avoid the circuit. The road had been very bad during the first part of the day, but the passage of the mountain, which was eight miles across, was very painful to the horses, as we were obliged to go over steep stony sides of hills and along the hollows and ravines, rendered more disagreeable by the fallen timber, chiefly pine, spruce pine and fir. We at length reached the creek having made twenty-three miles of a route so difficult that some of the party did not join us before ten o'clock. We found the account of the scantiness of game but too true, as we were not able to procure any thing during the whole of yesterday, and to-day we killed only a single pheasant. Along the road we observed many of the pine trees pealed off, which is done by the Indians to procure the inner bark for food in the spring.

Friday 13. Two of the horses strayed away during the night, and one of them being captain Lewis's, he remained with four men to search for them while proceeded up the creek: at the distance of two miles we came to several springs issuing from large rocks of a coarse hard grit, and nearly boiling hot. These seem to be much frequented as there are several paths made by elk, deer and other animals, and near one of the springs a hole or Indian bath, and roads leading in different directions. These embarrassed our guide, who mistaking the road took us three miles out of the proper course over an exceedingly bad route. We then fell into the right road, and proceeded on very well, when having made five miles we stopped to refresh the horses. . . . Other mountains covered with snow are in view to the southeast and southwest. We were somewhat more fortunate to-day in killing a deer and several pheasants which were of the common species, except that the tail was black.

Saturday 14. The day was very cloudy with rain and hail in the vallies, while on the top of the mountains some snow fell. We proceeded early, and continuing along the right side of Glade creek crossed a high mountain, and at the distance of six miles reached the place where it is joined by another branch of equal size from the right. Near the forks the Tushepaws have had an encampment which is but recently abandoned, for the grass is entirely destroyed by horses, and two fish weirs across the creek are still remaining; no fish were however to be seen. . . . The mountains which we crossed to-day were much more difficult than those of yesterday; the last was particularly fatiguing, being steep and broken by fallen timber, and thickly overgrown by pine, spruce, fir, hacmatack and tamarac. Although we had made only seventeen miles we were all very weary. The whole stock of animal food was now exhausted, and we therefore killed a colt, on which we made a hearty supper. From this incident we called the last creek we had passed from the south Colt-killed creek. The river itself is eighty yards wide, with a swift current, and a stony channel. Its Indian name is Kooskooskee.

Sunday 15. At an early hour we proceeded along the right side of the Koosk-ooskee over steep rocky points of land, till at the distance of four miles we reached an old Indian fishing place: the road here turned to the right of the water, and began to ascend a mountain: but the fire and wind had prostrated or dried almost all the timber on the south side, and the ascents were so steep that we were forced to wind in every direction round the high knobs which con-stantly impeded our progress. Several of the horses lost their foot-hold and slipped: one of them which was loaded with a desk and small trunk, rolled over and over for forty yards, till his fall was stopped by a tree. The desk was broken; but the poor animal escaped without much injury. . . .

. . . All around us are high rugged mountains, among which is a lofty range from southeast to northwest, whose tops are without timber, and in some places covered with snow. The night was cloudy and very cold, and three hours before daybreak,

Monday 16, it began to snow, and continued all day, so that by evening it was six or eight inches deep. This covered the track so completely, that we were obliged constantly to halt and examine, lest we should lose the route. In many places we had nothing to guide us except the branches of the trees which, being low, have been rubbed by the burdens of the Indian horses. The road was, like that of yesterday, along steep hill sides, obstructed with fallen timber, and a growth of eight different species of pine, so thickly strewed that the snow falls from them as we pass, and keeps us continually wet to the skin, and so cold, that we are anxious lest our feet should be frozen, as we have only thin mocca-sins to defend them.

. . . We had now made thirteen miles. We were all very wet, cold, and hungry but although before setting out this morning, we had seen four deer, yet we could not procure any of them, and were obliged to kill a second colt for our supper.

Tuesday 17. Our horses became so much scattered during the night, that we were detained till one o'clock before they were all collected. We then continued our route over high rough knobs, and several drains and springs, and along a ridge of country separating the waters of two small rivers. The road was still difficult, and several of the horses fell and injured themselves very much, so that we were unable to advance more than ten miles to a small stream, on which we encamped.

We had killed a few pheasants, but these being insufficient for our subsistence, we killed another of the colts. This want of provisions, and the extreme fatigue to which we were subjected, and the dreary prospects before us, began to dispirit the men. It was therefore agreed that captain Clarke should go on ahead with six hunters, and endeavour to kill something for the support of the party. . . .

Wednesday 18. . . . we were detained till after eight o'clock by the loss of one of our horses which had strayed away and could not be found. We then proceeded, but having soon finished the remainder of the colt killed yesterday, felt the want of provisions, which was more sensible from our meeting with no water, till towards nightfall we found some in a ravine among the hills. By pushing on our horses almost to their utmost strength, we made eighteen miles.

We then melted some snow, and supped on a little portable soup, a few canisters of which, with about twenty weight of bears oil, are our only remaining means of subsistence. Our guns are scarcely of any service, for there is no living creature in these mountains, except a few small pheasants, a small species of gray squirrel, and a blue bird of the vulture kind about the size of a turtle dove or jay, and even these are difficult to shoot.

Thursday 19. . . . Three miles beyond this last branch of Hungry creek we encamped, after a fatiguing route of eighteen miles. The road along the creek is a narrow rocky path near the borders of very high precipices, from which a fall seems almost inevitable destruction. One of our horses slipped and rolling over with his load down the hill side, which was nearly perpendicular and strewed with large irregular rocks, nearly a hundred yards, and did not stop till he fell into the creek: we all expected he was killed, but to our astonishment, on taking off his load, he rose, and seemed but little injured, and in twenty minutes proceeded with his load. Having no other provision we took some portable soup, our only refreshment during the day. This abstinence, joined with fatigue, has a visible effect on our health. The men are growing weak and losing their flesh very fast: several are afflicted with the dysentery, and erruptions of the skin are very common.

Friday 20. Captain Clarke went on through a country as rugged as usual till on passing a low mountain he came at the distance of four miles to the forks of a large creek. Down this he kept on a course south 60° west for two miles, then turning to the right, continued over a dividing ridge where were the heads of several little streams, and at twelve miles distance descended the last of the rocky mountains and reached the level country. A beautiful open plain partially supplied with pine now presented itself. . . .

Saturday, [February 21, 1806,] and proceeded towards the flats. The mortification of being obliged to tread back our steps, rendered still more tedious a route always so obstructed by brush and fallen timber, that it could not be passed without difficulty and even danger to our horses. One of these poor creatures wounded himself so badly in jumping over fallen logs that he was rendered unfit for use, and sickness has deprived us of the service of a second. At the pass of Collins's creek we met two Indians, who returned with us about half a mile, to the spot where we had formerly slept in September, and where we now halted to dine and let our horses graze. These Indians had four supernumerary horses, and were on their way to cross the mountains. They had seen Drewyer and Shannon, who they said would not return for two days. We pressed them to remain with us till that time, in order to conduct us over the mountains, to which they consented, and deposited their stores of roots and bread in the bushes at a little distance. After dinner we left three men to hunt till our return, and then proceeded; but we had not gone further than two miles when the Indians halted in a small prairie, where they promised to remain at least two nights, if we did not overtake them sooner. We left them, and about seven in the evening found ourselves at the old encampment on the flats; and were glad to find that four hunters whom we had sent ahead, had killed a deer for supper. . . .

Tuesday 24, . . . *Set* out on a second attempt to cross the mountains. On reaching Collins's creek, we found only one of our men, who informed us that a short time before he arrived there yesterday, the two Indians, tired of waiting, had set out, and the other four of our men had accompanied them as they were directed. After halting, we went on to Fish creek, the branch of Hungry creek, where we had slept on the nineteenth instant.

In the evening the Indians, in order as they said to bring fair weather for our journey, set fire to the woods. As these consist chiefly of tall fir trees, with very numerous dried branches, the blaze was almost instantaneous, and as the flame mounted to the tops of the highest trees, resembled a splendid display of fireworks. In the morning,

Wednesday, 25, one of our guides complained of being sick, a symptom by no means pleasant, for sickness is generally with an Indian the pretext for abandoning an enterprise which he dislikes. He promised, however, to overtake us, and we therefore left him with his two companions, and set out at an early hour. At eleven o'clock we halted for dinner at the branch of Hungry creek, where we found our two men, who had killed nothing. Here too we were joined, rather unexpectedly by our guides, who now appeared disposed to be faithful to their engagements. The Indian was indeed really sick, and having no other covering except a pair of moccasins and an elk skin dressed without the hair, we supplied him with a buffaloe robe.

In the evening we arrived at Hungry creek, and halted for the night about a mile and a half below our encampment of the sixteenth.

Thursday, 26. Having collected our horses, and taken breakfast, we set out at six o'clock, and pursuing our former route, at length began to ascend, for the second time, the ridge of mountains. . . . The whole country was completely covered with snow, except that occasionally we saw a few square feet of earth, at the roots of some trees, round which the snow had dissolved. We passed our camp of September 18, and late in the evening reached the deserted spot, and encamped near a good spring of water. It was on the steep side of a mountain, with no wood and a fair southern aspect, from which the snow seems to have melted for about ten days, and given place to an abundant growth of young grass, resembling the green sward. . . .

In the night there came to the camp a Chopunnish, who had pursued with a view of accompanying us to the falls of the Missouri. We now learnt that the two young Indians whom we had met on the twenty-first, and detained several days, were going merely on a party of pleasure to the Ootlashoots, or as they call them, Shallees, a band of Tushepahs, who live on Clarke's river, near Traveller's-rest. Early the next morning,

Friday, 27, we resumed our route over the heights and steep hills of the same great ridge. At eight miles distance we reached an eminence where the Indians have raised a conic mound of stone, six or eight feet high, on which fixed a pole made of pine, about fifteen feet. Here we halted and smoked for some time at the request of the Indians, who told us, that in passing the mountains with their families, some men are usually sent on foot from this place to fish at the entrance of Colt creek, whence they rejoin the main party at the glade on the head of the Kooskooskee. From this elevated spot we have a commanding view of the surrounding mountains, which so completely close us, that although we have once passed them, we almost despair of ever escaping from them without the assistance of the Indians. The marks on the trees which had been our chief dependence, are much fewer and more difficult to be distinguished than we had supposed; but our guides traverse this trackless region with a kind of instinctive sagacity; they never hesitate, they are never embarrassed; yet so undeviating is their step, that wherever the snow has disappeared for even a hundred paces, we find the summer road. With their aid the snow is scarcely a disadvantage, for although we are often obliged to slip down, yet the fallen timber and the rocks, which are now covered, were much more troublesome when we passed in the autumn. . . . As for ourselves, the whole stock of being gone, we distributed to each mess a pint of bear's oil, which, with boiled roots, made an agreeable dish. We saw several black-tailed or mule-deer, but could not get a shot at them, and were informed that there is an abundance of in the valley, near the fishery, on the Kooskooskee. The Indians also assert that in the mountains to our right are large numbers of what they call white buffaloe or mountain sheep. Our horses strayed to some distance to look for food, and in the morning,

Saturday, 28, when they were brought up, exhibited rather a gaunt appearance. The Indians, however, promised that we should reach some good grass at noon, and we therefore set out after an early breakfast. Our route lay along the dividing ridge, and across a very deep hollow, till at the distance of six miles we passed our camp of the fifteenth of September. A mile and a half further we passed the road from the right, immediately on the dividing ridge, leading by the fishery. We went on as we had done during the former part of the route over deep snows, when having made thirteen miles we reached the side of a mountain, just above the fishery, which having no timber, and a southern exposure, the snow had disappeared, leaving an abundance of fine grass. Our horses were very hungry as well as fatigued, and as there was no other spot within our reach this evening, where we could find any food for them, we determined to encamp, though it was not yet midday. But as there was no water in the neighbourhood, we melted snow for cooking, and early in the morning,

Sunday, 29, continued along the ridge which we have been following for several days, till at the end of five miles it terminated; and now bidding adieu to the snows in which we have been imprisoned, we descended to the main branch of the Kooskooskee. . . .

33. TECUMSEH AND THE WESTERN INDIAN CONFEDERATION

The Louisiana Purchase and Lewis and Clark's long expedition did not solve the basic problem of how to get land occupied by powerful Native Nations into the hands of white settlers. Several times, Native leaders successfully organized large confederations that challenged the US Army. In 1809, Tecumseh, a Shawnee warrior and a powerful speaker, gathered up Indian warriors from as far north as Canada and as far south as the Carolinas to take a stand against the US Army. Furious over bitterly fought treaties that took away most of what is now Michigan, Indiana, and Illinois, they planned a series of coordinated attacks on US forts and towns in the Midwest. Rumors about what might happen, the numbers of warriors, and which tribes had joined in terrified white settlers. In the end, the US Army destroyed Tecumseh's village before he could fully organize, but the threat was real. In this speech Tecumseh demands that Governor William Henry Harrison return land. He explains how different Indian and white ideas about ownership are, but he also warns that if Indians unite, they can and will defeat the US Army, because Indians at this point had nothing to lose. How does Tecumseh differentiate common use of land versus private ownership? Why does he think the treaties are invalid? Why does he mention Christianity at the end?

Speech by Tecumseh to William Henry Harrison[1]

Houses are built for you to hold councils in. Indians hold theirs in the open air. I am a Shawnee. My forefathers were warriors. Their son is a warrior. From them I take my only existence. From my tribe I take nothing. I have made myself what I am. And I would that I could make the red people as great as the conceptions of my own mind, when I think of the Great Spirit that rules over us all. I would not then come to Governor Harrison to ask him to tear up the treaty [the 1795 Treaty of Greenville, which gave the United States parts of the Northwest Territory].

But I would say to him, "Brother, you have the liberty to return to your own country." You wish to prevent the Indians from doing as we wish them, to unite and let them consider their lands as a common property of the whole. You take the tribes aside and advise them not to come into this measure. You want by your distinctions of Indian tribes, in allotting to each a particular place, to make them war with each other. You never see an Indian endeavor to make the white people do this. You are continually driving the red people, when at last you will drive them into the great lake [Lake Michigan], where they can neither stand nor work.

Since my residence at Tippecanoe, we have endeavored to level all distinctions, to destroy village chiefs, by whom all mischiefs are done. It is they who sell their land to the Americans. Brother, this land that was sold, and the goods that was [sic] given for it, was only done by a few. In the future we are prepared to punish those who propose to sell land to the Americans. If you continue to purchase them, it will make war among the different tribes, and, at last I do not know what will be the consequences among the white people.

Brother, I wish you would take pity on the red people and do as I have requested. If you will not give up the land and do cross the boundary of our present settlement, it will be vary hard and produce great trouble between us.

The way, the only way to stop this evil, is for the red people to unite in claiming a common and equal right in the land, as it was at first, and should be now—for it was never divided, but belongs to all.

No tribe has the right to sell, even to each other, much less to strangers.

Sell a country?! Why not sell the air, the great sea, as well as the earth? Did not the Great Spirit make them all for the use of his children?

How can we have confidence in the white people? We have good and just reasons to believe we have ample grounds to accuse the Americans of injustice, especially when such great acts of injustice have been committed by them upon our race, of which they seem to have no manner of regard, or even to reflect.

---

1. Transcribed 1810, American Rhetoric, Online Speech Bank, www.americanrhetoric.com/speeches/nativeamericans/chieftecumseh.htm.

Army, however, did not have the manpower to enforce removal or to protect eastern tribes from western Indians. Many nations migrated back to their original homelands, deciding that fighting for their homelands was better than risking the unfamiliar and dangerous situation in the West.

The situation of the Sauk Indians, one of the tribes that signed treaties and moved west "voluntarily," demonstrates the complexities involved. Black Hawk, a war chief of the Sauk, who had never agreed to a treaty, refused to submit. In 1832, after one winter in his new home in Iowa, he led unhappy members of his tribe back east to plant corn in Illinois, their traditional homeland. The white American settlers who had bought up the Sauk lands believed they were being invaded. Illinois militia and federal troops drove the Indians back over the Mississippi River, slaughtering hundreds. As a result, the Sauk lost their land in Iowa and were removed to Indian Territory in the West.

By the mid-1830s many Indians had been resettled on lands in what would become Indian Territory, later Oklahoma. A few communities, notably the Cherokee and the Creeks, who were the most successful landowners, resisted. President Jackson, and later President Martin Van Buren, sent in federal troops to move remaining Native people forcibly. The Cherokees were herded along the infamous 1838 Trail of Tears, a forced winter march that killed nearly a quarter of them. Removal was a human tragedy on a vast scale. Thousands of Indians died from hunger and exposure during the process, which split some Indian nations into those who resisted and those who urged submission. Many Native nations ended up with inferior, unfamiliar land, making survival heroic. Removal revealed deep moral flaws in federal Indian policy and the limits to ideals about equality in the early republic.

These documents focus on expansion, and its tangled story of government policy, and *Indian removal,* a term that meant forced exodus and war. A set of letters from Indian girls being trained as teachers in a missionary school demonstrates the methods schools used to train their Indian students. Andrew Jackson's official statements about the policy of removal lay out how he justified such actions, while letters from army officials charged with implementing the policy reveal its difficulties. Black Hawk, a Sauk war chief, expresses his opposition to US policy.

34. CHEROKEE EDUCATION AND ASSIMILATION

Letters from Cherokee Women to Their Missionary Patrons
1828[1]

Christian missionaries played an important role in the national project of "civilizing" the Cherokees and other tribes living on the southern frontier. Protestant

---

1. "Letters from Cherokee Women to Their Missionary Teachers," ed. Theda Purdue. *Journal of Cherokee Studies* 4 (1979), 4–9.

groups built mission houses in many Cherokee towns but were frustrated by their lack of success at conversion. To solve the problem, missionaries focused on children and required that they be taken to boarding schools far from the influence of their Cherokee culture and family. One of the earliest of these schools, the Brainerd Mission, was founded in Chattanooga, Tennessee in 1817 by Quakers, but with funding from many Protestant groups. Teachers at the school encouraged their students to thank their benefactors. These letters, from female students at Brainerd, were all written in 1828. What do these letters tell you about the effect of missionaries on Cherokee culture? What was the relationship of these students with other Native people and their families? What practical skills were they learning at school

Elizabeth Taylor to Miss Abigail Parker
June 26, 1828

As we often write to our teachers friends she has requested me to write a few lines to you. She wishes me to give you an idea of the customs of the Cherokees, as she has not time. I am willing to do it because I think when christians know how much we need the means of knowledge, they will feel the importance of sending missionaries.—The unenlightened parts of this nation assemble for dances around a fire. The one that goes before sings; a woman follows after having herself adorned with shells which make a rattling noise when she dances. The others follow after, dancing around a fire in a ring, and keep up their amusements all night. In like manner the men dance the night before their ball plays. The next day when the two parties are collected at the ball ground, the side that excels receives horses, kegs, guns, clothing &c. from the other party. When they wish it to rain, they will send for a conjurer who will throw a black cat into the water, hang up a serpent &c.

Likewise when they are sick, they get one to blow and throw cold water on them and mutter over talk that cannot be understood. . . . Every year when the green corn, beans, &c are large enough to eat, they dance one night and torture themselves by scratching their bodies with snakes teeth before they will eat any.

When they go to each others houses, they will stand and peep through the fence, till some one goes out and inquires what they wish. Their living consist chiefly of pounded corn, sweet potatoes, and some meat. Their dishes are made by themselves of clay, first hardned by burning, then glazed by the smoke of meal bran; eight or ten will often get around one of these on the ground, with one wooden spoon, one will take a mouthful and pass it on to the other.

Many about this station are more civilized. Some come to meeting and appear as well as white people. Others dress in the Indian manner with maucassins for shoes, and handerchiefs round their heads for turbans.

But I have learned that the white people were once as degraded as this people; and that encourages me to think that this nation will soon become enlightened.

Sally M. Reece to Reverend Daniel Campbell
July 25, 1828

First I will tell you about the Cherokees. I think they improve. They have a printing press, and print a paper which is called the Cherokee Phoenix. They come to meeting on Sabbath days. They wear clothes which they made themselves.

Some though rude, have shoes and stockings. They keep horses, cows, sheep, and swine. Some have oxen. They cultivate fields. They have yet a great many bad customs but I hope all these things will soon be done away. They have thought more about the Saviour lately. I hope this nation will soon become civilized and enlightened. There are 25 girls in school at Brainerd. Mary Ann and Electa goes to school. They are not Cherokees. They are the daughters of Mr. John Vail, one of the missionaries.

I am now under the care of Mr and Mrs Fernal. They live down to the creek when Mr Dean used to live. Catharine my sister stays there too. My parents comes here to meeting on Sabbaths. My Father thinks is a great privelege to learn to read. He can read but Mother cannot I should like to tell you how my Father's house is situated. It is surrounded with hills. There are trees in the door yard. I take pleasure in sitting under them to attend to my work. And [there is] an orchard back of the house. A road [runs] between the house and field where the travellers pass. They very often call to stay all night. I help Mother to take care of my Brothers and sisters. My Father works in the field Mother spins and weaves.

Nancy Reece to Reverend Fayette Shepherd
December 25, 1828

I will tell you something of our happy school, so you may know how we shall feel if we should be separated from each other, and from our teachers and other missionaries. Miss. Ames has twenty-nine scholars one more is expected which will make the school full. The studies in our school are Reading, Spelling, Writing, Geography, Arithmetick, two have begun to study grammar. Eight new scholars have entered school this year. Part of them cannot talk english, and Miss Ames is obliged to have me interpret for her. I have a class of the younger children in Sabbath school. I ask those children who do not talk english if they understood the sermon that was read and they say they do not but when my father comes on sabbath days he talks in Cherokee. Then they tell me a great [deal] he says. I try to tell them how to spend the sabbath day and tell them where they will go when they die if they are not good. When they first enter school if they are asked these questions, they often say they don't know.

When school hours are over, the girls attend to domestick concerns and learn to make their own clothes and the clothes of the boys so they can do such work when they go home, to assist their parents. They can then take care of their houses and their brothers and sisters and perhaps can learn their parents something that they do not understand.

We have a society on Saturdays we work two hours to try to get some money for the heathen who have not had missionaries as we have. Miss Sargent generally comes in and reads to us.

The boys chop wood and in the summer help about the farm and some that have left school are learning the black smiths trade. Miss Sargent goes into their school room evenings to teach them, and sometimes they set with her in her room. . . .

I do not think that all the people are friends to the Cherokees. Miss. Ames has been reading a part of the Presid. message. Perhaps he does not like the laws of the Indian tribes for he says "This state of things requires that a remedy should be provided." Miss. Ames has been talking to the scholars and she felt bad and told them that they must get a good education soon as they can, so they can teach if they should be removed where they could not attend school and says that we must try to get religion for all the instructors ought to be christians. It seems that it will be a trying season to us and the missionaries if we should be separated from them, but she says if God suffers it to be, we ought not to complain, for it will be for the best. I have been talking to the children about it and one says "if the white people want more land let them go back to the country they came from," another says "they have got more land than they use, what do they want to get ours for?"

35. THE PLACE OF INDIANS IN THE REPUBLIC

Andrew Jackson, who served as president from 1828 to 1836, was the chief instigator of the policy of removal. Jackson had a long history of confrontation with Native nations, from his childhood in frontier Tennessee to his military service in the Creek War of 1813–14. As the first backcountry resident to be elected president, Jackson took western matters seriously and recognized the challenge Indian land claims posed to white settlement. He wanted to make it clear that the United States and the needs of its white citizens overrode the claims of sovereign Indian tribes. Along with his secretary of war, Lewis Cass, Jackson developed the policy of removal, engineered the passage of the 1830 Indian Removal Act, and executed its harsh outcome. The documents excerpted here are from two State of the Union messages, in which he outlined his reasons for supporting and implementing the act. How did Jackson justify taking land from the Indians? What benefits did he see in the policy of removal? How did this policy change the relationship between Native nations and the US government?

Andrew Jackson

Second Annual Message to Congress
December 6, 1830[1]

. . . It gives me pleasure to announce to Congress that the benevolent policy of the Government, steadily pursued for nearly thirty years, in relation to the removal of the Indians beyond the white settlements is approaching to a happy consummation. Two important tribes have accepted the provision made for their removal at the last session of Congress, and it is believed that their example will induce the remaining tribes also to seek the same obvious advantages.

. . . It will separate the Indians from immediate contact with settlements of whites; free them from the power of the States; enable them to pursue happiness in their own way and under their own rude institutions; will retard the progress of decay, which is lessening their numbers, and perhaps cause them gradually, under the protection of the Government and through the influence of good counsels, to cast off their savage habits and become an interesting, civilized, and Christian community. . . .

Humanity has often wept over the fate of the aborigines of this country, and Philanthropy has been long busily employed in devising means to avert it, but its progress has never for a moment been arrested, and one by one have many powerful tribes disappeared from the earth. To follow to the tomb the last of his race and to tread on the graves of extinct nations excite melancholy reflections. But true philanthropy reconciles the mind to these vicissitudes as it does to the extinction of one generation to make room for another. In the monuments and fortresses of an unknown people, spread over the extensive regions of the West, we behold the memorials of a once powerful race, which was exterminated or has disappeared to make room for the existing savage tribes. Nor is there anything in this which, upon a comprehensive view of the general interests of the human race, is to be regretted. Philanthropy could not wish to see this continent restored to the condition in which it was found by our forefathers. What good man would prefer a country covered with forests and ranged by a few thousand savages to our extensive Republic, studded with cities, towns, and prosperous farms, embellished with all the improvements which art can devise or industry execute, occupied by more than 12,000,000 happy people, and filled with all the blessings of liberty, civilization, and religion?

The present policy of the Government is but a continuation of the same progressive change by a milder process. The tribes which occupied the countries now constituting the Eastern States were annihilated or have melted away to make room for the whites. The waves of population and civilization are rolling to the westward, and we now propose to acquire the countries occupied by the red men of the South and West by a fair exchange, and, at the expense of the

---

1. James D. Richardson, *A Compilation of the Messages and Papers of the Presidents,* 1789–1908, v. 2 (Bureau of National Literature and Art, 1908).

United States, to send them to a land where their existence may be prolonged and perhaps made perpetual. Doubtless it will be painful to leave the graves of their fathers; but what do they more than our ancestors did or than our children are now doing? To better their condition in an unknown land our forefathers left all that was dear in earthly objects. . . . Can it be cruel in this Government when, by events which it can not control, the Indian is made discontented in his ancient home to purchase his lands, to give him a new and extensive territory, to pay the expense of his removal, and support him a year in his new abode? How many thousands of our own people would gladly embrace the opportunity of removing to the West on such conditions! If the offers made to the Indians were extended to them, they would be hailed with gratitude and joy.

yes, it can.

And is it supposed that the wandering savage has a stronger attachment to his home than the settled, civilized Christian? Is it more afflicting to him to leave the graves of his fathers than it is to our brothers and children? Rightly considered, the policy of the General Government toward the red man is not only liberal, but generous. He is unwilling to submit to the laws of the States and mingle with their population. To save him from this alternative, or perhaps utter annihilation, the General Government kindly offers him a new home, and proposes to pay the whole expense of his removal and settlement. . . .

well, they have been there longer . . .

Seventh Annual Message to Congress
Washington, December 7, 1835[1]

. . . The plan of removing the aboriginal people who yet remain within the settled portions of the United States to the country west of the Mississippi River approaches its consummation. It was adopted on the most mature consideration of the condition of this race, and ought to be persisted in till the object is accomplished, and prosecuted with as much vigor as a just regard to their circumstances will permit, and as fast as their consent can be obtained. All preceding experiments for the improvement of the Indians have failed. It seems now to be an established fact that they can not live in contact with a civilized community and prosper. . . . In the discharge of this duty an extensive region in the West has been assigned for their permanent residence. It has been divided into districts and allotted among them. Many have already removed and others are preparing to go, and with the exception of two small bands living in Ohio and Indiana, not exceeding 1,500 persons, and of the Cherokees, all the tribes on the east side of the Mississippi, and extending from Lake Michigan to Florida, have entered into engagements which will lead to their transplantation.

The plan for their removal and reestablishment is founded upon the knowledge we have gained of their character and habits, and has been dictated by a

---

1. James D. Richardson, *A Compilation of the Messages and Papers of the Presidents, 1789–1908*, v. 2 (Bureau of National Literature and Art, 1908)

spirit of enlarged liberality. A territory exceeding in extent that relinquished has been granted to each tribe. Of its climate, fertility, and capacity to support an Indian population the representations are highly favorable. To these districts the Indians are removed at the expense of the United States, and with certain supplies of clothing, arms, ammunition, and other indispensable articles; they are also furnished gratuitously with provisions for the period of a year after their arrival at their new homes. In that time, from the nature of the country and of the products raised by them, they can subsist themselves by agricultural labor, if they choose to resort to that mode of life; if they do not they are upon the skirts of the great prairies, where countless herds of buffalo roam, and a short time suffices to adapt their own habits to the changes which a change of the animals destined for their food may require. Ample arrangements have also been made for the support of schools; in some instances council houses and churches are to be erected, dwellings constructed for the chiefs, and mills for common use. . . . And besides these beneficial arrangements, annuities are in all cases paid, amounting in some instances to more than $30 for each individual of the tribe, and in all cases sufficiently great, if justly divided and prudently expended, to enable them, in addition to their own exertions, to live comfortably. . . .

Such are the arrangements for the physical comfort and for the moral improvement of the Indians. The necessary measures for their political advancement and for their separation from our citizens have not been neglected. The pledge of the United States has been given by Congress that the country destined for the residence of this people shall be forever "secured and guaranteed to them." A country west of Missouri and Arkansas has been assigned to them, into which the white settlements are not to be pushed. No political communities can be formed in that extensive region, except those which are established by the Indians themselves or by the United States for them and with their concurrence. A barrier has thus been raised for their protection against the encroachment of our citizens, and guarding the Indians as far as possible from those evils which have brought them to their present condition. . . .

36. INDIAN REMOVAL AND ITS HUMAN COST

The Choctaws, who lived as farmers in Mississippi, were the first Indians to be removed from their homelands under the new policy. Factions of the tribe ceded land to the US government in 1820 and again in 1830 with the Treaty of Dancing Rabbit Creek. In return for their land in Mississippi, the Choctaws were promised new land in Indian Territory, a cash payment, tools, housing, and schools in the new settlements, as well as assistance with moving. The army, given the task of moving the Indians, faced resistance from a significant number of Choctaw people. These letters between officials in Washington responsible for the grand scheme of removal and the military officers supervising the daily details of moving hundreds of people reveal both the complex logistics of the move and the deep resistance of many of the Choctaws. What kinds of problems did army officials expect to have in the removal process? What were the most serious difficulties they actually encountered? In what ways do these documents hint at how the Choctaws felt about removal?

Army Correspondence about the Choctaw Removal
1834[1]

General George Gibson to Lieutenant L. F. Carter

Office Commissary General Subsistence,

Washington, December 27, 1830.

Sir: On receipt of this, you will proceed with as little delay as practicable to Kiamitia, or the nearest point where it is supposed the body of Choctaws now about emigrating westward will select their settlement. On your reaching the settlement, you will take a list of such as have recently arrived, as well as those who may hereafter arrive at their destination: and, that you may prevent confusion and disorder, you will organize them into companies of fifty or one hundred, each company, who will receipt to you for the rations, and distribute them to the company. The ration to consist of one and a half pounds of beef or pork, one pint of corn, or an equivalent in corn-meal or flour, and two quarts of salt, to every hundred rations. In the performance of this duty, every care and economy must be practiced consistent with the good of the service in which you will be engaged, taking special pains to treat the emigrants with all the kinds ness and civility in your power in order that they may be induced to remain, and, as agriculturists, to become useful to themselves and to the Government; and also, that no unfavorable impressions may be carried back to their nation that will have the slightest tendency to discourage the emigration of the main body. To prevent fraud issues to them beyond the period limited by the treaty, every caution is to be used; and you are authorized to employ as your assistants such confidential whites and Indians as you may consider essential to his service. In the event of the ratification of the treaty, other more extensive arrangements will necessarily be made. You will make yourself acquainted with the resources of the country bordering on the Choctaw settlements, and communicate freely with me on the best mode of supplying any deficiency beyond what the country will afford. Permit me to repeat, that too much care and vigilance in obtaining, from time to time, a correct registry of the emigrants cannot be practiced by you. Their names, description, &c., to avoid imposition, should be particularly required. Two thousand dollars have been placed to your credit in the Branch

---

1. *Correspondence on the Subject of the Emigration of Indians Between the 30th November, 1831 and the 27th December, 1833* (Washington, D.C. Duffereen, 1834), 5–6, 14–15, 414–415.

Bank of the United States at New Orleans, for which you can draw in such amounts as you may require. Further sums will be placed to your credit in the same bank. You will be careful in taking receipts for all expenditures; and, in making out your returns and quarterly accounts, you will keep them distinct from any other; these being expressly for this purpose alone.

Respectfully,

Your most obedient servant,

GEO. GIBSON, C.G.S.

J. H. Hook to Lieutenant S. V. R Ryan

Office Commissary General Subsistence,

Washington, June 21, 1831.

Sir: You will find enclosed a copy of the Choctaw treaty.

Many small parties of Choctaws will no doubt precede the main body intended to be removed the present year: these will of course be provided for. Several of these parties have already reached the station of Lieutenant Stephenson, and are supplied with provisions by him. You have been incidentally apprized in a copy of a letter to Lieutenant Stephenson, enclosed to you on the 27th April, of the necessity of keeping a roll of the Indians. It deemed proper to direct your attention particularly to that part of the 16th article of the treaty in which the United States bind themselves to furnish the Indians and "their families with ample corn and beef for twelve months after reaching their new homes." The principal object of the roll to be kept by you is to prevent, as far as possible, the support of any of these Indians beyond that period.

Lieutenant Stephenson has been told in reply to certain queries, which reply was also enclosed to you in a letter of 4th June instant, that rations would be issued to slaves, the property of the emigrating Indians. This is the construction given to the word *families* above mentioned. The Indians and their slaves will be organized into companies of from fifty to one hundred, and a captain appointed by themselves from each company, to whom the provisions will be issued. Each ration to consist of one and a half pounds of beef or pork, and a pint of corn and or equivalent of corn meal or flour, with two quarts of salt to the hundred rations. You can, when it may become necessary, establish several places of issue in the nation. The persons whom you may employ in these agencies will be strictly responsible to you; and care will be taken that they issue promptly, and with due regard to the convenience of the Indians, are especially recommended, that the reports returned from the first emigrants may encourage rather than retard the spirit of emigration. . . .

Respectfully, &c.

J.H. HOOK, Acting C.G.S.

William Armstrong to General George Gibson

Choctaw Agency, September 14, 1833.

Sir: Since I had the honor of addressing you, I have had a council with a number of the Indians of Leflore's district. I find them much opposed to the emigrating; yet, I hope and believe, a favorable impression as to their removal was made with a good number. As I had been through their new country west, I could speak securely to them, and advise their removal, even to those who, under the treaty, had acquired land. But, strange as it is. It is also true, that there are a large party who seem almost determined to remain, not one whom have a foot of land. This is owing to some three or four leading captains who, themselves, are entitled to land, either given them in the treaty, or have taken the five years' stay, which will give them land. To those captains I appealed in as strong language as I could, and informed them that the laws were extended over them, and that they could not protect their warriors against the laws; that, although they themselves had land, their people had not; that the Government were anxious for them to remove; that this was the last they would be emigrated at the expense of the United States. I explained the advantages of their county west, with all the benefits arising from the treaty, and the many articles that would be furnished, and the ten thousand dollars to be divided amongst those who had no land here given them by the treaty. Finally, I urged every consideration to induce them to go. I assure you it is distressing to me to find that those people are so blind to their own interest; yet I shall not relax in my exertions. To-morrow I set out for Nituchache's district, and will have a council there on the 26th. There is opposition to the emigration in that district. I have with me good interpreter, and go from house to house, and endeavor to start them off. We shall avoid the heavy expenses by keeping out the wagons until we discover the probably number of Indians we shall have to remove. Nothing shall be left undone to them off, and with the least possible expense to the Government. I will keep you advised of our movements, and hope by the 25th of the month to give you a better account. I will be here again on that day.

Respectfully, your obedient servant,

WM. ARMSTRONG,
Sup. Choc. removal.

37. WAR IN THE OLD NORTHWEST: BLACK HAWK'S ACCOUNT OF REMOVAL WEST

Black Hawk, a Sauk warrior, led the faction of his nation that refused to be peaceably removed. In 1832, after one winter in Iowa, during which they faced attacks from other Indian nations and starvation from failed crops, Black Hawk led a group of Sauks back to plant corn in their traditional Illinois homeland.

US officials and local farmers refused to meet with the returning Sauks. Black Hawk's warriors successfully battled local militia and held out for nearly a year. Finally, the US Army chased the Sauk into southern Wisconsin, and as the remaining villagers tried to flee across a river, the army and its Dakota and Menominee allies massacred many. A few Sauk straggled back to Iowa, but Black Hawk was captured. He dictated this memoir to a minister while in a Virginia prison. What is Black Hawk hoping for his people at this point? How has his travel through the eastern United States affected his view?

Black Hawk

From *Life of Ma-Ka-Tai-Me-She-Kia-Kiak or Black Hawk, Dictated by Himself*
1833[1]

. . . That fall I paid a visit to the agent, before we started to our hunting grounds, to hear if he had any good news for me. He had news! He said that the land on which our village stood was now ordered to be sold to individuals; and that, when sold, *our right* to remain, by treaty, would be at an end, and that if we returned next spring, we would be *forced* to remove!

We learned during the winter, that *part* of the lands where our village stood had been sold to individuals, and that the *trader* at Rock Island had bought the greater part that had been sold. The reason was now plain to me, why *he* urged us to remove. His object, we thought, was to get our lands. We held several councils that winter to determine what we should do, and resolved, in one of them, to return to our village in the spring, as usual; and concluded, that if we were removed by force, that the *trader*, agent, and others, must be the cause; and that, if found guilty of having us driven from our village, they should be *killed!* The trader stood foremost on this list. He had purchased the land on which my lodge stood, and that of our *grave yard* also! . . .

Our women received bad accounts from the women that had been raising corn at the new village—the difficulty of breaking the new prairie with hoes—and the small quantity of corn raised. We were nearly in the same situation in regard to the latter, it being the first time I ever knew our people to be in want of provision.

I prevailed upon some of Ke-o-kuck's band to return this spring to the Rock river village. Ke-o-kuck would not return with us. I hoped that we would get permission to go to Washington to settle our affairs with our Great Father. I visited the agent at Rock Island. He was displeased because we had returned to our village, and told me that we *must* remove to the west of the Mississippi. I told him plainly that we *would not!* I visited the interpreter at his house, who advised me to do as the agent had directed me. I then went to see the trader,

---

1. *Black Hawk: An Autobiography,* ed. Donald Jackson (Urbana: University of Illinois Press, 1964), 104–115.

and upbraided him for buying our lands. He said that if he had not purchased them, some person else would, and that if our Great Father would make an exchange with us, he would willingly give up the land he had purchased to the government. This I thought was fair, and began to think that he had not acted as badly as I had suspected. We again repaired our lodges, and built others, as most of our village had been burnt and destroyed. Our women selected small patches to plant corn, (where the whites had not taken them within their fences,) and worked hard to raise something for our children to subsist upon.

I was told that, according to the treaty, we had no *right* to remain upon the lands *sold,* and that the government would *force* us to leave them. There was but a small portion, however, that *had been sold;* the balance remaining in the hands of the government, we claimed the right (if we had no other) to "live and hunt upon, as long as it remained the property of the government," by a stipulation in the same treaty that required us to evacuate it *after* it had been sold. This was the land that we wished to inhabit, and thought we had the best right to occupy. . . .

I would here remark, that our pastimes and sports had been laid aside for the last two years. We were a divided people, forming two parties. Ke-o-kuck being at the head of one, willing to barter our rights merely for the good opinion of the whites; and cowardly enough to desert our village to them. I was at the head of the other party, and was determined to hold on to my village, although I had been *ordered* to leave it. But, I considered, as myself and band had no agency in selling our country—and that as provision had been made in the treaty, for us all to remain on it as long as it belonged to the United States, that we could not be *forced* away. I refused, therefore, to quit my village. It was here, that I was born—and here lie the bones of many friends and relations. For this spot I felt a sacred reverence, and never could consent to leave it, without being forced therefrom. . . .

The winter passed off in gloom. We made a bad hunt, for want of the guns, traps, &c. that the whites had taken from our people for whisky! The prospect before us was a bad one. I fasted, and called upon the Great Spirit to direct my steps to the right path. I was in great sorrow—because all the whites with whom I was acquainted, and had been on terms of friendship, advised me so contrary to my wishes, that I begun to doubt whether I had a *friend* among them.

Ke-o-kuck, who has a smooth tongue, and is a great speaker, was busy in persuading my band that I was wrong—and thereby making many of them dissatisfied with me. I had one consolation—for all the women were on my side, on account of their corn-fields.

On my arrival again at my village, with my band increased, I found it worse than before. . . . In this mood, I called upon the *trader,* who is fond of talking, and had long been my friend, but now amongst those advising me to give up my village. He received me very friendly, and went on to defend Ke-o-kuck in what he had done, and endeavored to show me that I was bringing distress on our women and children. . . . After thinking some time, I agreed, that I could honorably give up, by being paid for it, according to our customs; but told him, that I could not make the proposal myself, even if I wished, because it would be dishonorable in me to do so. He said he would do it, by sending word to the great chief at St. Louis, that he could remove us peaceably, for the amount stated, to the west side of the Mississippi. A steam boat arrived at the island during my stay. After its departure, the *trader* told me that he had "requested a war chief, who is stationed at Galena, and was on board of the steam boat, to make the offer to the great chief at St. Louis, and that he would soon be back, and bring his answer." I did not let my people know what had taken place, for fear they would be displeased. I did not much like what had been done myself, and tried to banish it from my mind.

After a few days had passed, the war chief returned, and brought for answer, that "the great chief at St. Louis would give us *nothing!*—and said if we did not remove immediately, we should be *drove off!*"

I was not much displeased with the answer brought by the war chief, because I would rather have laid my bones with my forefathers, than remove for any consideration. Yet if a friendly offer had been made, as I expected, I would, for the sake of my women and children, have removed peaceably.

I now resolved to remain in my village, and make no resistance, if the military came, but submit to my fate! I impressed the importance of this course on all my band, and directed them, in case the military came, not to raise an arm against them. . . .

Our women had planted a few patches of corn, which was growing finely, and promised a subsistence for our children—but the *white people again commenced ploughing it up!*

I now determined to put a stop to it, by clearing our country of the *intruders.* I went to the principal men and told them, that they must and should leave our country—and gave them until the middle of the next day, to remove in. The worst left within the time appointed—but the one who remained, represented, that his family, (which was large,) would be in a starving condition, if he went and left his crop—and promised to behave well, if I would consent to let him remain until fall, in order to secure his crop. He spoke reasonably, and I consented. . . .

The war chief arrived, and convened a council at the agency. Ke-o-kuck and Wà-pel-lo were sent for, and came with a number of their band. The council house was opened, and they were all admitted. Myself and band were then sent for to attend the council. When we arrived at the door, singing a *war song,* and armed with lances, spears, war clubs and bows and arrows, as if going to battle, I halted, and refused to enter—as I could see no necessity or propriety in having the room crowded with those who were already there. If the council was convened for us, why have others there in our room? The war chief having sent all out, except Ke-o-kuck, Wà-pel-lo, and a few of their chiefs and braves, we entered the council house, in this war-like appearance, being desirous to show the war chief that we were *not afraid!* He then rose and made a speech.

He said:

["The president is very sorry to be put to the trouble and expense of sending a large body of soldiers here, to remove you from the lands you have long since ceded to the United States. Your Great Father has already warned you repeatedly, through your agent, to leave the country; and he is very sorry to find that you have disobeyed his orders. Your Great Father wishes you well; and asks nothing from you but what is reasonable and right. I hope you will consult your own interest, and leave the country you are occupying, and go to the other side of the Mississippi."

I replied: "That *we* had never sold our country. We never received any annuities from our American father! And *we* are determined to hold on to our village!"

The war chief, apparently angry, rose and said:—"Who is *Black Hawk?* Who is *Black Hawk?*"

I responded:

"I am a *Sac!* my forefather was a Sac! and all the nations call me *a* SAC!!"

The war chief said:

"I came here, neither to *beg* nor *hire* you to leave your village. My business is to remove you, peaceably if I can, but *forcibly* if I must! I will now give you two days to remove in—and if you do not cross the Mississippi within that time, I will adopt measures to *force* you away!"

I told him that I never could consent to leave my village, and was determined not to leave it! . . .

All our plans were now defeated. We must cross the river, or return to our village and await the coming of the war chief with his soldiers. We determined on the latter: but finding that our agent, interpreter, trader, and Ke-o-kuck, (who were determined on breaking my ranks,) had seduced several of my warriors to cross the Mississippi, I sent a deputation to the agent, at the request of my band, pledging myself to leave the country in the fall, provided permission was given us to remain, and secure our crop of corn, then growing—as we would be in a starving situation if we were driven off without the means of subsistence.

The deputation returned with an answer from the war chief, "that no further time would be given us than that specified, and if we were not then gone, he would remove us!"

I directed my village crier to proclaim, that my orders were, in the event of the war chief coming to our village to remove us, that not a gun should be fired, nor any resistance offered. That if he determined to fight, for them to remain quietly in their lodges, and let him *kill them if he chose!* . . .

Some of our young men who had been out as *spies,* came in and reported, that they had discovered a large body of mounted men coming towards our village, who looked like a *war party.* They arrived, and took a position below

Rock river, for their place of encampment. The great war chief entered Rock river in a steam-boat, with his soldiers and one big gun. . . .

The war chief appointed the next day to remove us! I would have remained and been taken prisoner by the *regulars*, but was afraid of the multitude of *pale faces*, who were on horseback, as they were under no restraint of their chiefs.

We crossed the Mississippi during the night, and encamped some distance below Rock Island. The great war chief convened another council, for the purpose of making a treaty with us. In this treaty he agreed to give us corn in place of that we had left growing in our fields. I touched the goosequill to this treaty, and was determined to live in peace.

The corn that had been given us, was soon found to be inadequate to our wants; when loud lamentations were heard in the camp, by our women and children, for their *roasting-ears, beans*, and *squashes*. To satisfy them, a small party of braves went over, in the night, to steal corn from their own fields. They were discovered by the whites, and fired upon. Complaints were again made of the depredations committed by some of my people, *on their own corn-fields!* . . .

FURTHER READING

Gordon-Reed, Annette. *The Hemingses of Monticello: An American Story.* New York: W. W. Norton, 2008.

Green, Michael, and Theda Perdue. *The Cherokee Nation and the Trail of Tears.* New York: Penguin, 2008.

Guyatt, Nicholas. *Bind Us Apart: How Enlightened Americans Invented Racial Segregation.* New York: Basic Books, 2016.

Meacham, Jon. *American Lion: Andrew Jackson in the White House.* New York: Random House, 2009.

O'Brien, Jean M. *Firsting and Lasting: Writing Indians Out of Existence in New England.* Minneapolis: University of Minnesota Press, 2010.

Perdue, Theda. *Cherokee Women: Gender and Culture Change, 1700–1835.* Lincoln: University of Nebraska Press, 1999.

Prucha, Frances Paul. *The Great Father: The United States Government and the American Indians.* 2 vols. Lincoln: University of Nebraska Press, 1984.

Trask, Kerry. *Black Hawk and the Battle for the Heart of America.* New York: Holt, 2007.

Wallace, Anthony F. C. *The Long Bitter Trail: Andrew Jackson and the Indians.* New York: Hill and Wang, 1993.

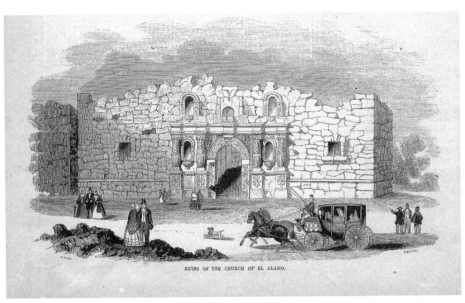

RUINS OF THE CHURCH OF EL ALAMO.

The old Alamo Mission in San Antonio, 1854. When Anglo-Americans and a few Mexican Texans rebelled against Mexico and formed an independent nation in Texas in 1836, Mexico and the United States allowed the rebellion to unfold. The Texas revolution was quickly normalized as a natural progression, rather than as a revolution that overthrew a legitimate government. When this happened in New Mexico a year later, the reaction was very different, and the rebellion was crushed. No images exist of the actual 1836 battle at the Alamo, a disaster for the people inside, but this image of the battle was one of the first printed depictions. How does this image work to romanticize what happened? Why would tourists be interested in the crumbling building in the 1850s?

Gleason's Pictorial Drawing Room Companion, Boston, Massachusetts.

Early Republics

New Nations Test their Borders

The United States was only one of several republics in North America that experimented with new forms of government in the early nineteenth century. The Republic of Mexico, new nations in Central and South America, and the British Dominion of Canada struggled to create nations and citizens. Part of that struggle involved controlling the western part of North America. During the first half of the 1800s, these new nations all claimed parts of the American West as frontier, borderland, and "empty land," where they planned to expand, colonize, and settle. Of course, none of these were empty, and each new republic had to conquer and incorporate indigenous people and find sources of land and labor that would allow their nations to expand. Claiming that a nation "owned" a piece of land and actually establishing control over that land turned out to be two very different things. The first was easy and the second very difficult.

In 1822, the United States of America found itself with a new revolutionary neighbor, the brand new United States of Mexico or Estados Unidos Mexicanos. Similar in size, population, and national ambition to the United States, Mexico had spent nearly fifteen years fighting for its independence against Spain. It began as Europe fell apart. Mexican-born Spaniards found they were far more loyal to their Mexican homeland than to foreign kings or queens, who rarely visited or provided military support. When the king of Spain, busy defending Spain from Napoleon, demanded new taxes and new loyalty from New Spain, elite Mexicans revolted. In that same revolutionary moment, indigenous Mexicans, increasingly rebellious and influenced by radical Catholic priests like Father Miguel Hidalgo y Costilla, demanded to be full members of the new nation.

In 1810, Father Hidalgo led an army of poor and indigenous Mexicans to spectacular and surprising victories in what is now northern Mexico. Marching under the flag of the Virgin de Guadelupe, thirty thousand people tramped toward Mexico City and drove the Spanish and Mexican Army into retreat. They didn't take the city, and Father Hidalgo and numerous other rebels were executed. However, the power of indigenous Mexicans and their military success ensured that Mexico would have to take their demands seriously. In 1821, the long struggle against Spain ended, and a new Mexican nation emerged out of Spain's North American territories. Much like their counterparts in the United States, new citizens disagreed about who should be a citizen and how the government should be run. And, just as in the United States, the political battles for Mexico began in earnest with independence. In 1824, Mexican citizens restructured the country as a federal republic with nineteen states and four territories in a new written constitution. Whether the new nation of Mexico would be conservative or liberal, Catholic or secular, a monarchy or a republic was yet to be determined.

One of the first challenges the unstable Mexican government faced was trouble on its northern borders in Texas, New Mexico, and California. One of the new Mexican states was Coahuila y Tejas, which combined the sparsely populated Spanish provinces of Texas and Coahuila, and another was Alta California. Before New Spain had been overthrown, Spanish administrators had begun experiments in colonization using missions and civilian colonists to settle among large Indian populations living in these border regions. The idea was to create a large buffer zone to protect interior Mexico and its mines and cities from expansionistic and ambitious invaders from the United States and from powerful indigenous raiders. In California and New Mexico, sheep and cattle ranchers were threatened by horse-mounted Indians, who raided settlements and stole people and animals. Californians demanded more local government and military support. Beginning in 1831, Californians drove out several appointed governors, and in 1836 they initiated a more serious rebellion. After declaring themselves independent from Mexico, the Californians chose Juan Bautista Alvarado as their governor. The revolt ended when the central government in Mexico agreed to make Alvarado the governor of the Department of California.

In Texas, perhaps the most isolated region of the Mexican north, significant numbers of Anglo-American and European colonists had been invited to become Mexican citizens and to do the work of protecting and developing that border region. US residents began settling in eastern Texas in the 1820s and soon developed communities that did not resemble the Catholic and Spanish-speaking world that Spanish and Mexican officials had envisioned. Beginning with Moses and Stephen Austin's colony in the Mexican state of Coahuila y Tejas, Anglo-American communities demanded representative government, protection from Indian raiding, and the right to own slaves. Mexican officials and government inspectors warned that rebellion brewed.

Meanwhile, the United State was on its own expansionist binge. The 504 million acres obtained in the Louisiana Purchase weren't enough to absorb the nation's astonishing growth. The middle decades of the nineteenth century were characterized by almost constant expansion as the United States acquired land on its western borders through warfare and diplomacy. In 1820, Mexico and the United States were about the same size: the United States held 1.9 million square miles of land and 9.6 million people, and Mexico had 1.8 million acres with about 7 million inhabitants. Soon, however, the United States would demand the Pacific Northwest and also begin eyeing valuable Pacific ports in Mexico's Northern California.

Mexico's growing size and continuing instability looked risky to the prickly United States, which certainly couldn't control its own citizens from marching over borders illegally, grabbing Indian land, and even setting up their own countries in Mexico and British Canada. As people in Latin America began to demand independence everywhere, many politicians in the United States worried about where this might lead. As revolts and coups erupted, European nations attempted to stop local independence movements to serve their own interests. In 1823, President James Madison insisted that all of Latin America was essential to US interests and that any greedy European interests that intervened there would be sorry. The Monroe Doctrine made a grand declaration of US power and interest, but in the 1820s and 1830s, it had little ability to do more than make sweeping claims enforced with only vague threats.

In the Pacific Northwest, however, US residents began moving into territory still claimed by Great Britain, Russia, and Mexico. Traders from those nations had long cruised the coasts to trade with Native people for furs, and large settlements of former fur traders, French, Indians, Hawaiians, and Russians studded what is now British Columbia, Washington, and Oregon. A few Anglo-American missionaries moved into those regions, part of a worldwide swell in evangelical religion. Like Anglo settlers in Texas and New Mexico, they began to complain about how they were treated. Trouble was coming.

The documents in this chapter examine a global trend of independence movements that often took older governments, even ones that claimed to be republics, by surprise. Father Hidalgo's electrifying call for all of Mexico to revolt against Spain shocked Spanish leaders for its radical language and its inclusion of Mexico's indigenous peoples. President James Madison's speech about US interest in Latin America demonstrates Anglo-American worries about instability. Similarly, the excerpt from General Mier y Terán's report describes the unstable situation brewing in Texas. In an 1837 letter, a local priest in New Mexico tries to explain a violent revolt against the new nation of Mexico. Finally, an Anglo-American missionary living illegally in British Oregon writes a letter describing her challenges with native converts in 1837.

38. MEXICAN REVOLUTIONS AND US RESPONSES 1810 REVOLUTION

Don Miguel Hidalgo y Costilla, or Miguel Hidalgo, was a Mexican Catholic priest who worked to incite the Mexican War of Independence. In his famous "Cry of Dolores," given in a small town on September 16, 1810, he called on poor Mexicans everywhere to rebel against European-born Spaniards. Hidalgo gathered an army of ninety thousand, including indigenous people and Mexican-born mixed-race people, who marched across Mexico with great success. Finally, professional Spanish troops defeated them, and on January 17, 1811, they executed Father Hidalgo. This speech, delivered by Hidalgo at his trial, urges his people to continue fighting. How does Hidalgo use Catholic and Republican ideals to support his position? How does he use ideas about race and class?

Father Miguel Hidalgo
Agrarian Reform and Edict against Slavery
1810[1]

DON MIGUEL HIDALGO Y COSTILLA, Generalisimo of America, &c. By the present [document] I order the Judges and Justices of the district of this Capital to proceed immediately to the collection of rents due up to today, by the tenants of the lands pertaining to the Native Communities, so that being entered in the national Treasury the lands may be delivered to the said Natives for their cultivation, without being able to rent them in the future, then it is my will, that its use be only for the Natives in their respective Villages. Given in my general Barracks of Guadalajara on December 5, 1810. Miguel Hidalgo Ordered by H[is] H[ighness] Generalisimo Lic. Ignacio Rayón Secretary

Miguel Hidalgo, Mr. Commander General D. Nemesio Salcedo. The Br. D. Miguel Hidalgo, contained in the afore mentioned, asked that His Majesty that by reason of his goodness, he receive and widely circulate this statement with contentment, so that my conscience may be relieved. Royal Hospital, May 18, 1811. Miguel Hidalgo

---

1. From Henry Rupp Wagner Collection, Yale University Library, reprinted in Hugh M. Hamill, *The Hidalgo Revolt: Prelude to Mexican Independence* (Gainesville, University of Florida Press, 1966).

countries is called the lowest class—the very poor and very ignorant. The naturalized North Americans in the town maintain an English school, and send their children north for further education; the poor Mexicans not only do not have sufficient means to establish schools, but they are not of the type that take any thought for the improvement of its public institutions or the betterment of its degraded condition. Neither are there civil authorities or magistrates; one insignificant little man—not to say more—who is called an *alcalde*, and an *ayuntamiento* that does not convene once in a lifetime is the most that we have here at this important point on our frontier; yet, wherever I have looked, in the short time that I have been here, I have witnessed grave occurrences, both political and judicial. It would cause you the same chagrin that it has caused me to see the opinion that is held of our nation by these foreign colonists, since, with the exception of some few who have journeyed to our capital, they know no other Mexicans than the inhabitants about here, and excepting the authorities necessary to any form of society, the said inhabitants are the most ignorant of Negroes and Indians, among whom I pass for a man of culture. Thus, I tell myself that it could not be otherwise than that from such a state of affairs should arise an antagonism between the Mexicans and foreigners, which is not the least of the smoldering fires which I have discovered. Therefore, I am warning you to take timely measures. Texas could throw the whole nation into revolution.

The colonists murmur against the political disorganization of the frontier, and the Mexicans complain of the superiority and better education of the colonists; the colonists find it unendurable that they must go three hundred leagues to lodge a complaint against the petty pickpocketing that they suffer from a venal and ignorant alcalde, and the Mexicans with no knowledge of the laws of their own country nor those regulating colonization, set themselves against the foreigners, deliberately setting nets to deprive them of the right of franchise and to exclude them from the ayuntamiento. Meanwhile, the incoming stream of new settlers is unceasing; the first news of these comes by discovering them on land already under cultivation, where they have been located for many months; the old inhabitants set up a claim to the property, basing their titles of doubtful priority, and for which there are no records, on a law of the Spanish government; and thus arises a lawsuit in which the alcalde has a chance to come out with some money. In this state of affairs, the town where there are no magistrates is the one in which lawsuits abound, and it is at once evident that in Nacogdoches and its vicinity, being most distant from the seat of the general government, the primitive order of things should take its course, which is to say that this section is being settled up without the consent of anybody. . . .

In spite of the enmity that usually exists between the Mexicans and the foreigners, there is a most evident uniformity of opinion on one point, namely the separation of Texas from Coahuila and its organization into a territory of the federal government. This idea, which was conceived by some of the colonists who are above the average, has become general among the people and does not fail to cause considerable discussion. In explaining the reasons assigned by them for this demand, I shall do no more than relate what I have heard with no addition of my own conclusions, and I frankly state that I have been commissioned by some of the colonists to explain to you their motives, notwithstanding the fact that I should have done so anyway in the fulfillment of my duty.

They claim that Texas in its present condition of a colony is an expense, since it is not a sufficiently prosperous section to contribute to the revenues of the state administration; and since it is such a charge it ought not to be imposed upon a state as poor as Coahuila, which has not the means of defraying the expenses of the corps of political and judicial officers necessary for the maintenance of peace and order. Furthermore, it is impracticable that recourse in all matters should be had to a state capital so distant and separated from this section by deserts infected by hostile savages. Again, their interests are very different from those of the other sections, and because of this they should be governed by a separate territorial government, having learned by experience that the mixing of their affairs with those of Coahuila brings about friction. The native inhabitants of Texas add to the above other reasons which indicate an aversion for the inhabitants of Coahuila; also the authority of the *comandante* and the collection of taxes is disputed. . . .

The whole population here is a mixture of strange and incoherent parts without parallel in our federation: numerous tribes of Indians, now at peace, but armed and at any moment ready for war, whose steps toward civilization should be taken under the close supervision of a strong and intelligent government; colonists of another people, more progressive and better informed than the Mexican inhabitants, but also more shrewd and unruly; among these foreigners are fugitives from justice, honest laborers, vagabonds and criminals, but honorable and dishonorable alike travel with their political constitution in their pockets, demanding the privileges, authority and officers which such a constitution guarantees.

41. ANGLOS, MEJICANOS, AND INDIOS: REBELLIONS CRUSHED IN NEW MEXICO

A Catholic priest living in Taos, Father Antonio Martinez was shocked when members of his parish, Native, Anglo, and Mexican Catholics, organized a rebellion against the New Mexican government. Tired of paying taxes; being forced to serve in the army; and receiving no help against Navajo, Ute, and Comanche nations, local sheep and cattle ranchers had simply had enough. Instead of listening to their complaints and providing the local funding and political control they wanted, the Mexican government appointed a haughty outsider, Albino Perez, as their new governor. When Perez instituted new taxes, they formed an army that included Native men from local Pueblos and long-

time New Mexican farmers. They marched to Santa Fe and killed Perez. Such a revolt had to be met with a powerful response. A large Mexican army was dispatched, and after a long campaign the conspirators were hung in public in downtown Santa Fe. How does Martinez explain what happened? What kinds of forces does he see operating? Does he defend the Mexican government?

Father Antonio Martinez
Letter to His Bishop
Santa Fe
1837[1]

Most Excellent Señor Bishop Don José Antonio de Zubiría.

Taos, September 25, 1837.

My venerated lord of all my esteem.

I must tell you, your excellency, about the occurrences of the present year and why I must beg you that if I have to continue serving in the ecclesiastical ministry, it not be in the curacy of Taos, as I will present explain plainly, and that I am determined to leave promptly for any other place whatever, or remain unemployed in my home.

This is the case: An incident, strange but hardly remote from the turbulent character of the inhabitants of the Villa of Santa Cruz de la Cañada who have always been the sewage of New Mexico, happened at the end of August: a mob arose in that place, only because one of the Abréus, the prefect, suspended the alcalde of that villa, and the sad consequence was that they killed the governor, Don Alvino Pérez, his secretary, the three Abréus, and others to the number of eighteen, on the eighth, ninth, and tenth of August; but although all the inhabitants of this department were in agreement, for the sake of peace and quiet, that news of the deed would be reported, offering some of them pardon for their actions and awaiting the answer and resolution of the Supreme Government; still all this was not enough but that the same people and my parishioners, the inhabitants of the plaza of San Francisco del Rancho, emulating that which possessed the aforesaid to commit the horrible deed that I imputed to them, although they had conspired they were not the movers, they started a revolution a second time, in order to commit hostilities against those who aided and obeyed the last government, atrocious and wretched purposes touching upon matters of the church; so then I heard something about it, notwithstanding it was kept secret from me, but I had very positive news the second of the month that they were assembling hastily with weapons in order to come and attack my brothers at my house and three other persons of the plaza of San Fernando in opposition to me and to pillage them, so that I could do nothing else but leave, fleeing in the morning of the

---

1. Archivo General de la Nación (Mexico) Justicia, tomo 138, legajo 48, 166–168.

same day with a brother of mine whom they had persecuted because he was sub-prefect, and I prepared to go to the city of Santa Fe to be free of this danger, but then when they assumed I would flee, they had me followed, probably with orders to kill me if they caught up with me, which they did not succeed in doing, and so passed the first and second of the month, after which they wrote me proposing that I not be anxious, that I come to my curacy without fear. In view of such an offer I returned in five days along with the governor who had been named, and was well received by the said mob or reunión; it was intimated to me that I had not admitted to a disavowal of the government but in order to afford me rest from certain illnesses caused by the roads and conveyances, it was necessary that they inform the reunión and get permission from the entire reunión, and so I was granted a limit of two days, after which I went to the said place and on the eleventh of the month I was made to appear in a room in which they had a table with the city councilmen around it, and on all sides were rows of men with their weapons ready and lacking only that they were pointed at me: In this way they made me give up the collection of sacramental fees, and the charges for baptisms, marriages and burials; they wanted to eliminate the contributions toward the church building funds, and bury all the dead in the church, to which I said that this was not in my jurisdiction, that if they attempted it by violence and force, I alone could not defend against it, that they would take full responsibility for it and that they themselves would be held responsible to the supreme powers; and they resolved that the church building funds would not be collected and they seized the church of El Rancho, Chapel of San Francisco of Assisi as they had already determined to do, and they buried a corpse by the steps of the chancel and followed this by doing whatever occurred to them which I could not prevent for no less a reason than I was threatened with death if I opposed it; they made me put this cession in writing, and they gave me a similar document for written evidence and for my safety saying that they would take responsibility for burying in the church and that the church funds would not be paid in all of Taos.

As I already knew this matter that they touched upon from previous experience, I told two men, one a city councilman and the other the secretary of the reunión, that doing these things in this way would incur excommunication and interdiction by the church of this place, and this I believe encouraged them even more to carry out their endeavor and with great stubborness they proceeded: I repeated the same thing to them in the said meeting where I appeared, saying to them that they would not wish to suffer such ecclesiastical punishment, and they said that they would not wish it but that they will not pay obventions nor contributions to church building funds, and that they would be buried in the churches, that for this reason they had made their decree and would continue to support it.

For this, the obventions, church funds and church burial, all the humble people were adamant, with only a few exceptions and those from the sensible people of stature, but of these substantial people the only known conspirators to date are named Córdoba, sons of one Abán Córdoba, deceased, whose two nephews are in jail in Santa Fe because they were those of the first uprising who also had influence in the second, all of them were; one of them being represented among the city councilmen of this place; and so it remains for order to be reestablished as is going to be done in the present time, neither am I determined henceforth to make such collection nor even that of the first fruits [*primicias*] since they are rejecting that entirely and are determined not to pay them; this is well proved with the example that from then until now, of seven burials, twelve baptisms and four marriages, only one of the married couples has asked me what fees they ought to pay, to whom I told about said cession and that I would receive them only if they were freely offered, and he paid a pledge and offered to pay up what he owed.

42. MISSIONARIES ON THE BORDER: AMERICANS IN BRITISH OREGON

Narcissa Whitman was part of an enthusiastic corps of young, educated New Englanders who felt a religious calling to save Native peoples in the West. Part of a Methodist mission to the Flathead and Spokane nations, who lived in the British-controlled Oregon country, Whitman and her husband set up a church in the isolated Walla Walla Valley. Supported by the British Hudson Bay Company, which hoped the missionaries might provide schools and churches for everyone, the Whitman mission lasted for nearly ten years. Preaching to the Cayuse and Walla Walla nations in English, and insisting that local Indians send their children to work in mission orchards and fields, the Whitmans eventually wore out their welcome. A measles epidemic in 1846, which devastated native children at the mission, pushed local Indians to attack and kill everyone in the Whitman's extended household. This letter, written by Whitman to her sister, lays out some of the troubles the missionaries faced. What frustrates Narcissa most about her situation? How does she intend to reach her Indian audience? Has her stay in Oregon changed any of her ideas about life in Oregon?

Narcissa Whitman
Letter from Oregon
1837[1]

March 30, 1837

Dear Parents, Brothers and Sisters:—Again I can speak of the goodness and mercy of the Lord to us in an especial manner. On the evening of my birthday,

---

1. Reprinted in *Marcus Whitman, Crusader*, ed. Archer Butler Hulbert, vol. 6, part 1 (Colorado Springs: D. C. Hulbert, 1936), 267–77.

March 14th, we received the gift of a little daughter—a treasure invaluable. During the winter my health was very good, so as to be able to do my work. About a week before her birth, I was afflicted with an inflammatory rash, which confined me mostly to my room. After repeated bleeding, it abated very considerably. Mrs. Pambrun had been with me two weeks previous to this, and had been much out of health. She, with my husband, dressed the babe. It would have made you smile to see them work over the little creature. Mrs. P. never saw one dressed before as we dress them, having been accustomed to dress her own in the native style. I was able to lend a helping hand and arrange the clothes for them, etc. Between us all, it was done very well. She slept very quiet that night, but the next night she cried very hard. All the reason of it was that she was hungry, and we did not think to feed her soon enough. On the second day I dressed her alone, sitting in the bed, and have ever since. I slept but little the two first nights, but since have got my usual sleep. She is a very quiet child, both night and day—sleeps all night without nursing more than once, sometimes not at all.

Thus, you see, beloved sisters, how the missionary does in heathen lands. No mother, no sister, to relieve me of a single care—only an affectionate husband, who, as a physician and nurse, exceeds all I ever knew. He was excessively pressed with care and labor during the whole time of my confinement. I received all the attention I required of him. He had my washing and the cooking to do for the family. . . . During the same week we were thronged with company, for the whole camp of Indians had arrived. . . . All this, with the care of four men and two boys that know little or nothing about work, just at the commencement of plowing[???] etc., requires many steps for one man alone. It was a very great mercy that I have been able to take the whole care of my babe, and that she is so well and quiet. The little stranger is visited daily by the chiefs and principal men in camp, and the women throng the house continually, waiting an opportunity to see her. Her whole appearance is so new to them. Her complexion, her size and dress, etc., all excite a deal of wonder; for they never raise a child here except they are lashed tight to a board, and the girls' heads undergo the flattening process . . . [Fee-low-ki-ke, a kind, friendly Indian, called to see her the next day after she was born. Said she was a Cayuse te-mi (Cayuse girl), because she was born on Cayuse waitis (Cayuse land). He told us her arrival was expected by all the people of the country—the Nez Perces, Cayuses and Walla Wallapoos Indians, and, now she has arrived, it would soon be heard of by them all, and we must write to our land and tell our parents and friends of it. The whole tribe are highly pleased because we allow her to be called a Cayuse girl.] We have beautiful weather here this month. Travel here is as pleasant as May in New York.

May 2nd. 1837.— The opportunity of sending home has come to hand, but I have been able to write but little. Mr. McLeod leaves soon with an expedition to Rendezvous, the same as last year. We can send letters very safely to Rendezvous, so long as this expedition goes, but the great uncertainty lies in the expedition of the American Fur Company. This year we are safe enough in sending Mr. Gray has made up his mind to go home this fall. . . . He will meet Mr. McLeod at Rendezvous, if his life is preserved. It would have been agreeable for us to have known of his going, immediately when he went from here, that we might have sent some things home by him. We have been here so short a time, however, that we should not have been able to send many things. His present determination is to return in two years, when we shall expect letters in abundance. We are all very well at present. I believe I was up and dressed the day the babe was a week old, and in a day or two after was about the house, and the next Sabbath walked out of doors. The weather is very mild and beautiful—so much so, that I do not require a fire in my room but a small part of the time. Fine, healthy atmosphere—no danger of nervous affections here. . . . Mrs. P. remained with me until Friday of the second week, when she left her daughter, about twelve years of age, with us, for the purpose of being taught to read, etc. It being impossible for me to obtain permanent help here, husband wrote to V. for an orphan girl. Dr. McLoughlin sent us one by express. She arrived the first of April. Is entirely unacquainted with every kind of work, neither can she speak the English language. Said to be sixteen, but she is not larger than a girl of twelve years. You have no idea how difficult it is to realize any benefit from those who do not understand you. During the winter, husband had two men only to assist him—Nina and Green. Green returns to the mountains again this spring, and Mr. Spalding has sent us Jack again. These two Owyhees will remain with us we know not how long. Here we are lost again, because they speak a different language. They are the best for labor of any people this side of the mountains. The Indians do not love to work well enough for us to place any dependence upon them. . . .

The third Sabbath after my babe was born, the weather was too cold to hold our meeting out of doors. So many Indians had come recently that it was impossible for all to get into our house. It was concluded best to go to the young chief Tow-en-too-e's lodge. I went, with the babe, to assist in singing. Found it a very convenient place, and completely filled. His part of it was remarkably clean and neat. Several families join their lodges together, making a long hall. In this way they hold great numbers. Their lodges are made of skins and rush mats, and, with a fire in the center, they are very warm and comfortable. The single lodges are put up in the same way. . . .

Indeed, I should not attempt to sing with them, were it not for the assistance my husband renders. You will recollect, when he was in Angelica, he could not sing a single tune. Now he is able to sing several tunes, and lead the school in them. This saves me a great deal of hard singing. I have thought many times if the singers in my father's family could have the same privilege, or were here to assist me in the work, how much good they could do. I was not aware that singing was a qualification of so much importance to a missionary. While I was in Vancouver, one Indian woman came a great distance with her daughter, as she said, to hear me sing with the children. The boys have introduced all the tunes they can sing alone into their morning and evening worship—these they sing very well. To be at a distance and hear them singing them, one would almost forget he was in a savage land.

May 3.—. . . There has been much sickness, both at Vancouver, Walla Walla, and here, and some deaths. The Indians here had but just begun to break ground for planting, when many of them were taken sick with an inflammation of the lungs. This was severe upon them, and threw them in great consternation. The old chief Umtippe's wife was quite sick, and came near dying. For a season they were satisfied with my husband's attention, and were doing well; but when they would overeat themselves, or go into a relapse from unnecessary exposure, then they must have their te-wat doctors; say that the medicine was bad, and all was bad. . . . When the te-wats were called, husband had nothing more to do with them. Their sickness commenced about the first of April, and, through the great mercy of God to us, none of them died to whom medicine was administered. . . .

Notwithstanding all our trials, yet our situation is enviable to Brother and Sister Merrell's. We have not their difficulties to contend with. No alcohol here to destroy men's lives; neither do they steal. I have let my clothes remain out over night, feeling just as safe in doing it as I used to in Prattsburgh. There is another circumstance which makes our situation very agreeable. There is not a man, woman, and scarcely a child, but what is well covered, and many of them have changes of garments. Some are dressed entirely in cloth made in American style. Those who wear only a shirt and leggins, wear a blanket or Buffalo skin over their shoulders. The women and girls' dresses are made entirely of skin. . . .

But it is time for me to think of closing, as I am unable to write without her on my lap. She is now seven weeks old, and weighs thirteen pounds. We have given her the names of our mothers, Alice Clarissa. We both have a sister of the same name also. We think she resembles her grandmother Clarissa very considerably as well as her mother. O, the responsibilities of a mother! To be a mother in heathen lands, among savages, gives feeling that can be known only to those who are such. You see our situation. If ever we needed your prayers and sympathies, it is at the Present time. . . .

. . . Who will come over and help us? Weak, frail nature cannot endure excessive care and anxiety any great length of time, without falling under it. I refer more particularly to my husband. His labor this spring has affected his health considerably. His old complaint in his side affects him occasionally. We both fail of writing as much as we desire. He is unable to write to any of my friends, and so am I to his, and wish you would copy my letters and send to his friends. He has requested the same of them, with regard to his letters.

Our love to you all, and the dear church of Christ. Farewell.

Narcissa Whitman.

P.S.—You are indebted to little Alice Clarissa's quiet disposition for this sheet. I have no cradle yet, and she has lain in my lap all day; for she does not like to be where she cannot see her mother, long at a time. She receives many kisses for her grandparents, uncles and aunts, every day. She is now in bed with her father, sleeping sweetly. She is pleasant company for me, here alone. . . .

FURTHER READING

Allen, Debra J. *Historical Dictionary of U.S. Diplomacy from the Revolution to Secession.* Lanham, MD: Rowman and Littlefield, 2012.

Archer, Christon I. *The Birth of Modern Mexico, 1780–1824.* Lanham, MD: Rowman and Littlefield, 2007.

Greenberg, Amy. *Manifest Manhood and the Antebellum American Empire.* Cambridge: Cambridge University Press, 2005.

Jeffrey, Julie Roy, ed. *Where Wagons Could Go: Narcissa Whitman and Eliza Spaulding.* Lincoln: University of Nebraska Press, 1997.

Lecompte, Janet. *Rebellion in Río Arriba, 1837.* Albuquerque: University of New Mexico Press, 1985.

Miller, Robert R. *Juan Alvarado, Governor of California, 1836–1842.* Norman: University of Oklahoma Press, 1998

Reséndez, Andrés. *Changing National Identities at the Frontier: Texas and New Mexico, 1800–1850.* Cambridge: Cambridge University Press, 2004.

Russell, Phillip. *The History of Mexico: From Pre-conquest to Present.* London: Routledge, 2011.

Truett, Samuel, and Elliott Young, eds. *Continental Crossroads: Remapping U.S.-Mexico Borderlands History.* Durham, NC: Duke University Press, 2004.

Van Young, Eric. *The Other Rebellion: Popular Violence, Ideology, and the Mexican Struggle for Independence, 1810–1821.* Palo Alto, CA: Stanford University Press, 2002.

Advertisement, Double Ve Waist, Young Ladies' Style 92. This corset, a required part of the attire for middle-class women and girls, was made of whalebone stays. Those whalebones came from a worldwide whale-hunting industry that employed hundreds of thousands of sailors, mostly young men apprenticed unwillingly to ship's captains. Hunting whales was dangerous, but far more men were killed cutting up whales and deboning them on ship deck. These stiff undergarments broke women's ribs when they were cinched too tightly or the wearer fell awkwardly. They made women have the hourglass figures required by nineteenth-century fashions. What other nineteenth-century fashion items involved unfree labor? When you imagine whaling, what images come to mind? How does the image portray wearing a corset as ordinary or even necessary?

Godey's Lady's Book and Magazine, New York (February 1853).

In contrast, Texas, the most southern of the western states, entered the Union as a slave state, and slavery remained crucial to its economy. By 1861, nearly a third of its population was black. Most of these African Americans labored as slaves in the cotton, rice, and sugarcane regions, but a significant number worked on isolated farms in frontier areas. In addition, Galveston and Houston each had a large population of urban slaves, who worked as house servants or as artisans making clothing or leather or metal goods. This pattern was similar to Southern slavery but with important exceptions. Because the Mexican border lay to the south and the sparsely populated frontier to the west, slaves in Texas had more opportunities to escape. By 1855, more than four thousand fugitive slaves lived south of the border, where they were welcomed by Mexican officials.

Enslaving Indian and Hispanic people remained legal long after plantation slavery ended. Called indenture, adoption, or guardianship, this form of slavery affected thousands of young native Californians, Texans, New Mexicans, and Arizonans, who labored in mines, in households and on farms, where they weren't paid and which they couldn't leave. Slavery also became a fixture in Indian Territory, where a tradition of slaveholding already existed. Tribes from the Deep South, who had long held slaves and used them to work the land, took their slaves with them when they were removed to Indian Territory in the 1830s. By 1861, African Americans made up nearly 15 percent of the territory's population. The Native American tradition of slavery, however, more often allowed slaves to buy their own freedom and to become part of tribal life. As a result of this greater openness and freedom, mixed-raced people became central to society in Indian Territory (which eventually became Oklahoma).

Slavery was hardly a Southern aberration. Slavery in its many forms endured, and even flourished in the West, belying the notion of natural geographic or cultural barriers to its practice. The selections in this chapter reflect the diverse forms of slavery in the American West and the political debates that slavery provoked. The Missouri Compromise, a set of laws passed by Congress in 1819 and 1820, demonstrates the dangerous political quagmire revealed every time slavery was discussed. Finally, in two pieces of legislation, the Mormon leader Brigham Young outlines the dangers of using Indians as slaves in Utah in the 1850s. A trial transcript from a Cherokee courtroom demonstrates the way ideas about slavery among that Native nation differed from those of the American South. Finally, Mary Lawrence's description of the harsh lives young sailors led on Pacific whaling ships shows us another version of unfree labor.

AS YOU READ: Think about the similarities and differences in slavery between the West and the South. Did "frontier conditions" affect how slavery developed? How do we think about the enslavement of and by Native people and the range of unfree lives that people lived in the West? How does gender figure into the story of captivity and enslavement?

43. WESTERN STATEHOOD AND THE SLAVERY CRISIS

Although politicians attempted to keep slavery out of national politics, slavery in the western territories added by the Louisiana Purchase remained a burning issue. Proslavery advocates insisted that expansion was crucial to the economic and social health of the nation, while antislavery activists regarded the institution and its expansion as threats to the American ideal of free labor. A crisis arose in 1818, when Missouri, the first truly western state, petitioned to enter the Union as a slave state. In a complex set of petitions and amendments, Congress admitted Missouri as a slave state and Maine as a free state but limited further expansion of slavery in the territories to those regions south of the Missouri border. The compromise solved the immediate conflict but satisfied no one entirely. The following documents are excerpts from the acts and amendments preceding the final compromise granting statehood to Missouri. Why do you think the Missouri Enabling Act was so careful to specify Missouri's boundaries? How did the Thomas Amendment solve the problem of dividing up the Louisiana Purchase? Why was the issue of escaping slaves so important? Why did politicians in Missouri want to outlaw the presence of free blacks?

The Missouri Compromise
1819–21

A Debate on the House Floor
February 13, 1819[1]

. . . Mr. Meigs, of New York, spoke as follows: Mr. Chairman, I assure the Committee that I shall not detain them long by my observations upon this question; nor should I now undertake to consume the fifteen or twenty minutes which I shall allot to myself, if it was not for the somewhat peculiar situation in which I am placed.

It is well known that the Legislature of the respectable State which I have the honor in part to represent, has requested the Representatives of that State, upon this floor, to vote for the restriction upon Missouri, now under consideration.

I have examined, attentively, the mass of argument which has been so laboriously accumulated on this question; and never, perhaps, was there on any occasion so much exhausted as on this. But, sir, I freely own that I cannot, in conscience or judgment, consent to impose this restriction upon Missouri.

There is a wonderful singularity in the present controversy, which destroys all confidence in the weight and value of that process of mind which we so proudly dignify with the title of reasoning. Sir, I never yet knew that reason and

---

1. 13 February, Journal of the House of Representatives, Dec. 1, 1817 to April 20, 1818, 15th Cong., 2nd Session. S. set 4, 272; Annals of the Congress of the United States, 26 Jan. 1820, 17 Feb. 1820, 16th Congress, Ist. Sess.

logic were to be found on this side or that of a parallel of latitude or longitude. What is the fact in this case? Why, sir, the parallel of latitude of 39 degrees almost precisely marks the division between the reason and argument of the North and South. That line of demarcation separates the slaveholding from the non-slaveholding States. On the south side of that line we find the climate and soil adapted to slaves, and there are the slaves; on the north side of that line we discover that the soil and climate require no slaves, and, therefore, few or no slaves are found. . . .

Reason divided by parallels of latitude! Why, sir, it is easy for prejudice and malevolence, by aid of ingenuity, to erect an eternal impenetrable wall of brass between the North and South, at the latitude of thirty-nine degrees! But, in the view of reason, there is no other line between them than that celestial arc of thirty-nine degrees which offers no barrier to the march of liberal and rational men. . . .

Sir, we have been now for a long time occupied in this debate, mis-spending our time and the public money. I feel well assured that the body of the people will judge our conduct rightly. They are able critics. Yes, sir, even in matters of sub-lime art, even in those works which none can execute, all are critics! They deter-mine, at a glance of the eye, what is good and beautiful in architecture, in statuary, in painting, and, what is to them still more easy, what is good in governments and constitutions. They will soon ask us, what is the controversy about? Did you, from motives of policy and regard for the welfare of the whites, propose to remove the growing black race from this country? No. Did you, actuated by humane considerations for the unfortunate slaves, propose to redeem them from their bondage, and restore them to liberty and the land of their fathers? No. What then? Did you propose to draw such lines of restriction around the slave population as would ere long starve them out, and so prevent their becoming dangerous to the whites? If you did, remember that such is the increasing kindness of the slaveholders, so ameliorated the condition of the slave, that not one slave, not one child less will be born, and not one can die by starvation. Sir, the truth is, that nothing has yet been proposed beneficial either to the white or black race in all this long-drawn debate. Give me leave to say, sir, that this consideration induced me to introduce the resolution which now lies upon the table, devoting the public lands to the emancipation and colonization of the unfortunate slaves. If we want some object upon which to exhaust our enthusiasm, here is one worth it all. Not the subjugation of a people, but the redemption of a nation/. . . .

A Debate on the Senate Floor
January 20, 1820

The Senate resumed, as in Committee of the Whole, (Mr. Burrill in the Chair,) the consideration of the Missouri question.

Mr. King, of New York, again rose and spoke more than one hour in support of the opinions which he had previously advanced on the right and expediency of restricting Missouri as to slavery, and in answer to the gentlemen who had replied to his previous remarks. . . .

Mr. Smith said: . . . The discontent of the people was still kept up; he believed we were never to hear the last of it. The gentleman had reiterated in every speech he had made before the Senate. If the people were let alone, they would do right. But, it is found to be expedient to keep up the excitement by some means, because they are a necessary instrument in this business, if they can be brought to bear on it. . . . Their artillery is next turned upon the South and the West, and the pretext is, opposition to the extension of slavery. The people are led to believe that the Southern and Western States are endeavoring to open afresh the African slave trade, and the North and East were to be swallowed up by Africans. If the real fact had been stated, that the question was nothing more than whether the citizens of the United States who now lived in Missouri, and owned slaves, should be at liberty to keep them there, or whether they should be set free over their masters' heads, the subject would have been a plain one, and the people would have reasoned for themselves. Therefore, it is necessary to magnify the impending evil, or the people would have retained their senses, and this farce could not have been [kept] up. . . .

Mr. S. said this declaration of the gentleman could receive no reply, because it deserved none but such as would not be tolerated by the rules of that Senate. The gentleman had, with the same deliberate composure, told the Senate,

> the people who held slaves were indolent and inactive. They had slaves to work for them; therefore, they would not work for themselves. By this means, the energies of the Government must become enfeebled and relaxed. The Northern people attended to their own business; they were always engaged in some active employment.

Mr. President, is this a language for a gentleman to utter in this Hall, in his Senatorial character, who ought to employ all the faculties of his mind, and all the powers of his eloquence, to appease every ferment that should, in any degree, tend to relax the bonds of this Union? Instead of this, the gentleman has sought every opportunity to indulge all the fanciful arguments of his imagination, that could lead to rouse unfriendly and hostile feelings between different sections of the nation. But the gentleman is under an egregious mistake in his facts. The people of the South and West are as much in the habit of industry as any people in America. There are few persons among them, whether they own slaves or not, who are not so. Where he got his information he did not relate, but it is probable he got it from some pamphlet writer. The gentleman himself, perhaps, had little to do but to attend bank meetings, and look, now and then, into the management of his bank stock. This could give him no great deal to boast of, as respected industrious habits, whatever other habits he might inspire. He says,

> these gentlemen who wish to extend slavery to Missouri, are obliged to be constantly on the watch against the insurrection of their own slaves. They were alarmed at the toll of every bell.

This was as unfounded as any position he had advanced. We had nothing to fear, sir, if unprincipled incendiaries would mind their own business, and let our slaves alone. If the gentleman pursued the course he had set out on, he might succeed in producing this state of things in time; but he ought to be amongst the last to tell us of it, as he had been amongst the first to excite it. Almost all the gentlemen who had opposed the admission of Missouri, and especially the gentleman from New York, had urged, with much zeal, the impolicy of extending slavery, because it destroyed your military character. He says,

> if you tolerate this extension of slavery, you must diminish your white population in proportion, and, in time of war, instead of supplying their proportion of military strength, the free States will have to defend your country, and protect the slaveholding States at the same time.

Mr. President, all the resolutions of the crossroad meetings, and of the town meetings, and of the primary assemblies, and all the pamphlet writers, from Marcus to Mr. *Philadelphia*, had held the same language. Sir, during the Revolutionary war, the people of the slaveholding States fought your principal battles, and found no inconvenience from their slaves; their slaves were useful, and participated with their masters, in many respects, in the burdens of the war. These gentlemen of the Senate, and among them the gentlemen of New York, and these resolvers, and the pamphlet writers, had all been silent about the military strength of the nation, whilst we were engaged in our last war. As a test of the military strength furnished from the different sections of the Union, it would not prove, to their satisfaction, the correctness of their position. . . .

The Thomas Amendment
February 17, 1820

The following amendment, offered by Mr. Thomas, and pending when the Senate adjourned yesterday, being still under consideration:

"*And be it further enacted,* That the sixth article of compact of the ordinance of Congress, passed on the thirteenth day of July, one thousand seven hundred and eighty-seven, for the government of the territory of the United States northwest of the river Ohio, shall, to all intents and purposes be, and hereby is, deemed and held applicable to, and shall have full force and effect in and over, all that tract of country ceded by France to the United States, under the name of Louisiana, which lies north of thirty-six degrees and thirty minutes north latitude, excepting only such part thereof as is included within the limits of the State contemplated by this act."

Mr. Thomas withdrew this amendment, and offered the following as a new section:

"*And be it further enacted,* That, in all that territory ceded by France to the United States, under the name of Louisiana, which lies north of thirty-six degrees and thirty minutes north latitude, excepting only such part thereof as is included within the limits of the State contemplated by this act, slavery and involuntary servitude, otherwise than in the punishment of crimes whereof the party shall have been duly convicted, shall be and is hereby forever prohibited: *Provided, always,* That any person escaping into the same, from whom labor or service is lawfully claimed in any State or Territory of the United States, such fugitive may be lawfully reclaimed and conveyed to the person claiming his or her labor or service as aforesaid." . . .

The Missouri Enabling Act
March 6, 1820[1]

Be it enacted by the Senate and House of Representatives of the United States of America, in Congress assembled, That the inhabitants of that portion of the Missouri territory included within the boundaries hereinafter designated, he, and they are hereby, authorized to form for themselves a constitution and state government, and to assume such name as they shall deem proper; and the said state, when formed, shall be admitted into the Union, upon an equal footing with the original states, in all respects whatsoever.

Sec. 2. And be it further enacted, That the said state shall consist of all the territory included within the following boundaries, to wit: Beginning in the middle of the Mississippi river, on the parallel of thirty-six degrees of north latitude; thence west, along that parallel of latitude, to the St. Francois river; thence up, and following the course of that river, in the middle of the main channel thereof, to the parallel of latitude of thirty-six degrees and thirty minutes; thence west, along the same, to a point where the said parallel is intersected by a meridian line passing through the middle of the mouth of the Kansas river, where the same empties into the Missouri river, thence, from the point aforesaid north, along the said meridian line, to the intersection of the parallel of latitude which passes through the rapids of the river Des Moines, making the said line to correspond with the Indian boundary line; thence east, from the point of intersection last aforesaid, along the said parallel of latitude, to the middle of the channel of the main fork of the said river Des Moines; thence down and along the middle of the main channel of the said river Des Moines, to the mouth of the same, where it empties into the Mississippi river; thence, due east, to the middle of the main channel of the Mississippi river; thence down, and following the course of the Mississippi river, in the middle of the main channel thereof, to the place of beginning. . . .

Sec. 3. And be it further enacted, That all free white male citizens of the United States, who shall have arrived at the age of twenty-one years, and have

---

1. *U.S. Statutes at Large,* ed. Richard Peters, v. 3 (Boston: Charles Little and James Brown, 1848), 545.

Said Molly and her descendants, now who are the only descendants of said Molly, had been and are claimed to be the property of one Molly Hightower, who has come into the said Nation and set up claim by Bill of Sale for said Sam Dend [or Dent] to said Hightower's Father, who was also an Indian trader and who lived many years near the descendants of said and never advanced or set up any claim to the said descendants that the present petitioner Chunestutee, alias Isaac Tucker, and his mother Chickawa was aware off in these fore mentioned natives, as we has ever be conscious. The Council and authorities of the Cherokee Nation as also we the subscribers, members of the same clan, ask and require of our council and head men for assistance and for Council to resist this oppression and illegal wrong attempted to be practiced on our Brother and Sister by the Hightower in carrying into slavery Two of whom have ever been and considered native Cherokee. We feel that the attempt is of cruel grievance to us and ask of your honorable bodies redress in the protection and defence of the two a fore mentioned members of our clan and your petitioners will ever pray & &c

> *The Doctor*
> *The Ola thegh his mark*
> *Chunestutee alias Bucks Horn his mark*
> *Isaac Tucker his mark*
> *Chickaw ne Molly her mark*
> *Charles Buffington*
> *Chickedincuan his mark*

This Day appeared before me Daniel McCoy, one of the Judges of the Supreme Court of the Cherokee Nation, the Big Half Breed, John Watts, the Tiger and the White Path who being duly sworn and saith that to the best of their knowledge and belief, that the mother of Edward & Isaac Tucker, Molley, was surrendered and delivered up when a girl some time previous to the Revolutionary War by a white named Samuel Bend [Dent or Dend] to the authorities of the Cherokee Nation for certain important considerations, & that said Molly was then emancipated and adopted into the clan composing the Deer family, agreeably to the then existing usages & customs of said Nation, & since that time she has continued in the Nation & enjoyed the liberty of freedom & that her two sons Edward & Isaac Tucker were born at the beloved town called Echota on the Tennessee River & has ever been free & resided in the Nation.

Sworn to and subscribed to before me at Red Clay this 18th October 1833.

> *Daniel McCoy Signed*
> *Big Half Breed his mark*
> *J. S. Court White Path his mark*
> *Jno. Watts his mark*
> *Tiger his mark*

I certify that the above to be a correct copy of the original handed to the said Isaac Tucker.

18th Oct. 1833 Charles Vann, Clerk, Supreme Court

46. UNFREE LABOR ON THE SEAS

Mary Chipman Lawrence headed out to sea as the wife of a ship captain in 1856. Accompanied by her four-year-old daughter and a ship full of young, indentured sailors, she sailed to the Pacific. Mary spent nearly four years at sea, as her husband and his crew hunted whales, and visited Hawaii, the Bering Sea, the coast of California, and Mexico. Young men signed onto whaling ships and became the property of the captain, who could beat, starve, abandon, and drown them. The first piece of the selection describes Mrs. Lawrence's excitement at being at sea and her efforts to maintain comfort and status for her family; the second part gives a sense of the danger and hard work involved for the crew. From this selection, can you get any sense of what life was like for sailors? What were the cultural and economic factors that made this work so dangerous? Is this different from being an enslaved worker like the African Americans described in the congressional debates around the Missouri Compromise?

Mary Chipman Lawrence
Three Years on a Whaling Ship
1856[1]

New Bedford to the Sandwich Islands: November 1856–April 1857

November 25 [and 26]. As this is my first experience in seafaring life, I have thought it advisable to attempt keeping a Journal, not for the purpose of interesting anyone out of my own private family, but thinking it might be useful to myself or my child for fixture reference. We left New Bedford on the morning of the twenty-fifth of November, 1856, with a sad heart, knowing not whether we should ever behold the faces of friends near and dear to us again on earth. God grant we may all meet in that better land where the parting tear is never shed, the word good-by never spoken. We had a good wind from the eastward and a fine sail down the bay, out into the wide ocean which is to be my home for months and years to come. Went on deck before dark to take my last look at my native land. With what different feelings shall I behold it should I be permitted to return.

The next day was sick more or less throughout the day. Got over it before night, but Minnie's seasickness lasted throughout the next day, We were very for-

---

1. *The Captain's Best Mate: The Journal of Mary Chipman Lawrence on the Whaler Addison, 1856–1860*, ed. Stanton Gardner. https://archive.org/details/captainsbestmate00lawr_0

tunate in getting over it as we did, for we had exceedingly rough weather for ten days, a constant gale from the west. Not much transpired during that time except the ordinary duty on board ship. Each one had as much as he could do to look out for himself. As for Minnie and myself, we were obliged to sit in our bed the whole time, except as we went on deck. It was of no use for us to attempt to sit up in the cabin, for we were tossed from one side to the other without the least mercy.

November 27. Thanksgiving at home. What a pity we could not have remained at home until after that event. We all thought we should relish a plate of Grandma's nice turkey for dinner as we were sitting on deck but had no appetite for anything they had here. I delight to be on deck and watch the ocean in its varying moods. Truly, "they that go down to the sea in ships, that do business in great waters, see the works of the Lord and his wonders in the deep. For he commandeth and raiseth the stormy wind, which lifteth up the waves thereof. They mount up to the heaven and go down again into the depths." It sometimes seems impossible that we can live through it, but our gallant ship rides along fearlessly. It is grand beyond anything I ever witnessed, sublimity itself.

December 1. The first day of winter seems not much like it with us. How I should enjoy a calm day. Think I shall get accustomed to gales if this continues much longer . . . . Pleasant breeze and just warm enough for comfort. Went on deck immediately after breakfast to view old Ocean in another aspect. Everything is smiling and serene; one would never suspect the treachery that lurks in his bosom. Everything seems changed. This is one of the most delightful moments of my life. I do not wonder that so many choose a sailor's life. It is a of hardship, but it is a life full of romance and interest. As I went on deck, the first sight that greeted my eyes was the pigs and chickens running about at large on deck. Altogether they made an appearance so homelike that I could hardly realize that I was thousands of miles away from home.

December 21. For the last ten days nothing of interest has transpired. During the most of our passage the sea has been rather rough and the wind not very favorable. Occasionally we catch a glimpse of a distant vessel, and as we are going different directions, they soon vanish, and we are left alone, a solitary speck on the ocean. Several days ago several dolphins were following the ship for some time, but they did not succeed in catching any of them, to my disappointment. Flying fish are very plenty. One flew over the side of the ship one day, and the steward cooked him for my breakfast. Was very nice; tasted some like a fresh herring. Have seen none of those monsters of the deep yet, although occasionally we hear from the masthead the cry of "There blows!"

December 22. We are now nearly to the line. It is very warm indeed, not much, I imagine, like the weather at home. Minnie enjoys herself very much, running about on deck and making new acquaintances. Her little heart swells sometimes when she thinks of her dear friends she left behind. Yesterday I broke a wishbone with her, she wished that she could see Aunt Susan.

Lower California: November 1858–April 1859

November 30. After a long period of silence I again resume my writing. Left Honolulu today after being a resident of that goodly city for a period of seven weeks. Our stay was prolonged so much beyond our usual time on account of repairing our ship, which has been thoroughly done, and now we think she is in a sound condition and will prove seaworthy. May she for the future keep clear of all ice, shoals, rocks, and quicksands and bear us safely on until we shall reach the port of home.

Time passed very pleasantly to us while in port. Minnie's delight was unbounded at meeting with children again of her own age, which she found at Mr. Whitney's, where we boarded, also at Mr. Damon's, where we occupied a room. We formed many pleasant acquaintances, especially among captains and their ladies, at one time there being twenty-one ladies in port. Three of the ladies came in with infants that were born at sea in the northern regions during the season: Mrs. Smith of the *Eliza F. Mason* has a son, Mrs. Green of the *Sheffield* a daughter, and Mrs. Taber of the *Adeline* a son. They are called young "bowheads" by the captains.

We received an abundant supply of letters while in port, more than we could reasonably have expected, and they were mostly filled with good tidings with the exception of our dear niece Celia Maria, whom we left in the full bloom of health and vigor and who is now in all human probability fast passing away. God help those parents if called so soon to part with their only child. I can hardly endure the thought that we can never look on her bright face again, but there is consolation in the thought that our loss will be her exceeding gain; in her young days she gave herself up to her Heavenly Father and, we trust, has ever since been an humble follower of the meek and lowly Jesus. I sent letters home to all the family on both sides, having an opportunity of sending by three different mails.

December 25. Minnie hung up her stocking as usual last night and was fortunate in finding it quite well filled with the usual supply of candies, nuts, and oranges, also a book and transparent slate from me, and a $2.50 gold piece from her papa. A few days ago Mr. Forsyth, our mate, gave her a very pretty little spyglass, which she said she should call her Christmas present too.

We are now bound to the coast of California for mussel diggers, if we can find them, and for wood. After undergoing repairs it was too late to go on New Zealand where we would like to have gone, but it may be all for the best for us to come here. Yesterday saw a ship supposed to be a merchantman from

The US-Mexico War

In the 1840s, annexation of land became war between nations. War and the threat of more war brought Texas, the Southwest, California, and the Pacific Northwest into the borders of the United States. By 1850, the United States had acquired more than three times the land and nearly four times the population of Mexico. Although many Americans regarded the annexation of territory as natural, even preordained by God, this growth came at a high social, military, and political cost. The United States now extended from the Atlantic to the Pacific, but it took the Texas Revolution, the Mexican War, and finally the Civil War to absorb these contested regions into the national fabric. The nation's center moved steadily west. St. Louis and New Orleans became the most important US ports. The Mississippi no longer seemed to be a national boundary. During the 1820s and 1830s Anglo-American traders, fur trappers, and farmers began moving beyond the borders of the Louisiana Purchase into areas claimed by Mexicans, English, Russians, and Indians. Sometimes they were invited in as trading partners and family members, but at other times they simply squatted, traded illegally, or invaded.

Texas and New Mexico offer good examples of the complex situations that led to war. Before 1821, when the Mexican Revolution ended the Spanish empire's hold in

North America, the Spanish forbade Americans to enter New Spain. Recognizing the prodigious land hunger of white Americans, they didn't want them around as traders or settlers. But the overextended empire could rarely police its borders. After the revolution, however, the new Mexican government decided to change policy and to accept American trade and settlement, hoping that new residents would strengthen and populate their vast northern border. For example, in 1821, young Stephen F. Austin negotiated with the Mexican territorial governor in San Antonio to start a colony in Texas populated by slave-owning white Americans. In the same year, William Bucknell led the first trade caravan from St. Louis to Santa Fe, initiating a significant trading relationship between Mexico and the United States along what would come to be known as the Santa Fe Trail. This policy change ended the economic isolation of the Southwest, but it also brought in the aggressive and ambitious norteamericanos that Mexican officials had always feared. By 1830, more than seven thousand Americans outnumbered the three thousand Mexicans in Texas and New Mexico.

In 1835, a new administration in Mexico decided to impose stricter controls over Texas. American and Mexican Texans protested their loss of autonomy. When the government responded with armed soldiers, Texans declared themselves independent and went to war to uphold their revolution. After the dramatic loss of the Alamo, where Davy Crockett and 186 men fought and were killed by the Mexican army, Texans joined the revolution in droves. They soon routed the larger Mexican army, and Texas became an independent republic in 1836. Anglo-Texans immediately petitioned the United States for annexation, but because of the divisiveness of the slavery issue and fear of war with Mexico, they were refused.

California, with its Pacific ports and supposedly Mediterranean climate, lured nations, big trading companies, sailors, and immigrants, becoming an important center of international trade. Along the California coast and on inland ranches, a few Anglo-Americans married Mexican women or became Mexican citizens, so that they could own land. California's indigenous people, numerous and varied, controlled inland California. They provided a source of labor for some industries but also became expert horsemen and herders, part of an entire economy based on raiding horses, mules, sheep, and humans.

Beginning in the early 1840s, US politicians and merchants began to make aggressive moves to take California. In 1842, after hearing rumors of a US war with Mexico, US Navy Commodore Jones took his warships into Monterrey harbor and demanded that the local community surrender. No state of war existed, no fighting had begun between the two nations, but it took Jones two days to realize his mistake, get his men back onto his ships, and leave. He refused to apologize, and neither did the US government. Two years later, another US official sent by President Polk arrived in California. Lt. John C. Frémont, the famous pathfinder, planned to "explore" California while aiding and supporting a group of Americans bent on causing a Texas-style rebellion in California. The Bear Flag Revolt began in Northern California, when a group of American settlers and John C. Frémont's soldiers kidnapped some Mexican leaders and raised a new flag.

However, real war soon superseded that rag-tag event, when in 1845, after the election of James K. Polk, the United States annexed Texas. However, the Texas the United States intended to annex was far larger than the Republic of Texas and included a border stretching all the way to the Rio Grande. Mexicans were already angry over events in Texas and California, when Polk made the situation worse by sending a delegation to Mexico City to buy California and New Mexico. At the same time, he sent four thousand troops into the disputed border area, actively provoking war with Mexico. Tension mounted as Mexican and US troops stared at each other across the Rio Grande. The inevitable happened: the troops fired on each other and President Polk immediately declared war.

Battle soon spread to New Mexico and California. US troops from Missouri led by General Stephen Watts Kearny headed toward Santa Fe and Los Angeles. He arrived in New Mexico mostly unchallenged, because the Mexican army, focused on Texas and central Mexico, had left its New Mexican and Californian citizens unprotected. Few soldiers remained to take a stand. However, once Mexican citizens realized what US control would mean, a series of very challenging rebellions occurred in both New Mexico and California. A brutal uprising in Taos shocked U.S officials, and a group of Mexican Californians, led by Jose María Florez, and acting without Mexican support, began a siege of Los Angeles, forcing the US garrison there to retreat.

Once additional US troops arrived, along with naval support, they took those Mexican northern border states. The main part of the war now shifted to Mexico itself. After a series of victories on both land and sea, General Winfield Scott marched his troops into Mexico City and delivered President Polk's demands for peace. Two years of war, approximately ninety-seven million dollars, thirteen thousand American lives, and fifty thousand Mexican lives had been spent to settle this border dispute. By this time, many people in the United States demanded all of Mexico, but the Treaty of Guadalupe Hidalgo, signed in February 1848, did not go that far, much to Polk's annoyance. For a payment of fifteen million dollars, Mexico ceded its northern provinces, which included California, New Mexico, Arizona, Nevada, Utah, and the Rio Grande border for Texas. Organizing these acquisitions both politically and socially, however, remained difficult. Native nations, like the Comanche, Wichita, and Apaches, however, still controlled territory at the heart of the region. Debate over how to negotiate with these powerful warriors, the role of formerly Mexican citizens, and the place of slavery took decades to resolve.

The selections in this chapter look at the causes and results of the US war with Mexico. In the first selection, two US senators argue on the Senate floor about the dangers of expansion. Hoping to push California toward a revolution, Secretary of State James Buchanan sent this secret message to an official in California. The Treaty of Guadalupe Hidalgo that ended the war and gave the United States a great swath of land also included promises to the Mexican government that they would stop the devastating Indian raiding that had essentially stopped movement in Texas and northern Mexico. Finally, a young woman from New Mexico, Teresina Bent, remembers her father's murder during an uprising in Taos over the unrest created by the Mexican war.

47. OPPOSING VIEWS OF EXPANSION INTO MEXICO

As the Mexican War shifted from sudden war to sudden peace, and Americans realized what this might mean for the nation, government officials argued about what its result should be. Southern politicians, especially slaveholders, who had convinced the government and the army to fight for slavery in Texas, now began clamoring for all of Mexico. As military victory became inevitable, this position, seen as extreme before the war, suddenly looked reasonable. Southerners envisioned a new empire for slavery; Northerners and Westerners hoped for land and mineral wealth for everyone. On the other hand, others argued that annexing Mexico was impractical and dangerous because of its alien culture and political traditions. They made racial arguments about the impossibility of absorbing millions of Mexicans and Indians. Included here are the 1848 speeches of two senators, John Calhoun of South Carolina and John Dix of New York, that illuminate the debate over annexing Mexico. How did ideas about race and ethnicity affect both arguments? Why did John Calhoun, a passionate supporter of slavery, oppose the incorporation of Mexico? Why do John Dix's arguments make incorporation sound natural?

John Calhoun and John Dix
Congressional Debate over Incorporating Mexico
1848[1]

[John Calhoun]

Sir, we have heard how much glory our country has acquired in this war. I acknowledge it to the full amount, Mr. President, so far as military glory is concerned. The army has done nobly, chivalrously; they have conferred honor on the country, for which I sincerely thank them. . . .

---

1. The Congressional Globe, 4 January 1848, 30th Congress, 1st Session, 98–99.

Now, sir, much as I regard military glory; . . . it is without example or precedent, either to hold Mexico as a province, or to incorporate her into our Union. No example of such a line of policy can be found. We have conquered many of the neighboring tribes of Indians, but we never thought of holding them in subjection—never of incorporating them into our Union. They have either been left as an independent people amongst us, or been driven into the forests.

I know further, sir, that we have never dreamt of incorporating into our Union any but the Caucasian race—the free white race. To incorporate Mexico, would be the very first instance of the kind of incorporating an Indian race; for more than half of the Mexicans are Indians, and the other is composed chiefly of mixed tribes. I protest against such a union as that! Ours, sir, is the Government of a white race. The greatest misfortunes of Spanish America are to be traced to the fatal error of placing these colored races on an equality with the white race. That error destroyed the social arrangement which formed the basis of society. The Portuguese and ourselves have escaped—the Portuguese at least to some extent—and we are the only people on this continent which have made revolutions without being followed by anarchy. And yet it is professed and talked about to erect these Mexicans into a Territorial Government, and place them on an equality with the people of the United States. I protest utterly against such a project.

Sir, it is a remarkable fact, that in the whole history of man, as far as my knowledge extends, there is no instance whatever of any civilized colored races being found equal to the establishment of free popular government, although by far the largest portion of the human family is composed of these races. And even in the savage state we scarcely find them anywhere with such government, except it be our noble savages—for noble I will call them. They, for the most part, had free institutions, but they are easily sustained amongst a savage people. Are we to overlook this fact? Are we to associate with ourselves as equals, companions, and fellow-citizens, the Indians and mixed race of Mexico? Sir, I should consider such a thing as fatal to our institutions. . . .

I come now to the proposition of incorporating her into our Union. Well, as far as law is concerned, that is easy. You can establish a Territorial Government for every State in Mexico, and there are some twenty of them. You can appoint governors, judges, and magistrates. You can give the people a subordinate government, allowing them to legislate for themselves, whilst you defray the cost. So far as law goes, the thing is done. There is no analogy between this and our Territorial Governments. Our Territories are only an offset of our own people, or foreigners from the same regions from which we came. They are small in number. . . . It is entirely different with Mexico. You have no need of armies to keep your Territories in subjection. But when you incorporate Mexico, you must have powerful armies to keep them in subjection. You may call it annexation, but it is a forced annexation, which is a contradiction in terms, according to my conception. You will be involved, in one word, in all the evils which I attribute to holding Mexico as a province. In fact, it will be but a Provincial

Government, under the name of a Territorial Government. How long will that last? How long will it be before Mexico will be capable of incorporation into our Union? Why, if we judge from the examples before us, it will be a very long time. Ireland has been held in subjection by England for seven or eight hundred years, and yet still remains hostile, although her people are of kindred race with the conquerors. A few French Canadians on this continent yet maintain the attitude of a hostile people; and never will the time come, in my opinion, Mr. President, that these Mexicans will be heartily reconciled to your authority. They have Castilian blood in their veins—the old Gothic, quite equal to the Anglo-Saxon in many respects—in some respects superior. Of all nations of the earth they are the most pertinacious—have the highest sense of nationality—hold out longest, and often even with the least prospect of effecting their object. On this subject also I have conversed with officers of the army, and they all entertain the same opinion, that these people are now hostile, and will continue so.

But, Mr. President, suppose all these difficulties removed; suppose these people attached to our Union, and desirous of incorporating with us, ought we to bring them in? Are they fit to be connected with us? Are they fit for self-government and for governing you? Are you, any of you, willing that your States should be governed by these twenty-odd Mexican States, with a population of about only one million of your blood, and two or three millions of mixed blood, better informed, all the rest pure Indians, a mixed blood equally ignorant and unfit for liberty, impure races, not as good as the Cherokees or Choctaws?

We make a great mistake, sir, when we suppose that all people are capable of self-government. We are anxious to force free government on all; and I see that it has been urged in a very respectable quarter, that it is the mission of this country to spread civil and religious liberty over all the world, and especially over this continent. It is a great mistake. None but people advanced to a very high state of moral and intellectual improvement are capable, in a civilized state, of maintaining free government; and amongst those who are so purified, very few, indeed have had the good fortune of forming a constitution capable of endurance. It is a remarkable fact in the history of man, that scarcely ever have free popular institutions been formed by wisdom alone that have endured. . . .

[John Dix]

Mr. President, it was my wish to address the Senate on the resolutions offered by the Senator from South Carolina. . . . I believe it would be in the highest degree unjust to ourselves, possessing, as we do, well-founded claims on Mexico, to withdraw forces from her territory altogether, and exceedingly unwise, as a matter of policy, looking to the future political relations of the two countries, to withdraw from it partially, and assume a line of defence, without a treaty of peace. On the contrary, I am in favor of retaining possession, for the present, of all we have acquired, not as a permanent conquest, but as the most effective means of bringing about, what all most earnestly desire, a restoration of peace. . . .

Sir, no one who has paid a moderate degree of attention to the laws and elements of our increase, can doubt that our population is destined to spread itself across the American continent, filling up, with more or less completeness, according to attractions of soil and climate, the space that intervenes between the Atlantic and Pacific oceans. This eventual, and, perhaps, in the order of time, this not very distant extension of our settlements over a tract of country, with a diameter, as we go westward, greatly disproportioned to its length, becomes a subject of the highest interest to us. On the whole extent of our northern flank, from New Brunswick to the point where the northern boundary of Oregon touches the Pacific, we are in contact with British colonists, having, for the most part, the same common origin with ourselves, but controlled and moulded by political influences from the Eastern hemisphere, if not adverse, certainly not decidedly friendly to us. The strongest tie which can be relied on to bind us to mutual offices of friendship and good neighborhood, is that of commerce; and this, as we know, is apt to run into rivalry, and sometimes becomes a fruitful source of alienation.

From our northern boundary, we turn to our southern. What races are to border on us here, what is to be their social and political character, and what their means of annoyance? Are our two frontiers, only seven parallels of latitude apart when we pass Texas, to be flanked by settlements having no common bond of union with ours? Our whole southern line is conterminous, throughout its whole extent, with the territories of Mexico, a large portion of which is nearly unpopulated. The geographical area of Mexico is about 1,500,000 square miles, and her population about 7,000,000 souls. The whole northern and central portion, taking the twenty-sixth parallel of latitude as the dividing line, containing more than 1,000,000 square miles, has about 650,000 inhabitants—about two inhabitants to three square miles. The southern portion, with less than 500,000 square miles, has a population of nearly six and a half millions of souls, or thirteen inhabitants to one square mile. The aboriginal races, which occupy and overrun a portion of California and New Mexico, must there, as everywhere else, give way before the advancing wave of civilization, either to be overwhelmed by it, or to be driven upon perpetually contracting areas, where, from a diminution of their accustomed sources of subsistence, they must ultimately become extinct by force of an invincible law. We see the operation of this law in every portion of this continent. We have no power to control it, if we would. It is the behest of Providence that idleness, and ignorance, and barbarism, shall give place to industry, and knowledge, and civilization. The European and mixed races, which possess Mexico, are not likely, either from moral or physical energy, to become formidable rivals or enemies.

The bold and courageous enterprise which overran and conquered Mexico, appears not to have descended to the present possessors of the soil. Either from the influence of climate or the admixture of races—the fusion of castes, to use the technical phrase—the conquerors have, in turn, become the conquered. The ancient Castilian energy is, in a great degree, subdued; and it has given place, with many other noble traits of the Spanish character, to a peculiarity which seems to have marked the race in that country, under whatever combinations it is found—a proneness to civil discord, and a suicidal waste of its own strength.

With such a territory and such a people on our southern border, what is to be the inevitable course of empire? It needs no powers of prophecy to foretell. Sir, I desire to speak plainly; why should we not, when we are discussing the operation of moral and physical laws, which are beyond our control? As our population moves westward on our own territory, portions will cross our southern boundary. Settlements will be formed within the unoccupied and sparsely-peopled territory of Mexico. Uncongenial habits and tastes, differences of political opinion and principle, and numberless other elements of diversity will lead to a separation of these newly-formed societies from the inefficient government of Mexico. They will not endure to be held in subjection to a system, which neither yields them protection nor offers any incentive to their proper development and growth. They will form independent States on the basis of constitutions identical in all their leading features with our own; and they will naturally seek to unite their fortunes to ours. The fate of California is already sealed: it can never be reunited to Mexico. The operation of the great causes, to which I have alluded, must, at no distant day, detach the whole of northern Mexico from the southern portion of that republic. . . .

48. CREATING A GLORIOUS WAR IN CALIFORNIA

President James Polk watched developing tensions in Mexican California over active US efforts to get control over its West Coast ports. He sent clear messages to government officials in California that they were to take action the moment any kind of unrest or rebellion began in California. Hoping to support a revolution that someone else started rather than attacking California as an aggressor, Polk sent this message, through his secretary of state, to the man who served as American counsel to Mexico. Thomas Larkin, a long-time resident and businessman in Monterey, began working secretly to convince a group of Anglo-Americans and Spanish-speaking Californians that a coup and peaceful annexation to the United States would be the best path for California. How does Buchanan explain what Larkin is supposed to do? How does Buchanan justify such actions, and what kinds of arguments does he use to persuade Larkin to take on this illegal job?

Secretary of State James Buchanan
Secret Message to Thomas Larkin, American Counsel to
Mexico in California
1845[1]

TO MR. LARKIN.

DEPARTMENT OF STATE, WASHINGTON,
OCTOBER 17TH, 1845.

THOMAS O. LARKIN, ESQUIRE,
Consul of the United States at Monterey.

SIR:

I feel much indebted to you for the information which you have communicated to the Department from time to time in relation to California. The future destiny of the country is a subject of anxious solicitude for the Government and people of the United States. The interests of our commerce and our whale fisheries on the Pacific ocean demand that you should exert the greatest vigilance in discovering and defeating any attempts which may be made by foreign governments to acquire a control over that country. In the contest between Mexico and California we can take no part, unless the former should commence hostilities against the United States; but should California assert and maintain her independence, we shall render her all the kind offices in our power, as a sister Republic. This Government has no ambitious aspirations to gratify and no desire to extend our federal system over more territory than we already possess, unless by the free and spontaneous wish of the independent people of adjoining territories. The exercise of compulsion or improper influence to accomplish such a result, would be repugnant both to the policy and principles of this Government. But whilst these are the sentiments of the President, he could not view with indifference the transfer of California to Great Britain or any other European Power. The system of colonization by foreign monarchies on the North American continent must and will be resisted by the United States. It could result in nothing but evil to the colonists under their dominion who would naturally desire to secure for themselves the blessings of liberty by means of republican institutions; whilst it must prove highly prejudicial to the best interests of the United States. Nor would it in the

1. *The Works of James Buchanan,* ed. and comp. John Bassett Moore, vol. 6 (Philadelphia: Lippincott, 1909), 275–78.

end benefit such foreign monarchies. On the contrary, even Great Britain, by the acquisition of California, would sow the seeds of future war and disaster for herself; because there is no political truth more certain than that this fine Province could not long be held in vassalage by any European Power. The emigration to it of people from the United States would soon render this impossible.

I am induced to make these remarks in consequence of the information communicated to this Department in your despatch of the 10th July, last. From this it appears that Mr. Rea, the Agent of the British Hudson Bay Company, furnished the Californians with arms and money in October and November, last, to enable them to expel the Mexicans from the country; and you state that this policy has been reversed, and now no doubt exists there, but that the Mexican troops about to invade the province have been sent for this purpose at the instigation of the British Government; and that "it is rumored that two English houses in Mexico have become bound to the new General to accept his drafts for funds to pay his troops for eighteen months." Connected with these circumstances, the appearance of a British Vice Consul and a French Consul in California at the present crisis, without any apparent commercial business, is well calculated to produce the impression, that their respective governments entertain designs on that country which must necessarily be hostile to its interests. On all proper occasions, you should not fail prudently to warn the Government and people of California of the danger of such an interference to their peace and prosperity; to inspire them with a jealousy of European dominion, and to arouse in their bosoms that love of liberty and independence so natural to the American Continent. Whilst I repeat that this Government does not, under existing circumstances, intend to interfere between Mexico and California, it would vigorously interpose to prevent the latter from becoming a British or French Colony. In this they might surely expect the aid of the Californians themselves.

Whilst the President will make no effort and use no influence to induce California to become one of the free and independent States of this Union, yet if the people should desire to unite their destiny with ours, they would be received as brethren, whenever this can be done without affording Mexico just cause of complaint. Their true policy for the present in regard to this question, is to let events take their course, unless an attempt should be made to transfer them without their consent either to Great Britain or France. This they ought to resist by all the means in their power, as ruinous to their best interests and destructive of their freedom and independence.

I am rejoiced to learn that "our countrymen continue to receive every assurance of safety and protection from the present Government" of California and that they manifest so much confidence in you as Consul of the United States. You may assure them of the cordial sympathy and friendship of the President and that their conduct is appreciated by him as it deserves.

them to his home, disguising them as squaws, and set them to grinding corn on metates in his kitchen."

FURTHER READING

Cantrell, Greg. *Stephen F. Austin: Empresario of Texas*. New Haven, CT: Yale University Press, 2001.

DeLay, Brian. *War of a Thousand Deserts: Indian Raids and the U.S.-Mexican War*. New Haven, CT: Yale University Press, 2009.

Eisenhower, John S. D. *So Far from* God: *The U.S. War with Mexico, 1846–1848*. New York: Random House, 1989.

Foley, Neil. *Mexicans in the Making of America*. Cambridge, MA: Harvard University Press, 2014.

Greenberg, Amy. *A Wicked War: Polk, Clay, Lincoln, and the 1846 U.S. Invasion of Mexico*. New York: Vintage, 2013.

Howe, Daniel Walker. *What Hath God Wrought: The Transformation of America, 1815–1848*. New York: Oxford University Press, 2009.

Montejano, David. *Anglos and Mexicans in the Making of Texas, 1836–1986*. Austin: University of Texas Press, 1987.

Resendez, Andrés. *Changing National Identities at the Frontier: Texas and New Mexico, 1800–1850*. Cambridge: Cambridge University Press, 2004.

St. John, Rachel. *A Line in the Sand: A History of the Western U.S. Mexico Border*. Princeton, NJ: Princeton University Press, 2012.

West, Elliott. *The Contested Plains: Indians, Gold Seekers, and the Rush to Colorado*. Lawrence: University of Kansas Press, 1998.

Advertisement, A Ship to California, July 1849. This flyer advertising a ship to California is an example of the ways that people from all over the world learned about the Gold Rush. Travelers wanted a quick way to California, and ship travel seemed easier than taking a wagon train, even though in 1849 the trip to California meant going around the tip of South America. The cost of ship passage—$100 (which would be nearly $1,500 now)—is prominently displayed, but the flyer hides a lot of details about the cost and other challenges in fine print. Why does the flyer include so many details about wages in California? How would this have appealed to young men? Young women? Families? Who is organizing the trip?

G. F. Nesbit, printers. Boston.

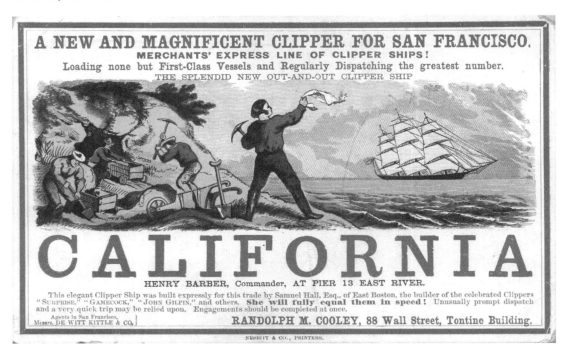

Westward Migration

Gold, Land, and Ambition

The western lands won by military conquest in the Mexican War and in negotiations with the British, combined with the stunning discovery of gold in California, offered Anglo-Americans a new range of possibilities and opportunities that affected them in intimate ways. More families moved west in search of opportunity, but many risked the health and safety of their loved ones in that search. Sometimes only a father or a brother or an uncle set out, leaving families with less male support and, frequently, less money coming into the household.

The dramatic family decision to go west tells us a lot about US national culture in the mid-nineteenth century. Crucial to this culture was the idea of individual ambition—the belief that anyone with good intentions who worked hard could be successful. But ambition took very different forms and was often limited by race and class. Women, of course, were supposed to support their male family member's ambitions, rather than having their own. The experience of migration is a useful case study of the notion that men and women, as well as white citizens and everyone else, should lead very different lives, a view that shaped the nation's ideology but was challenged by western migration.

As the frontier shifted west from the Old Northwest of Indiana and Ohio to the Mississippi Valley, and even to the Pacific Coast, this national culture found new modes of expression. Hoping to improve their future prospects, Anglo-American families moved constantly. When distances were great, people often wrote about the move in their diaries or in letters back to families and friends. These records provide a window on the hopes, dreams, and plans that often go unrecorded. If men and women harbored different hopes and saw the world in different ways, the decision to move and the experience itself vividly illuminated these differences.

The drive for land, which lured people to places like Oregon, Utah, and California, had a dynamic very different from the drive to find gold. Local western residents, Native peoples, and Mexicans or Canadians initially welcomed the newcomers, but their sheer numbers soon created tensions. Between 1840 and 1869, when the transcontinental railroad gave wealthy people a choice about travel, nearly 350,000 people traveled between the Mississippi River Valley and the Pacific Coast. Most were members of comfortable white midwestern farming families, who made their way together in wagons over what became known as the Overland Trail. Travel was slow, exhausting, and sometimes dangerous, and it was expensive. During the average seven-month trip, many wagon parties ran out of food, argued, and suffered illness and death. Men, usually the ones who made the decision to go, often appreciated the novelty and the sense of adventure that overland travel offered. For women, however, torn from their communities yet still tied to routines of cooking, childcare, and washing under difficult conditions, the trip was less of an adventure.

Another group looking for new opportunities was the Mormons, or the Church of Jesus Christ of Latter-Day Saints, one of many Christian sects formed during the great wave of religious revival that swept the United States in the 1820s and 1830s. Along with their leader, Joseph Smith Jr., the Mormons, who were subjected to religious persecution in Upstate New York, settled in Illinois and Missouri. There, they faced even greater hatred when Joseph Smith proclaimed the doctrine of polygamy, which allowed some men to have multiple wives. After Smith was murdered by an angry mob in 1846, the Mormons, now led by Brigham Young, decided to seek a safe haven in the isolated West. In the summer of 1847, Young took an advance team west and decided to settle the Mormons deep in Mexican territory, where he planned to build a Mormon city far from the interference of the United States. In 1848, nearly twelve thousand Mormons followed him, and over the next few years they build a prosperous agricultural community in the Great Basin Desert.

American history is full of ironies, and one of the greatest is the fact that because of the Mexican War and the California gold rush, the Mormon's remote desert haven almost immediately became part of a cosmopolitan new West within the United States. The California Gold Rush took the entire country by surprise. The discovery of gold in the foothills of the Sierra Nevada in January 1848 changed the world. By fall, the news had reached the settled part of the United States, and in the spring of 1849, the greatest mass migration in the nation's history began. The wealth was real. The first men to reach California, whether by ship or overland travel, could get rich on gold from the mountain streams. More than three hundred million dollars filled the pockets and knapsacks of the forty-niners between 1848 and 1855, with those who could afford to hire or enslave workers benefiting the most. But few people got rich. Very quickly white miners banded together to keep Native American, Chinese, and Latin American miners from taking up claims. While early comers had scooped up the easily panned gold, the remaining gold resources, hidden deep in the earth, required huge capital investments for complex mining and refining equipment to produce profits.

The Gold Rush changed the nation and the lives of participants forever. For native Californians, whether Indian or Mexican, the Gold Rush was a disaster, as white miners displaced, enslaved, or even murdered them. Overnight, San Francisco became a city, giving the United States a Pacific port and a place in the China trade. California, filled with a hundred thousand eager new miners, became a state in 1850, reigniting the debate over slavery that would bring on the Civil War. Hundreds of thousands of men left their families in search of a quick fortune in the West. Nearly everyone in the eastern parts of the United States knew someone who had gone. News of California and the trials of the journey filled the nation's newspapers, as anxious families awaited the return of their loved ones. Some never came back. They entered a world of male sociability, especially vivid in the West of Gold Rush towns, fur trade camps, and military forts, where men ate, slept, and played together.

Many miners returned home with nothing but the clothes on their backs and stories to tell. A lucky few returned with enough "rocks in their pockets" to remake their lives. The selections in this chapter are from the letters and diaries of people who traveled west. First, however, we have the 1850 law, drawn up at the first meeting of the California legislature, that ensured only white men could mine. Jean Rio Baker's diary offers a view of the Mormons on the final leg of their overland journey to Utah. J. D. Borthwick, a Scottish gold miner, surveys life in the California mountains in 1851. Finally, a series of letters between members of the Swain family depicts the life of a forty-niner and the family he left behind.

51. A GOLD RUSH FOR SOME

California became a territory and then a state in 1850. However, the administrative structures of a state, including courts, laws, and representative bodies to create laws, took a while to develop. Mining country along the foothills of the entire Sierra Nevada range of mountains was a chaotic and lawless place. One of the things that concerned new immigrants and miners was who should be permitted to mine and to make a fortune. In the first session of the new California legislature, new residents struggled to find legal language to limit mining to white citizens. Initially, they were concerned about French and Latin American companies, which brought teams of worker, giving them an unfair advantage over single white miners. In 1852, they passed a law prohibiting the Chinese from mining because those miners figured out loopholes in the first law. How does this legislation make the case about who should be able to mine? How does the legal language attempt to define white or citizen or American? How do you think the courts might perceive this law?

An Act to Regulate Mines and Foreign Miners
1850

AN ACT for the better regulation of the Mines and the government of Foreign Miners

Passed April 13 1850. The People of the State of California represented in Senate and Assembly do enact as follows:

l. No person who is not a native or natural born citizen of the United States or who may not have become a citizen under the treaty of Guadalupe Hidalgo, all native California Indians excepted, shall be permitted to mine in any part of this State without having first obtained a license so to do according to the provisions of this Act.

2. The Governor shall appoint a Collector of Licenses to foreign miners for each of the mining counties and for the county of San Francisco who before entering upon the duties of his office shall take the oath required by the Constitution and shall give his bond to the State with at least two good and sufficient sureties conditioned for the faithful performance of his official duties which bond shall be approved by the Governor and filed in the office of the Secretary of State.

3. Each Collector of Licenses to foreign miners shall be commissioned by the Governor.

4. It shall be the duty of the Comptroller to cause to be printed or engraved a sufficient number of licenses which shall be numbered consecutively and shall be in form following to wit:

"Number———(Date) A. B. a citizen of————age————years, complexion————is hereby licensed to work in the mines of California for the period of thirty days."

The Comptroller shall counter sign each of such licenses and shall transfer them to the Treasurer keeping an account of the number so transferred.

5. The Treasurer shall sign and deliver to each Collector of Licenses to foreign miners so many of the licenses mentioned in the preceding section as he shall deem proper and shall take his receipt for the same and charge him therewith Such collector and his sureties shall be liable upon his bond for the number so furnished him either for their return or the amount for which they may be sold and the moneys collected as herein provided shall be paid into the treasury as prescribed in this Act.

6. Every person required by the first section of this Act to obtain a license to mine shall apply to the Collector of Licenses to foreign miners and take out a license to mine for which he shall pay the sum of twenty dollars per month and such foreigners may from time to time take out a new license at the same rate per month until the Governor shall issue his proclamation announcing the passage of a law by Congress regulating the mines of precious metals in this State.

7. If any such foreigner or foreigners shall refuse or neglect to take out such license by the second Monday of May next it shall be the duty of the Collector of Licenses to foreign miners of the county in which such foreigner or foreigners shall be to furnish his or their names to the Sheriff of the county or to any deputy Sheriff whose duty it shall be to summon a posse of American citizens and if necessary forcibly prevent him or them from continuing such mining operations.

8. Should such foreigner or foreigners after having been stopped by a Sheriff or Deputy Sheriff from mining in one place seek a new location and continue such mining operations it shall be deemed a misdemeanor for which such offender or offenders shall be arrested as for a misdemeanor and he or they shall be imprisoned for a term not exceeding three months and fined not more than one thousand dollars.

9. Any foreigner who may obtain a license in conformity with the provisions of this Act shall be allowed to work the mines anywhere in this State under the same regulations as citizens of the United States.

10. It shall be the duty of each Collector of Licenses to foreign miners to keep a full and complete register of the names and description of all foreigners taking out licenses and a synopsis of all such licenses to be returned to the Treasurer.

11. Each license when sold shall be endorsed by the Collector selling or issuing the same and shall be in no case transferable and the Collector may retain out of the money received for each license the sum of three dollars which shall be the full amount of his compensation.

12. Each Collector of Licenses to foreign miners shall once in every two months and oftener if called upon by the Treasurer proceed to the seat of government,

settle with the Treasurer, pay over to that officer all moneys collected from for-eigners not before paid over and account with him for the unsold licenses remaining in his hands.

15. It shall be the duty of the Secretary of State immediately after the passage of this Act to have two thousand copies each in English and Spanish printed and sent to the mining districts for circulation.

52. THE MORMON TREK

After Brigham Young escorted the initial group of Mormons to what would become Utah in 1847, streams of Mormons poured into the successful commu-nity. Mormon missionaries recruited migrants from all over Europe, especially Great Britain. The strong pull of Mormon religious doctrine and the added attraction of ample land lured people in considerable numbers. In 1851, Jean Rio Baker, a widow with seven children, left her home in England hoping for a better life in Salt Lake City. She kept a diary of her trip from London to New Orleans, up the Mississippi to St. Louis, and across the plains to Utah. Baker's diary is unu-sual because it shows a woman operating as a family head and leader, but it also illustrates the help she received from other Mormon families. This selection describes the last, most difficult part of the journey and her first days in Salt Lake City. Did Baker enjoy the trip? What aspects of travel were most challenging? Did her gender affect her ability to make economic decisions? Compare her attitudes toward travel with those of William Swain or Mary Brewster (chapter 10).

Jean Rio Baker
Utah Diary Excerpts
1851[1]

[September] 11— Pretty good travelling all day, except the scarcity of grass, encamped on Pacific Creek, the wolves very troublesome all night, with their howling, which was accompanied by the barking of all the dogs in camp.

—12— Very heavy sandy roads all day.

—13— This morning the general strike took place, among Robins's team-sters, there has been dissatisfaction for some weeks, owing to the scantiness, and inferior quality of their rations, and Mr. Robins, refusing to make any improvement, the men shouldered their blankets, and set off intending to take

---

1. "Diary of a Trip from London to Salt Lake City," in *Covered Wagon Women, Diaries and Letters from the Western Trails,* 1840–1880, v. 3, ed. Kenneth Holmes (Glendale: Arthur H. Clark, 1984), 270–278.

J. D. Borthwick
"The Grizzly Bear Fight" and "The Gold Diggings Ball"
1857[1]

The Grizzly Bear Fight

"The Bear will be chained with a twenty-foot chain in the middle of the arena. The Bull will be perfectly wild, young, of the Spanish breed, and the best that can be found in the country. The Bull's horns will be of their natural length, and '*not sawed off to prevent accidents.*' The Bull will be quite free in the arena, and not hampered in any way whatever."

The proprietors then went on to state that they had nothing to do with the humbugging which characterised the last fight, and begged confidently to assure the public that this would be the most splendid exhibition ever seen in the country.

I had often heard of these bull-and-bear fights as popular amusements in some parts of the State, but had never yet had an opportunity of witnessing them; so, on Sunday the 15th, I found myself walking up towards the arena, among a crowd of miners and others of all nations, to witness the performances of the redoubted General Scott.

The amphitheatre was a roughly but strongly built wooden structure, uncovered of course; and the outer enclosure, which was of boards about ten feet high, was a hundred feet in diameter. The arena in the centre was forty feet in diameter, and enclosed by a very strong five-barred fence. From the top of this rose tiers of seats, occupying the space between the arena and the outside enclosure.

As the appointed hour drew near, the company continued to arrive till the whole place was crowded; while, to beguile the time till the business of the day should commence, two fiddlers—a white man and a gentleman of colour—performed a variety of appropriate airs.

The scene was gay and brilliant, and was one which would have made a crowded opera-house appear gloomy and dull in comparison. The shelving bank of human beings which encircled the place was like a mass of bright flowers. The most conspicuous objects were the shirts of the miners, red, white, and blue being the fashionable colours, among which appeared bronzed and bearded faces under hats of every hue; revolvers and silver-handled bowie-knives glanced in the bright sunshine, and among the crowd were numbers of gay Mexican blankets, and red and blue French bonnets, while here and there the fair sex was represented by a few Mexican women in snowy-white dresses, puffing their cigaritas in delightful anticipation of the exciting scene which was

1. J. D. Borthwick, *Three Years in California* (London: William Blackwood and Sons, 1857), 276–80, 303–5, 320–22.

to be enacted. Over the heads of the highest circle of spectators was seen mountain beyond mountain fading away in the distance, and on the green turf of the arena lay the great centre of attraction, the hero of the day, General Scott.

He was, however, not yet exposed to public gaze, but was confined in his cage, a heavy wooden box lined with iron, with open iron-bars on one side, which for the present was boarded over. From the centre of the arena a chain led into the cage, and at the end of it no doubt the bear was to be found. Beneath the scaffolding on which sat the spectators were two pens, each containing a very handsome bull, showing evident signs of indignation at his confinement. Here also was the bar, without which no place of public amusement would be complete. . . .

At last, after a final tattoo had been beaten on a gong to make the stragglers hurry up the hill, preparations were made for beginning the fight.

The bear made his appearance before the public in a very bearish manner. His cage ran upon very small wheels, and some bolts having been slipped connected with the face of it, it was dragged out of the ring, when, as his chain only allowed him to come within a foot or two of the fence, the General was rolled out upon the ground all of a heap, and very much against his inclination apparently, for he made violent efforts to regain his cage as it disappeared. When he saw that was hopeless, he floundered halfway round the ring at the length of his chain, and commenced to tear up the earth with his fore-paws. He was a grizzly bear of pretty large size, weighing about twelve hundred pounds.

The next thing to be done was to introduce the bull. The bars between his pen and the arena were removed, while two or three men stood ready to put them up again as soon as he should come out. But he did not seem to like the prospect, and was not disposed to move till pretty sharply poked up from behind, when, making a furious dash at the red flag which was being waved in front of the gate, he found himself in the ring face to face with General Scott.

The General, in the mean time, had scraped a hole for himself two or three inches deep, in which he was lying down. This, I was told by those who had seen his performances before, was his usual fighting attitude.

The bull was a very beautiful animal, of a dark purple colour marked with white. His horns were regular and sharp, and his coat was as smooth and glossy as a racer's. He stood for a moment taking a survey of the bear, the ring, and the crowds of people; but not liking the appearance of things in general, he wheeled round, and made a splendid dash at the bars, which had already been put up between him and his pen, smashing through them with as much ease as the man in the circus leaps through a hoop of brown paper. This was only losing time, however, for he had to go in and fight, and might as well have done so at once. He was accordingly again persuaded to enter the arena, and a perfect barricade of bars and boards was erected to prevent his making another retreat. But this time he had made up his mind to fight; and after looking steadily at the bear for a few minutes as if taking aim at him, he put down his head and charged furiously at him across the arena. The bear received him crouching down as low as he could, and though one could hear the bump of the bull's head and horns upon his ribs, he was quick enough to seize the bull by the nose before he could retreat. This spirited commencement of the battle on the part of the bull was hailed with uproarious applause; and by having shown such pluck, he had gained more than ever the sympathy of the people.

In the mean time, the bear, lying on his back, held the bull's nose firmly between his teeth, and embraced him round the neck with his fore-paws, while the bull made the most of his opportunities in stamping on the bear with his hind-feet. At last the General became exasperated at such treatment, and shook the bull savagely by the nose, when a promiscuous scuffle ensued, which resulted in the bear throwing his antagonist to the ground with his forepaws.

For this feat the bear was cheered immensely, and it was thought that, having the bull down, he would make short work of him; but apparently wild beasts do not tear each other to pieces quite so easily as is generally supposed, for neither the bear's teeth nor his long claws seemed to have much effect on the hide of the bull, who soon regained his feet, and, disengaging himself, retired to the other side of the ring, while the bear again crouched down in his hole.

Neither of them seemed to be very much the worse of the encounter, excepting that the bull's nose had rather a ragged and bloody appearance; but after standing a few minutes, steadily eyeing the General, he made another rush at him. Again poor bruin's ribs resounded, but again he took the bull's nose into chancery, having seized him just as before. The bull, however, quickly disengaged himself, and was making off, when the General, not wishing to part with him so soon, seized his hind-foot between his teeth, and, holding on by his paws as well, was thus dragged round the ring before he quitted his hold.

This round terminated with shouts of delight from the excited spectators, and it was thought that the bull might have a chance after all. He had been severely punished, however; his nose and lips were a mass of bloody shreds, and he lay down to recover himself. But he was not allowed to rest very long, being poked up with sticks by men outside, which made him very savagen. He made several feints to charge them through the bars, which, fortunately, he did not attempt, for he could certainly have gone through them as easily as he had before broken into his pen. He showed no inclination to renew the combat; but by goading him, and waving a red flag over the bear, he was eventually worked up to such a state of fury as to make another charge. The result was exactly the same as before, only that when the bull managed to get up after being thrown, the bear still had hold of the skin of his back.

In the next round both parties fought more savagely than ever, and the advantage was rather in favour of the bear: the bull seemed to be quite used up, and to have lost all chance of victory.

The conductor of the performances then mounted the barrier, and, addressing the crowd, asked them if the bull had not had fair play, which was unanimously allowed. He then stated that he knew there was not a bull in California which the General could not whip, and that for two hundred dollars he would let in the other bull, and the three should fight it out till one or all were killed.

This proposal was received with loud cheers, and two or three men going round with hats soon collected, in voluntary contributions, the required amount. The people were intensely excited and delighted with the sport, and double the sum would have been just as quickly raised to insure a continuance of the scene. A man sitting next me, who was a connoisseur in bear-fights, and passionately fond of the amusement, informed me that this was "the finest fight ever fit in the country."

The second bull was equally handsome as the first, and in as good condition. On entering the arena, and looking around him, he seemed to understand the state of affairs at once. Glancing from the bear lying on the ground to the other bull standing at the opposite side of the ring, with drooping head and bloody nose, he seemed to divine at once that the bear was their common enemy, and rushed at him full tilt. The bear, as usual, pinned him by the nose; but this bull did not take such treatment so quietly as the other: struggling violently, he soon freed himself, and, wheeling round as he did so, he caught the bear on the hindquarters and knocked him over; while the other bull, who had been quietly watching the proceedings, thought this a good opportunity to pitch in also, and rushing up, he gave the bear a dig in the ribs on the other side before he had time to recover himself. The poor General between the two did not know what to do, but struck out blindly with his fore-paws with such a suppliant pitiable look that I thought this the most disgusting part of the whole exhibition.

After another round or two with the fresh bull, it was evident that he was no match for the bear, and it was agreed to conclude the performances. The bulls were then shot to put them out of pain, and the company dispersed, all apparently satisfied that it had been a very splendid fight.

The reader can form his own opinion as to the character of an exhibition such as I have endeavoured to describe. For my own part, I did not at first find the actual spectacle so disgusting as I had expected I should; for as long as the animals fought with spirit, they might have been supposed to be following their natural instincts; but when the bull had to be urged and goaded on to return to the charge, the cruelty of the whole proceeding was too apparent; and when the two bulls at once were let in upon the bear, all idea of sport or fair play was at an end, and it became a scene which one would rather have prevented than witnessed.

Chapter XXI: A Ragged Camp and A Ball

If one can imagine the booths and penny theatres on a race-course left for a year or two till they are tattered and torn, and blackened with the weather, he

rather than to complain as regards Eliza's health. Four weeks ago I thought she would be no better, but now, by the providence of God, good care, and doctoring, she is better but still very unwell. I am giving her a syrup made of dandelion roots. . . .

While I am writing to one she has already forgotten, Eliza is trotting about the house with her playthings and coming to me occasionally to be taken up, which I have to do; and I let her oversee the writing, which she does with good grace by knocking my elbow now and then.

As to my own health: it is no better, if anything I think it is not quite as good as it was when you left. Not only my back, but my stomach troubles me very much; also I have a great deal of pain in my head, particularly on the top. I have not as yet had any of the sarsaparilla, but am taking a syrup compound of different roots which may be as good as sarsaparilla. Dr. Creswell tells me that I can not get well until I am willing to lie on my back for two months. My appetite is very poor and has been ever since I weaned Sis. The fact is, William, I feel bad every way, not only poor health but low spirits which I cannot get rid of. I cannot be reconciled to my lot. If I had known that I could not be more reconciled than I am, I should have tried hard to have kept you at home. My feelings are such that I can not describe them, and more than that, I try to conceal them as much as I can. I am quite confident that it wears on me. But let my feelings be what they will, I hope it will not trouble you. . . .

I received your letter of the 6th. Some one of us has been to the post office every day for two weeks. We began to think something had happened. I can tell you, my dear, that my soul rejoiced with unspeakable joy to read . . . your letter. My God bless you, my dear, in your undertaking. . . .

Good night—and farewell,
Sabrina

Youngstown, Sabbath afternoon
May 27, 1849

Dear Brother William,

Your letter dated Independence May 6 and 7 came to hand on Thursday, May 24, and gave us great pleasure to hear that you were "tolerably well." . . . We expect to get a full description of your outfit and company in your next.

We—the Roots, Baileys and Swains—were in a perfect fever of anxiety about you on account of the cholera. We watched the mail every day, and I never saw so long a two weeks as those between your St. Louis letter and your Independence letter. The latter has slightly relaxed the anxiety, but we still almost hold our breath, for we know the cholera will be with you to crossing the plains and probably in California. Do write as soon as you get there. . . .

The tenor of your last letter to Sabrina lacked the enthusiasm of former ones, although showing that your fortune thus far and your prospects for the future were good. I suppose the reason for this is that as it was Sabbath you had nothing else to do and surrendered yourself to thoughts of home and those you left behind you. But courage, William! We'll meet again, and I hope in better circumstances, although the parting and separation produce pain and anxiety. I wish I could telegraph you now, and tell you how we are, though I suppose you are three hundred miles out on the prairies. . . .

Sabrina is now back with us after her visit with her family and has been for two weeks, and I give you my honor I will do all I can to make her and Little Eliza comfortable and happy. Sabrina's health is, I think, some better than when you left. Little Sis is decidedly better. . . . She is quite cheerful and playful. But as Sabrina is writing, I will leave that story for her to tell. . . .

I wish I could this evening talk to you in your prairie tent. You are thought of here every day, and I may say every hour. Every day we wonder where poor William is, and we wish we could send you pancakes, baked potatoes, beans, and beef by telegraph. All this of course will do you no good, but nature will have her course. . . .

Will, I want you to write me everything about the country. Keep a pencil and paper in your pocket and note down everything, and when you write send it along. . . .

[George]

July 4
in camp for celebration,
eight miles below Fort Laramie

Dear Sabrina,

I have just left the celebration dinner table, where the company are now drinking toasts to everything and everybody and cheering at no small rate. I enjoy myself better in conversing with you through the medium of the pen. It is now some time since I wrote home, or at least since I wrote at any length, having written to you a line by a returning emigrant whom I met on the road and had just time to say that we were all well. But there is no certainty in sending letters by such conveyance. You may or may not have received some of the many letters I have sent you by traders and others, on many of which I have paid a postage of 25 cents.

I last wrote to George from Fort Kearny, and I will give you a sketch of our journey from that point. . . . We shall pass Fort Laramie tomorrow, where I shall leave this to be taken to the States. It will probably be the last time I can write until I get to my journey's end, which may take till the middle of October.

We have had uncommon good health and luck on our route, not having had a case of sickness in the company for the last four weeks. Not a creature has died, not a wagon tire loosened, and no bad luck attended us. . . .

The country is becoming very hilly; the streams rapid, more clear, and assuming the character of mountain streams. The air is very dry and clear, and our path is lined with wild sage and artemisia.

We had a fine celebration today, with an address by Mr. Sexton, which was very good; an excellent dinner, good enough for any hotel; and the boys drank toasts and cheered till they are now going in all sorts around the camp.

I often think of home and all the dear objects of affection there: of George; of dear Mother, who was sick; and of yourself and poor little Sister. If it were consistent, I should long for the time to come when I shall turn my footsteps homeward, but such thoughts will not answer now, for I have a long journey yet to complete and then the object of the journey to accomplish.

I am hearty and well, far more so than when I left home. That failing of short breath which troubled me at home has entirely left me. I am also more fleshy Notwithstanding these facts, I would advise no man to come this way to California. . . .

[William]

Sabbath, April 15, 1850
Foster's Bar, Yuba River
60 miles from Yuba City

Dear Sabrina and Mother,

When I last wrote you I was on the Feather River, but I now address you from the Yuba, about twenty-five miles from our cabin on that river. My absence from there has deprived me from receiving any letters since I last wrote and has also prevented me from writing as soon as I should, had I been at camp.

We have had considerable rain during the spring, and the rains in March became snow in the mountains. . . .

The great quantity of melting snow has caused very high water, which has thrown miners on their oars and really it has been a tiresome time. A great share of the weather is fine and pleasant, but the resting place of the "yellow boys" is far down in the waters. It is wearisome to one who is impatient to get at them and leave for a more congenial land, to mark the days as they drag their slow length along. . . .

I have occupied my time in prospecting over the miserable mountains and find it hard work which subjects a man to great exposure. The fact is, California has a miserable climate for mining: five months' rain, four months' high water, and three months' dry and good weather but very hot—almost too hot to work.

We are all here on the Yuba in good health. My health was never better and if it continues good through the summer I am confident of getting well paid for all my trouble on this long journey, and a little something handsome for the exposure and crucifixion of feeling I have undergone.

We finished our job on Feather River and tested it, although under great disadvantages. I am satisfied that it will *not pay* to work it out, but we intend to work part of it when the water goes down. Meanwhile, we shall prospect on this river till we find a place that suits us. We expect to go up this river soon and locate above here for the summer and I to profit by the experience we have had. Our job cost us a great deal and much hard work. Many a one has acquired a large fortune with half the exertion we have made, but we are not discouraged; on the contrary, we are confident of success. However, it is rather provoking to be disappointed in high hopes. . . .

But we are in good time for the mining season, and although we have no gold, we have our location on the Feather River, in which we might have sold a share for $1,000. But we would not cheat the fellow, as we did not believe the location to be worth much. I would rather have a clear conscience than $1,000. . . .

We have been at work on this bar some days, averaging $12 per day, but it won't do while the high water lasts. Prices are reasonable: flour, 35 cents per 1b.; fresh beef, 50 cents; salt pork, 60 cents; sugar, 70 cents; dried apples, $1. I have not eaten an apple since I left the Illinois River. All kinds of clothing is cheap here but boots and shoes. Boots are worth $25 to $30. I have two pair of J. Graves' boots yet and have not yet had to buy any clothing. We can board ourselves well here for $1.50 a day. . . .

I find this voyaging life disagreeable, as it is here today and there tomorrow and prevents me from hearing from home regularly or writing regularly and gives me a disagreeable feeling about the folks at home. I often feel as though I could not stay here, but reflection brings duty to my aid, and I solace myself with the thought that you are better off at home than I am here and that your wants will all be provided for. Still I feel very anxious to come home and see you all, little Sis in particular. May God grant that the long separation may prove to be for the comfort of us all through many years.

I am thankful to the Giver of good for the recovery of your health, Mother. May God grant that we may yet meet again and live for many years in the enjoyment of each other's society. I feel that I have not properly appreciated your kindness to me, and I have not properly estimated the value of a parent who has spent a life in caring for me and inculcating principles of justice, morality, and religion. Mother, I thank you for all those principles. Thanks can poorly pay for the years of trouble and hardship you have had, but it is all the tribute I can render at this distance from you.

I was sorry to hear of Sister's illness, but children are subject to such things, and I know that she will be taken care of. I am very sorry to hear, Sabrina, that you are troubled with your old complaint, spinal affection, and also with tooth-ache. Be careful of yourself; do not lift or do hard work.

You have kindly asked in your last letter if my expectations are being real-ized. My specific answer to your kind question is that my expectations are not realized. We have been unlucky—or rather, by being inexperienced, we selected a poor spot for a location and staked all on it, and it has proved worth nothing. Had it proved as it was expected when we took it up, I should have more than realized my most sanguine expectation, and I should have today been on my way to the bosom of my family in possession of sufficient means to have made them and me comfortable through life. But it is otherwise ordered; and I mostly regret the necessity of staying here longer. . . .

I was in hopes to have sent home a good pile of money before this time, but I am not able to at present. Still, my expectations are high, and in my opinion the excitement about the gold mines was not caused by exaggeration. In fact, I believe that greater amounts of gold have been and will be taken from the mines this summer than the gold news have told, and I would not today take less than $10,000 for my summer's work. . . . But were I to be unfortunate in all my business here and arrive at last at home without *one cent,* I should ever be glad that I have taken the trip to California. It has learnt me to have confidence in myself, has disciplined my impetuous disposition and has learnt me to think and act for myself and to look upon men and things in a true light. Notwith-standing all these favorable circumstances, it is a fact that no energy or indus-try can secure certain success in the business of mining; and it may perhaps be my lot after a summer of hardship and exposure to be but little better off than I am now. Be that as it may, I shall use my utmost endeavors to gain what money I can and do it honorably. Failing (if fail I should), I shall return home proud of honest and honorable effort.

In your letter, Sabrina, you have made frequent allusions to our little girl—her growth; her progress in walking, talking; her tricks of childhood; disposition; temper; attachments; etc., all of which are of great interest to me. I sympathize with you in the great responsibility devolving upon you alone in my absence, for with you I feel that the task of disciplining and guiding her mind is one of great care and anxiety and diligence, on which depends to great extent her disposition and happiness in future life. Be assured I would gladly share that task with you, knowing the weight of duty you feel, for I know that you properly estimate the relation of parent and child. And I also have the fullest confidence in your judgment and ability to train her aright. Having that confidence, I feel assured that you will do the best that can be done. I wish you always to be guided by your own judgment, irrespective of the opinions of either your own or my relatives in the discharge of duty to the child. . . .

Her physical development, too, I hope you will not neglect. It calls for far more care than parents usually bestow on their children's development. Be careful not to cripple the power of Nature by hampering it with close clothes; let them be such as will assist Nature in the creation of good physical system. Let her food be rather coarse and such that is easily digested, not too highly seasoned nor very salty. Milk is the best of all foods for young ones; and as little pork or grease as possible—it is the worst of all things for children except candies and sweets. Be sure not to allow her to sleep with a high pillow, for they cause round and stooped shoulders. Avoid anything that can have a tendency to induce curved spine. These will require your careful attention. . . .

I have much to say upon California in respect to the habits, customs, and morals of the miners, which will be embraced in my next two letters. I am sorry to say that on the subject of morality and religion, the miners are losing principle. Cut loose from restraints of society, men's principles are put to the test, and where surrounding influence is their foundation, they fall like leaves before the autumn blast. Swearing is very prevalent, and drinking and drunkenness a prominent feature in the mines. Temperance men are disregardful of their solemn pledge, and Sons of Temperance of their secret oaths of abstinence. Yesterday in returning down the river, in a walk of ten miles, I was invited by acquaintances to drink brandy no less than three times. But I find it the easiest thing in the world to refuse. The reply, "I thank you, I never drink any liquor" delivered in an emphatic and decided tone, hardly ever fails to stop all importuning, besides administering a silent rebuke, and I often glory in the momentary confusion of the drinker. . . .

Gambling too is another, I may say, of the prominent features of this country. It is now carried into the mines, and here in the mountains it is no unusual sight to see hundreds of dollars staked on the upturning of a certain card. I have known a gambler on this bar in one evening to rob the miners of $500 by their own wills. They are fools and need no pity. . . .

To such an extent does this vice exist that almost all participate in it. Many who were very careful to read a chapter in the Bible and pray every morning think it is no harm to deal monte in California; and one man, whom I am credibly informed was a Methodist minister at home, mines through the day and plays monte or some other game at night. Such men are not, thank heaven, the representatives of those principles taught in the Bible but rather of the depravity of human nature. . . .

[William]

November 14, 1850
Packet Ship *Mosconome*
500 m. from San Francisco

Dear George,

As I am on my passage home on this ship and there is cholera on board, there is a possibility that I may be attacked by it, and as I am in bad health, not

from the control of the United States in 1847, now found themselves at the center of national attention. The Mexican War had made Utah part of the United States, and the Gold Rush of 1849 had brought thousands of American travelers through Utah. In 1850 the Mormons applied to Congress to establish the state of Deseret, with Brigham Young as governor, but Congress saw this as a ploy to create a theocracy in which the Mormon Church could dictate all aspects of the lives of its citizens. Even though Utah had a large enough population to meet the requirements to become a state, Congress decided to make Utah a territory, which meant that its political leaders would be appointed by the president.

This decision, combined with the suspicion and hostility many Americans felt toward Mormons because of their clannishness and their practice of polygamy, intensified long-standing tensions. In 1857, convinced by his appointed officials in Utah that the Mormons were in actual rebellion against the United States, President James Buchanan sent in troops. The Mormons, with bitter memories of persecution and extermination at the hands of state officials, assumed that the troops were being sent to annihilate them and prepared for battle. Armed conflict was only narrowly avoided when negotiators convinced Mormon leaders to accept the authority of the US government in Utah.

Reading about these events, Northerners, Southerners, and Westerners worried about the specter of the federal government and the imposition and enforcement of unpopular laws. Some Americans took more direct action and began gathering up groups of followers to found their own "nations," where they could create their own rules about slavery, citizenship, or property ownership. A wave of filibusters and unofficial military invasions that challenged borders and national sovereignty spread out from the South and the West in the 1850s. Aspiring to create new empires where they could rule far from the authority of the United States, groups of US citizens sailed out of New Orleans, San Francisco, Los Angeles, and Charleston, hoping to foment revolution and mayhem in Mexico, Latin America, and the Caribbean.

The Mormon War, conflicts over slavery in the territories, and illegal filibusters foreshadowed what was to come. The election of 1860 featured two candidates from the western state of Illinois: Democrat Stephen Douglas, who remained convinced that popular sovereignty would solve the slavery question, and Republican Abraham Lincoln, who believed that slavery must be kept out of the West and that federal authority must be upheld. When Lincoln won, the South seceded from the Union, and once again the federal government sent troops to crush a regional rebellion.

The documents in this chapter highlight how the western territories brought the nation to the brink of Civil War and describe the unrelenting violence that characterized 1850s America. The Kansas-Nebraska Act forced the question of slavery back into the national arena. Letters from northern and southern settlers in Kansas reveal the depth of hatred between the two groups, as well as the horrific violence that occurred there. Two journalists, one in California and one in New York, describe the motives and personalities of disastrous filibusters. Finally, letters from Jesse Cove, a New Hampshire man serving in the Utah Expedition, uncover the divisions that made citizens willing to shoot at one another.

55. THE COMPROMISE OF POPULAR SOVEREIGNTY

When land-hungry settlers and railroad entrepreneurs began to demand the opening of the huge area between the Missouri River and the Rocky Mountains, the project immediately ran into two obstacles: the continuing presence of Native nations and the slavery question. According to federal law, all of this land had been designated in 1830 as a permanent Indian reserve, and the Missouri Compromise made it illegal to have slavery in any part of that vast territory. But Stephen A. Douglas, an Illinois senator and a great promoter of western development, proposed a series of laws that he claimed would solve both problems. He believed that the principle of popular sovereignty, allowing the citizens of a territory to decide the slavery issue for themselves, should operate in this region, which he designated as Nebraska. Douglas introduced legislation that used treaties to extinguish Indian land rights and created two new territories, Kansas and Nebraska. Once enough people had settled these territories, they could hold an election to determine the status of slavery by popular vote. The bill, excerpted here, passed narrowly, but it vaulted slavery in the territories to the center of political debate. How would proslavery and antislavery advocates each respond to the language in Douglas's bill? What would happen to Indians living in the region? Why didn't this solution solve the political problem of slavery?

The Kansas-Nebraska Act
1854[1]

Be it enacted by the Senate and House of Representatives of the United States of America in Congress assembled, That all that part of the territory of the United States included within the following limits, except such portions thereof as are hereinafter expressly exempted from the operations of this act, to wit: beginning at a point in the Missouri River where the fortieth parallel of north latitude crosses the same; thence west on said parallel to the east boundary of the Territory of Utah, on the summit of the Rocky Mountains; thence on said summit northward to the forty-ninth parallel of north latitude; thence east on said parallel to the western boundary of the territory of Minnesota; thence south-

---

1. An Act to Organize the Territories of Nebraska and Kansas, 1854, Record Group 11, General Records of the United States Government, National Archives.

ward on said boundary to the Missouri River; thence down the main channel of said river to the place of beginning, be, and the same is hereby, created into a temporary government by the name of the Territory of Nebraska; and when admitted as a State or States, the said Territory, or any portion of the same, shall be received into the Union with or without slavery, as their constitution may prescribe at the time of their admission. . . . *Provided further,* That nothing in this act contained shall be construed to impair the rights of person or property now pertaining to the Indians in said Territory, so long as such rights shall remain unextinguished by treaty between the United States and such Indians, or to include any territory which, by treaty with any Indian tribe, is not, without the consent of said tribe, to be included within the territorial limits or jurisdiction of any State or Territory; but all such territory shall be excepted out of the boundaries, and constitute no part of the Territory of Nebraska, until said tribe shall signify their assent to the President of the United States to be included within the said Territory of Nebraska, or to affect the authority of the government of the United States to make any regulations respecting such Indians, their lands, property, or other rights, by treaty, law, or otherwise, which it would have been competent to the government to make if this act had never passed. . . .

Sec. 5. And be it further enacted, That every free white male inhabitant above the age of twenty-one years who shall be an actual resident of said Territory, and shall possess the qualifications hereinafter prescribed, shall be entitled to vote at the first election, and shall be eligible to any office within the said Territory; but the qualifications of voters, and of holding office, at all subsequent elections, shall be such as shall be prescribed by the Legislative Assembly: *Provided,* That the right of suffrage and of holding office shall be exercised only by citizens of the United States and those who shall have declared on oath their intention to become such, and shall have taken an oath to support the Constitution of the United States and the provisions of this act. . . .

Sec. 10. And be it further enacted, That the provisions of an act entitled "An act respecting fugitives from justice, and persons escaping from the service of their masters," approved February twelve, seventeen hundred and ninety-three, and the provisions of the act entitled "An act to amend, and supplementary to, the aforesaid act," approved September eighteen, eighteen hundred and fifty, be, and the same are hereby, declared to extend to and be in full force within the limits of said Territory of Nebraska. . . .

Sec. 13. And be it further enacted, That the Legislative Assembly of the Territory of Nebraska shall hold its first session at such time and place in said Territory as the Governor thereof shall appoint and direct; and at said first session, or as soon thereafter as they shall deem expedient, the Governor and Legislative Assembly shall proceed to locate and establish the seat of government for said Territory at such place as they may deem eligible; which place, however, shall thereafter be subject to be changed by the said Governor and Legislative Assembly.

Sec. 14. And be it further enacted, That a delegate to the House of Representatives of the United States, to serve for the term of two years, who shall be a citizen of the United States, may be elected by the voters qualified to elect members of the Legislative Assembly, who shall be entitled to the same rights and privileges as are exercised and enjoyed by the delegates from the several other Territories of the United States to the said House of Representatives, but the delegate first elected shall hold his seat only during the term of the Congress to which he shall be elected. The first election shall be held at such time and places, and be conducted in such manner, as the Governor shall appoint and direct; and at all subsequent elections the times, places, and manner of holding the elections, shall be prescribed by law. The person having the greatest number of votes shall be declared by the Governor to be duly elected; and a certificate thereof shall be given accordingly. That the Constitution, and all Laws of the United States which are not locally inapplicable, shall have the same force and effect within the said Territory of Nebraska as elsewhere within the United States, except the eighth section of the act preparatory to the admission of Missouri into the Union, approved March sixth, eighteen hundred and twenty, which, being inconsistent with the principle of non-intervention by Congress with slavery in the States and Territories, as recognized by the legislation of eighteen hundred and fifty, commonly called the Compromise Measures, is hereby declared inoperative and void; it being the true intent and meaning of this act not to legislate slavery into any Territory or State, nor to exclude it therefrom, but to leave the people thereof perfectly free to form and regulate their domestic institutions in their own way, subject only to the Constitution of the United States. . . .

Sec. 19. And be it further enacted, That all that part of the Territory of the United States included within the following limits, . . . and the same is hereby, created into a temporary government by the name of the Territory of Kansas; and when admitted as a State or States, the said Territory, or any portion of the same, shall be received into the Union with or without slavery, as their Constitution may prescribe at the time of their admission; *Provided,* That nothing in this act contained shall be construed to inhibit the government of the United States from dividing said Territory into two or more Territories, in such manner and at such times as Congress shall deem convenient and proper, or from attaching any portion of said Territory to any other State or Territory of the United States. . . .

the fun all over before we came up. Titus had one man killed and one besides himself wounded. We took nineteen prisoners, Titus among the number, contrary to the wishes of a great many of the boys, but he begged so like a whipped puppy—so cringingly—that he was thought too goddamned mean, too despicable to notice sufficiently to kill him. One of his negroes, who was out at the stable during the fight, said, "Massa Titus wanted six abolitionists for breakfast! Yah! Yah! Gorra Massy! guess he get his belly full dis monin'!" . . .

I forgot to state that the old gun *Sacramento* first spoke at this place in favor of the Free-State cause, and also circulated several copies of the *Herald of Freedom*, amongst Titus' crowd. . . . During the fight it commenced raining, and fearing that our Sharps rifles would not be in fit trim for another fight until they were dried, Capt. Walker wouldn't allow us to march against Lecompton, as we desired him to do, and so we started back to Lawrence and arrived there safely without meeting with any adventure worthy of notice. . . .

Your affectionate brother
John Lawrie

Axalla John Hoole to His Family

Kansas City, Missouri, Apl. 3d., 1856

My Dear Brother

Here I am after two weeks travelling, and not in Kansas Territory yet, but it is only 1 1/2 miles off, and I can see into it. I feel a good deal tired of travelling, and we have concluded to rest here until to-morrow, when we will take the stage for Lawrence City, by way of Westport. . . .

It has cost me over $102 to get here, besides about $25 which I have spent for necessaries, &c. We have been quite well since we left—with the exception of one day that I had a headache and fever, caused I guess from losing so much sleep, and the fatigue of travelling. . . . I fell in company with a young man who had just married, from Georgia, who said he was going to Kansas, but there were other families along from Georgia, who were going to Missouri, and when they left the boat about 60 miles from here, he left with them and I was not sorry for it, as I did not fancy him much; neither did I fancy his wife. I would have but little to do with them—one objection I had to him was, he drank liquor –

The Missourians (all of whom I have conversed with, with the exception of one who, by the way, I found out to be an Abolitionist) are very sanguine about Kansas being a slave state & I have heard some of them say it *shall* be. I have met with warm reception from two or three, but generally speaking, I have not met with the reception which I expected. Everyone seems bent on the Almighty Dollar, and as a general thing that seems to be their only thought—There was a large box on one of the boats about a week ago coming up the river, which some of the Missourians thought contained Sharp's Rifles, so they sent a deputation to its destination, which was at this place, to have it opened. When they arrived here the person to whom it was consigned refused to let them open it, whereupon they opened it by force—when lo! it contained nothing but a piano. There was a box containing a cannon which a confounded Yankee opened, but closed it up again before any of them could examine it, saying that it was nothing but some cartwheels. . . .

Well, dear brother, the supper bell has rung, so I must close. Give my love to [the immediate family] and all the Negroes. . . . Excuse bad writing for I am very nervous. I am anxious to hear from home . . . direct to Lawrence City, Kansas Territory, as I shall leave word there for my letters to be forwarded to whatever place I go. Your ever affectionate brother,

Axalla.

Douglas City, K. T., Apl. 14th., 1856

My Dear Mother

. . . I came to this place last Saturday, after staying at that nasty Abolition town of Lawrence for a week. This is called a City, but there are only four little log houses in it, but it is laid out into lots for a town, and I expect one day it will be. The capital, Lecompton, is two miles from here, but they are going to build the state university at this place. It is situated close on the Kansas river, and I consider it the prettiest site for a town in the Territory. . . . They are wanting a school in Lecompton but I have not been able to make it up. The fact is, the people here seem to be so taken up with politics, that they can't take time to think of hardly anything else. There is a school wanting here at Douglas, but there is a young fellow from Georgia, who was ahead of me, but I am under the impression that he will not succeed, as there seems to be a sort of split in the neighborhood. If he fails, they say they will make up a good school for me. If I don't succeed in getting a school, I will go at the carpenter's trade which will pay, by-the-bye, better. . . . But I don't think I will ever like this country well enough to settle here, and I don't think, or at least I am afraid, it will be never be made a slave state, and if it is not, I will not live here on any conditions. . . .

My dear Mother, you need not be afraid. . . . This is a very good neighborhood. We are boarding with a good clever Methodist family. The circuit-rider stayed here last night. I had formed a very poor opinion of the morality of the Territory when I was at Lawrence, but I find the people up this way fare better. At Lawrence almost everyone I met was profane, but here it is quite different. I have not made use of an oath since I have been in the Territory, and I don't intend to be guilty of that practice any more if I can help it. Betsie makes me read the Bible sometimes, and I intend, when I can rent a house and go to ourselves, which I hope to do soon, to read it regularly. . . .

The people in this Territory have very poor houses, generally built of logs with rock chimneys. The one we are boarding in is three log houses built in a row—the middle one of which is the kitchen where the Negroes stay. They have four or five Negroes. If we stay here this summer, we will have plenty of ice as Mr. Ellison has put up a good deal of it. . . .

. . . Write me all the news, every little particular will be interesting to me. . . . Your ever affectionate son,

Axalla.

Douglas City, K. T., Apl. 27th., 1856

My Dear Brother

. . . I am still boarding at the above mentioned place with Mr. Elison and playing $3 a week apiece for myself and wife, but I have sent to Missouri for provisions which I expect here in a day or two, when I will go to housekeeping. I have two houses which I can rent, one of which we are occupying to sleep in. It is about a hundred yards from Mr. Elison's, where I eat. I commenced working at the carpenter's trade last Monday—I tried to get a school, but failed to get one worth my notice, so I concluded on the whole it was best for me to get at something else, and as a trade pays better than anything else, I went at the carpenter's. . . .

I have no fun here. Game is scarce. Mr. Elison's son killed a pelican in the river yesterday morning. I went out late in the evening and killed two squirrels, which is the first thing of any kind I have killed since I have been here. . . .

I still don't like this country, and I don't care how soon it is admitted as a state. The Governor sent the sheriff to take some men in Lawrence last Saturday (yesterday week) and the Lawrenceites rescued the prisoner from him. The sheriff came and reported to the Governor, who sent him back with four other men, but they also failed. The Governor then sent a dispatch to the fort for some soldiers; they came on Tuesday, and with the sheriff went to Lawrence on Wednesday and succeeded in taking six prisoners, but as they had not the most important one, they concluded that they would stay there all night. In the night the sheriff (Jones) with two or three other men went out of the tent to get some water, and while drawing it, the sheriff was shot at, the ball passing through his pantaloons behind his leg. They went into the tent, when a man came in pretending to be drunk. Jones told him to go out, that they had no use for him there. Then he left walking as steady and apparently as sober as any man. About five minutes after, Jones was shot through the tentcloth in the back, the ball entering near the backbone just below the shoulder blade. Jones drew his bowie knife, and attempted to rise, but could not. I hear that he was not dead last Friday evening, but there was very little hope for him. . . . There are scouting parties of Proslavery men out every night since Jones was shot. The Lawrenceites have threatened the life of Governor Shannon and several other Proslavery men. An attempt was made to burn the house of a Proslavery man, about a mile from here, on night before last, and a parcel went there last night to stand guard. The owner (Mr. Clark) is in Missouri, but his wife is at home. The same house was fired last fall, but was discovered soon enough to be put out. I don't expect anything else but a fight before long—the excitement is too great, and if Jones dies, it will be greater. . . .

You must write to me and tell me all the news about everything. . . . Tell me everything about people, farm, hogs, dogs, and everything else. Give my love to Mother, Sister, and all the Negroes, and my most sincere regards to all my friends. Tell Mother not to fret herself about me . . . I don't intend to risk myself to danger unnecessarily, but if my party needs my assistance, I will not shrink from what I consider my duty. . . . I subscribe myself, your ever affectionate brother till death,

Axalla.

Douglas, K. T., Augst. the 3d., 1856

My very dear Sister

. . . You must not think hard of me for not writing to you sooner, for I have so many of you to write to, that it would keep me all the time writing, if I undertook to write each one every week. . . . I am well now, but I can't get back my appetite. I had a very severe attack of the bilious fever. . . .

There are fewer snakes here than in Darlington. I have killed four rattlesnakes, three of them had only a button, but the other was a large one with nine rattles. My foot passed within a foot of his head, and he could have bit me with all ease, as I did not see him until I was by him, but they never strike without rattling—he did not rattle.

There are more insects about the house I live in than a little, crickets, spiders, cockroaches, granddaddies, &c. Yesterday Betsie and I burned and killed about a thousand of the last. They had got so troublesome that they were crawling over us at night; in the day they would collect in knots about the house, so I set a newspaper on fire and burned them. . . .

Plums are just commenced getting ripe. . . . There is no other fruit. Dried apples are worth $3 a bushel here. Watermelons are just getting ripe . . . one of my neighbors has some almost as large as my head. . . .

There is very little doing here. Money is scarce; a great many people want work done, but they have no money to pay with. Everyone seems to be resting on his oars, as the saying is. Nothing going on, except among some of the Abolitionists who are doing a good business stealing horses from Proslavery men. One of my neighbours (Mr. Elison) lost a very fine horse which he has been offered $135 for, which is a pretty big price for Kansas.

The Missourians are going to send 300 head of milk cows into the Ter. for the benefit of Southern immigrants. I was told the other day by one who is to have the distributing of them when they come, to come and pick me out one. Every Proslavery man who is keeping house and has no cow is entitled to one. Some men have gone after them now.

Well, my dear sister, I believe I have told you everything that I can think of that would interest you. . . . Betsie sends her love to you all. . . . Write soon to one who loves you dearly . . . .

Your affectionate brother, Axalla.

Lecompton, K. T., Augst. 27, 1856

My dear Sister

I rec'd yours of the 5th. inst. last week, but . . . I feel pretty well satisfied that my letters never get out of the Ter., no, nor this county, but are stopped in Lawrence; but I shall however make one more attempt, hoping that it may be overlooked and pass through—

You see from the heading that I am now in Lecompton. Last night two weeks ago the Abolitionists, about 250 or 300 strong attacked the little town of Franklin, or rather one house in the place in which there were 14 men (Proslavery). They demanded the arms of these 14 men which were refused, when they commenced firing upon the house, and, after a short time, were repulsed, but rallied and came again, were repulsed the second time. Then they set fire to a load of hay and rolled it against an adjoining house (the post office) when the 14 cried for quarter. Nearly all of the 14 made their escape without receiving a single wound, but of the Abolitionists, 32 were killed and wounded, 7 or 8 killed.

A few days after an army of 400 of the Murderers went to attack Col. Treadwell, who was making a settlement about 20 miles south of this, but he, hearing of their approach, abandoned his post and made his escape. Treadwell had only about 50 men and no ammunition. He sent to Lecompton for help and 18 started, but hearing that he had left, they turned back. On their return they fell into an ambuscade of the Abolitionists about 250 strong, but charged through them without losing a man, and only two were wounded slightly. The next morning the same band of villains attacked the house of Col. Titus, about 11/2 miles from here. Titus has 18 men, and after fighting with small arms for half an hour, they turned loose their cannon on his house and battered it down over his head. They took him and most of his men prisoners, after fighting to the last, Titus lost only one man killed, and himself and one more wounded. They were carried to Lawrence and after a few days were exchanged. Titus is from Florida and is a very brave man. On the morning the attack was made on Titus, the news came that 800 men were coming against Douglas, so we, 8 in number with our families, crossed over the river, but they did not come. The next day we returned, but not feeling safe there we came (after a few days) to this place, which has about 750 regulars to guard it. There are three families of us living in one house. There is a great deal of excitement here, but how long it will last no one can tell. Mo. is sending in men to help us, and it is high time they had come. This contest will decide the fate of Kansas and the Union. Lane is in the Ter. with a force of from 1500 to 2500 men. Gov. Shannon has resigned and the new governor has not come on, so the Lieut. Gov. Woodson is now the acting Gov.— I don't know what will be the plan of the present campaign, as the officers keep it a secret.

Betsie is well, but I have [had] slight fevers every day, for the last three or four days, caused, I guess, from excitement and standing guard. . . . I don't think you need be uneasy about me here as the regulars will guard this place, but if there is any fighting to be done, I intend to pitch in.

. . . Tell Mother not to be uneasy about me. I feel quite safe here and there will be such an influx of Missourians and other Southerners here in a few days that Lane can not hold them a dodge. . . .

Your Affectionate Brother,
Axalla.

57. INVASIONS AND FILIBUSTERS IN CALIFORNIA AND NICARAGUA

During the 1850's, political unrest in new republics was endemic. A symptom of this was the filibuster, a completely illegal invasion of a foreign nation by a group of adventurers taking advantage of what they saw as inept government. The word filibuster came from a Dutch word, vrijbuiter, *meaning robber or pirate. Dozens of groups bent on foreign invasion actually took off from US shores, but hundreds more were planned in smoky taverns and coffeehouses. Whether the location was Cuba, Baja California, Canada, Mexico, or Nicaragua, US residents believed they could provide better leadership and make better economic use of resources. They all believed that people living there would welcome their leadership. The two examples here, one in Sonora, Mexico, and one in Nicaragua, received wide national attention. In both cases, local people were horrified by the invaders and their plans and called in their own troops to protect their communities. The first example, Henry Crabbe's letter, was included in a memoir written by Horace Bell, a Southern California lawyer and local militia officer, who supported the idea of filibusters to increase American influence. The second example is an editorial from* Putnam's New Monthly Magazine. *What assumptions do we see in both documents about the governments of other nations? How did Henry Crabbe envision the entire episode in Sonora would turn out? How did the political issue of slavery drive William Walker and other filibusters?*

Horace Bell *Reminiscences*
Two Letters
1857[1]

On reaching the frontier town of Sonora, Crabbe was first made aware of Pesqueira's treachery, and that the compact between the two patriots was to be sealed with the blood of himself and his followers. He had gone too far to retreat. Crabbe was a man of true metal, and being in for it he determined to do or die. He accordingly issued a proclamation, here given word for word, setting forth his peaceful and legitimate object in coming, his determination to stay, his ability to defend himself if attacked and then pushed forward to Caborca.

Letter from Henry Crabbe

SONORA, March 26, 1857.
Don Jose Maria Redondo, Prefect of the District of Altar:

SIR: In accordance with the colonization laws of Mexico, and in compliance with several very positive invitations from the most influential citizens of Sonora, I have entered the limits of your State with one hundred companions and in advance of nine hundred others, in the expectation of making happy homes with and among you. I have come with the intention of injuring no one; without intrigues, public or private. Since my arrival I have given no indication of sinister designs, but on the contrary have made pacific overtures. It is true that I am provided with arms and ammunition, but you well know that it is not customary for Americans or any other civilized people to travel without them; moreover, we are about to travel where the Apaches are continually committing depredations. From one circumstance I imagine, to my surprise, that you are preparing hostile measures and collecting a force for destroying me and my companions. I know that you have given orders for poisoning the wells and have prepared to use the vilest and most cowardly measures. But bear in mind, sir, that whatever we may have to suffer shall fall upon the heads of you and those who assist you. I could never have believed that you would defile yourselves by such barbarous practices. I also know that you have not ceased to rouse against us, by mischievous promises, the tribe of Papagos, our best friends. But it is very likely that, considering my position, your expectations will be baffled. I have come to your country having a right to do so, and as has been shown, expecting to be received with open arms; but now I conceive that I am to encounter death among enemies destitute of humanity. As far as concerns my companions now here and about to arrive, I protest against any evil procedure toward them. You have your own course to follow, but bear this in

---

1. Horace Bell, *Reminiscences of A Ranger: Or, Early Times in Southern California* (Los Angeles, Yarnell, Caystile and Mathes, Printers, 1881).

mind: should blood be shed, on your head be it all and not on mine. Nevertheless, you can make yourself sure, and proceed with your hostile preparations. As for me, I shall lose no time in going to where I have for some time intended to go, and am only waiting for my party. I am the leader, and my intention is to obey the promptings of the law of nature and of self-preservation. Until we meet at Altar I remain,

> *Your obdt. servt.,*
> HENRY A. CRABBE

This letter is given to the Warden of Sonora, to be delivered without delay to the Prefect of Altar.

> *H. A. C.*

Ygnacio Pesquiera's Sonoran Response

Four days later Pesqueira issued the following modest *Proclama* to the gentle people of Sonora [Translation]:

YGNACIO PESQUEIRA,
Substitute Governor of the State and Commander-in-Chief of
the Forces of the Frontier, to His Fellow-Citizens:

FREE SONOREÑOS! TO ARMS, ALL!!

The hour has sounded, which I lately announced to you, in which you would have to prepare for the bloody struggle which you are about to enter upon.

In that arrogant letter you have just heard a most explicit declaration of war made by the chief of the invaders. What reply does it merit? That we march to meet him.

Let us fly, then, with all the fury of hearts intolerant of oppression, to chastise the savage Filibuster who has dared, in an unhappy hour, to tread our national soil, and to provoke, insensate, our rage.

Show no mercy, no generous sentiments, toward these hounds!

Let them be like wild beasts who, daring to trample under foot the law of nations, the right of States and all social institutions, dare to invoke the law of nature as their only guide, and to appeal to brute force alone.

Sonoreños, let our conciliation become sincere in a common hatred of this accursed horde of pirates, destitute of country, religion or honor.

Let the tri-colored ribbon, sublime creation of the genius of Iguala, be our only distinctive mark, to protect us from the enemy's bullets as well as from humiliation and affront. Upon it let us write the beautiful words, "LIBERTY OR DEATH," and henceforth it shall bear for us one more sentiment, the powerful, invincible bond that now unites the two parties of our State, lately divided by civil war.

We shall soon return covered with glory, having forever secured the welfare of Sonora, and having, in defiance of tyranny, established in indelible characters this principle; The people that wants liberty will have it.

Meanwhile citizens, relieve your hearts by giving free scope to the enthusiasm that oppresses them.

Viva Mexico! Death to the Filibusters.

Ygnacio Pesqueira.

Upon entering Caborca he was attacked in front, flank and rear, desperately fought his way to the plaza, and was there forced to assume the defensive, which was successfully maintained against twenty times his number for several days, and finally, under solemn guarantees and after more than half his men had been killed, and nearly if not all wounded, himself included, his ammunition exhausted, the house in which he had taken refuge burning over his head, Crabbe laid down his arms and surrendered. Within less than twelve hours the whole party, the well and the wounded, were murdered in the most barbarous manner. Their heads were severed from their mutilated bodies, and the head of Henry A. Crabbe was placed on a dish to adorn the head of the table at the grand dinner celebrated two days after the butchery, and over which his former ally, Ygnacio Pesqueira, presided. The bodies of his followers were left on the ground to be devoured by the swine, and of course in some degree contributed to the general weal of the good people of Caborca.

While Crabbe was besieged at Caborca a small party of about twenty men, under my Ranger comrade, Grant Oury, whose name I unfortunately omitted in naming the survivors of the Ranger company—Grant is now member of Congress from Arizona—started from Tucson to his relief, and reached the vicinity of the town just before the surrender, but could in no way aid him.

"Filibustering"
1857[1]

But suddenly, in our day, the Central American States have again become of vast importance, and their affairs challenge daily interest and attention.

At this moment (March, 1857) there is a freebooter in one of those states, in much sorer plight than the old pirate de Lussan, when he and his friends sacked Granada, or the earlier pirate, Morgan, who burnt Panama; and, although nearly two hundred years have passed—and even two hundred years ago in England, at war with Spain, the citizens of London did not publicly assemble to

---

1. *Putnam's New Monthly Magazine*, vol. 9 (April 1857), 427–34

express their sympathy for de Lussan—yet, in New York, to-day. in the chief city of a country that has nominally some especial Christian and democratic claims, the citizens are summoned to express, publicly, their hopes of the victory of de Lussan's successor, who has ordered the game Granada to be burnt to the ground. And as the old pirates coupled their carnage with *Te Deums,* the new ones consecrate theirs with poor sentimentality about the progress of the Saxon race and democratic equality.

At least, the old murderers of the Spanish main had the merit of cutting throats without canting. They wanted plate, and pieces of eight, and they said so plainly, and they butchered the inhabitants until they found them. Being anxious for information, and pressed for time, on one occasion, Lolonois, a French buccaneer of the seventeenth century, drew his cutlass and cut open the heart of one of the Spaniards who did not reply quickly enough, and, "pulling out his heart, began to bite and gnaw it with his teeth, like a ravenous wolf, saying to the rest, 'I will serve you all alike, if you show me not another way.'"

Walker had other objects than present booty merely; but the sufferings he has occasioned are a thousand-fold more dreadful than those usually recorded as the consequences of the old forays. And. to what end? Month after month, now for nearly two years, young men have been shipped by responsible agents in New York and New Orleans to Nicaragua, and for what purpose? Hundreds have gone—not three hundred remain above ground—by whose means—to what end? Was it a scheme of colonization in good faith? We have not seen a solitary man who believes so; but assuming it, then it has failed so disastrously that every city and village in the country should warn anybody, who intends to emigrate, of the facts. Was it a scheme of assistance to one of two contending parties, in good faith? Then why are both those parties in arms, to a man, against the invader? Having fulfilled his mission, or failed in it, why is he still lingering? Is all this blood, and grief, and desolation of a country, the consequence of commercial ambition! Then merchant princes are as inhuman as Indian caciques. Is it all part of an agitation to be used for the benefit of the great Christian blessing of slavery? Then its facts should be made patent to every voter in the land.

Walker, himself, is an adventurer in whose whole career there is not a solitary indication of ability. He is, we understand, a Tennesseean, about thirty-six or eight years of ago; who has studied law and medicine; has edited newspapers in New Orleans and San Francisco; practiced law in Marysville, California; and, in the year 1854, at the head of fifty or sixty missionaries of human progress and democratic equality. proclaimed himself President of Sonora, a small Mexican State bordering upon California. His presidency was very brief, and ended in a trial in California for a violation of the Neutrality Laws. He was acquitted; for the California of four years ago naturally judged such lapses lightly, and his services in the van of empire were not required again until he received, in the spring of 1855, a commission, as general in the army of Nicaragua, and a grant of 58,000 acres of land. On the 5th of May, in that year, he sailed for that country with fifty-six followers.

Nicaragua is one of the loveliest of tropical states; rich in natural products, and, upon its Pacific slopes, not unhealthy in climate; while, through its lake and river, it offers a convenient and rapid transit from sea to sea. Its government is nominally republican; but the languor and ignorance of its inhabitant, who are of mixed races, keep it in a semi-barbarous condition, without manufactures or industry, or any practical improvement of its natural advantages. It has been constantly embroiled in civil wars since the dissolution of the Central American Confederacy, in 1838. It is not necessary to state the details of these struggles. It is enough to know that, in the month of May, 1854, there had been a battle which resulted in the assumption of two governments in the country—the liberal, which had its headquarters at Leon, the old capital of Nicaragua, and the legitimist (as the government party called itself), which centred at Granada. The latter faction held the southern portion of the state; and the former occupied the northern. After the battle, in May, 1854, the liberals besieged Granada for ten months; but, in February, 1855, retired, and, pursued by the legitimists, a bloody battle was fought between the factions, at Massaya, which was disastrous to the liberals.

In May, 1855. Walker and his fifty-six men arrived from California, and, at the end of June, marched, with two hundred Nicaraguan liberals, upon Rivas, a city upon Lake Nicaragua, occupied by the legitimists. the attack was repulsed. Walker and his fifty-six men had taken up their position in a house, which the enemy fired, and the ex-president of Sonora and his men cut their way back to the coast of San Juan del Sur. There was some skirmishing during the summer; and, in October, at the head of two hundred Americans, and two hundred and fifty natives, Walker took possession of one of the Transit Company's steamers, at Virgin Bay, sailed to Granada, which lies upon the lake, and captured the city after a few shots, while the enemy were expecting him at Rivas, forty miles distant. A treaty followed between the two parties, and a government selected from both sides was constituted. Don Patricio Rivas, who had been an official under the legitimist rule, was made provisional president for fourteen months: Walker was commander-in-chief of the army; Corral, the legitimist general, was minister of war; Parker H. French, an ex California editor, minister of the Hacienda; Don Firmin Ferrer, a gentleman of Granada, minister of public credit; and General Maximo Xeres (who had been the predecessor of Walker in the command of the liberals), minister of foreign affairs. This government was recognized by Mr. Wheeler, minister of the United States, the only foreign minister then resident in Nicaragua. But, unfortunately, the new government commenced by shooting its minister of war, who was detected in treasonable correspondence with the enemy; and by sending Mr. French to Washington as minister, who was not recognized by the United States Government; and also by dispatching Major Louis Schlessinger as ambassador to Costa Rica, to propose a treaty of amity, which that state answered by declaring war upon Nicaragua—doubtless, regarding Walker as the small European states regarded Napoleon, as no less dangerous a friend than enemy.

• • •

And grave men and grave journals contemplate the ridiculous, and, in respect of others, tragical career of this incompetent Bombastes, and philosophize about the destiny of our country in overspreading the continent.

Mr. William Walker's personal views are as important as those of the old pirate Morgan, or his compeer Lolonois, or Roche Brasiliano, or Bartolomeo Portugues, or Captain Kidd; but any such man, used as a tool, becomes immediately important, and it is, therefore, quite worth while to know what was the meaning of this descent upon Nicaragua, if it meant anything beyond a personal scrabble for power and booty. Nor is it very difficult to ascertain.

We are far from supposing that Walker necessarily meant to keep the contract, because he signed it. His first necessity was munitions of war and money, and he was, doubtless, very willing to purchase them upon such easy terms as his word. If he did mean to keep the contract, it proves the ultimate intention which other events revealed; if he did not, it illustrates the quality of his honor. The Cuban movement in the United States, as explained and justified at Ostend by His Excellency, James Buchanan, the Hon. Pierre Soulé, and Mr. Mason, is no secret. It is notoriously a movement for the extension of slavery. It is not surprising, therefore, that some time subsequent to the signing of this contract, between Goicouria's agent and Walker, that eminent American citizen and lover of liberty, the Hon. Pierre Soulé, went to Nicaragua, and established relations with the Fillibuster.

By this time—the summer of 1856—the great contest between slavery and freedom upon this continent had been brought to open battle. For the first time in our political history, a vast party was organized upon the fundamental principle of no further slavery extension. The difference came to blows, and blood, and anarchy, in the territory of Kansas; and to the most searching and solemn debate and vote, throughout the country. The slavery party, accustomed to victory, were amazed at the vital earnestness of the struggle, and could with difficulty understand how a people, which had only made mouths at the fugitive slave law, and had only murmured protests against the repeal of the Missouri Compromise and the Kansas-Nebraska bill, should so suddenly take a lofty moral ground in politics, and declare that they valued the soul more than the body of the Union. In view of such surprising developments, the slave party naturally thought it might become necessary to relax their speed a little; it might even be politic to concede Kansas for the present, but the great policy of slavery extension must be sustained, oven at the cost of a rupture of the Union.

A general doctrine has long been current among sagacious slave-politicians that the extreme southern slave states might, one day, find it necessary to change their confederated relations, and form a slave republic, consisting of those states and the old Spanish provinces of Central America, which should abandon the northern states, and perhaps Canada, to the blight of freedom, while they advanced in a career of humanity and the Christian graces which slavery in the tropics would naturally develop. The Cuba movement is a fruit—let us rather say, a blighted blossom—of this theory, and, naturally, those who preferred their own tyranny to that of the Spaniards in Cuba, would wish well to the Walker war in Nicaragua; and the midsummer of 1856, therefore, finds Messrs. Soulé and Goicouria in full intelligence with the Fillibuster—the object of all, of course, being to extend the blessings of American laws and progressive popular institutions over those unhappy regions.

Now the simple history of this important matter is this: The Central American states became independent in 1821. In 1823 the federal constituent assembly met, and in April, 1824, abolished slavery and declared the slave-trade piracy. In 1838, the confederation was dissolved—each state became again independent and sovereign—but each recognized all the federal laws which were not incompatible with their own state constitutions. Those old laws had, therefore, precisely the same authority as the new ones. But the old laws were never "codified," and, consequently, there was great difficulty in knowing in detail what they were. Mr. E. George Squier, General Taylor's minister to Nicaragua, who has written a book about the country which contains a great deal of information, and who went up and down the land with his heart hankering and his mouth watering for it, and clearly in a constant droll panic, lest England should eat it up before America bit it—Mr. Squier writes to the London *Times* that "General" Walker has only "washed his slate," and that, by abrogating the federal decrease, he had not restored slavery, for slavery can only exist in virtue of positive laws. Now, whatever confusion there may have been in knowing the old laws, one law was simple and supreme—the one abolishing slavery—and if Walker had meant really to help the cause of human liberty, he would have excepted that, or would immediately have restored it. He did neither. Probably he thought—certainly his partisans in the United States thought—that, as slavery had always existed in those states by the Spanish law, the original status of the slave recurred by the abrogation of the law of abolition.

• • •

Such is an outline of the facts of the Walker foray into Nicaragua, which has so much occupied the newspapers during the last year, and has suggested so many reflections upon the destiny of this country. The chief mischief of the business is the fearful suffering which Walker's imbecility has entailed upon his followers. The destitution, starvation, agonized deaths, by loathsome diseases and mortified wounds, are dreadful to consider. There are no more piteous tales, in the history of any campaigner, than those told by impartial passengers across the country from California, as the result of their own observation.

The motives of the movement were, undoubtedly, many and complicated. The general intention of the Walker movement was to obtain absolute control of the government of Nicaragua, under a fair appearance of legal right; to be supported by the official recognition of the United States Government, by the pecuniary interest of a commercial company, by the popular sympathy of a spurious philosophy of manifest destiny, and the necessity of a short road to California, and by the general indifference of all who were not especially interested in the success of the effort. Thus Nicaragua was to be impregnated with American influences and interests; and, in the fullness of time, as a practically American state, comprising the shortest and safest transit to our western possessions and the vast Pacific commerce, she was to ask annexation and admittance into the Union, care having been taken from the beginning, that no "psalm-singing Yankees," but good Christian slaveholders, should have control of the elections and the state constitution.

This was, doubtless, the general intention, developing itself, of course, imperfectly, and modified by various circumstances. And, equally beyond doubt, this is a general intention of the extreme party of slavery in this country, which for the moment, and in Nicaragua, is disappointed. The plan includes Cuba and the islands of the Gulf, with Central America; and it implies war with Europe and a dissolution of the present Union. Its object is the extension of slavery into regions deemed more suitable to the institution than some of the cooler slave states, and in which a languid climate will be the most subtle ally of the sophistries and sins of the system. It is easy to see, for instance, that slavery would flourish much more luxuriantly in the ignorance of the Tropics than in Virginia begirt with intelligence and freedom. This is the great object; and its philosophy is the doctrine that the superior Saxon race, leading the van of civilization, must and ought to overspread the continent and displace the barbarism of Central America as it supplanted the savages of North America.

That it is the design of Providence to subdue this continent and the world to intellectual and moral light and liberty, we have no doubt. That the ways of Providence, in accomplishing its designs, are often inexplicable, we equally believe. That God is present in history, and that no great event occurs without that presence, is as much a necessary faith as that no sparrow falls to the ground without his care. All this is simply to say that God is God, and rules in the universe. But to assume that it is the divine intention a thing should be done, because we can do it, is a little dangerous. Such a doctrine is dear and convenient to every wrong-doer, and is as good an argument in the mouth of Cain as in that of the Holy Inquisition. It is very evident in history that the race, has gradually advanced from the East toward the West, its moral condition improving with its march. The great experiment of popular government about to be tried, the new world was discovered, and the pilgrims arrived upon its shores. Belonging to the superior race they were, in the divine order, to supplant the inferior. Now will any man contend that any individual pilgrim who, having helped to entrap the Indians into a war, then went to Saybrook and helped slay the Pequots, was less a murderer—he the individual Pilgrim who shot the individual Pequot—because, in the order of Providence, the Saxon race was to overspread this continent? If the argument is valid, every crime is justified. If a man is found murdered in his room, it was, doubtless, the divine design that the man should be murdered. Shall we then regard the murderer as the instrument of God?

There is still, happily, a moral sentiment in this country, which is distinctively American, and honors that name so much, that it would willingly fight rather than see it desecrated. That sentiment was fully aroused and interested in the recent presidential election, and will not again fall into political indifference. So long as a country of popular institutions has a conscience, represented by a considerable body of voters, that country is safe. Within the last two years—as we believe—we, as a people, have passed the greatest peril with which we were ever threatened. The repeal of the Missouri Compromise, and the Kansas-Nebraska bill, were the high-water marks of a slave despotism. Those waters were happily driven back, before the harvests of the future were totally submerged. The shock, which the good sense and patriotism of the country received, showed itself in the vital excitement of the presidential election, and scored itself upon our history in that prodigious combined vote of the opposition, amounting to more than two millions, against the eighteen hundred thousand that elected Mr. Buchanan. The great battle is still to be fought, day by day, but that shock will keep the public conscience alive. Men who have hitherto scorned politics will now consent to mingle in them, conscious that politics can be purified only by mingling principle with them. That process develops a patriotism of which "General" Walker is not a representative; which loves its country as the great means of future civilization and human progress; and that patriotism would fight to the death rather than that country should, by a single meanness or crime, dishonor its divine intention, and disappoint forever the secret hope of humanity.

We repeat, the great battle is still to be fought; and, if we thought so last summer, how much more so now, after our new President's inaugural and the decision of the Supreme Court of the United States in the Dred Scott case. The maddest dogma of Mr. Calhoun has now received the deliberate sanction of the highest official legal authority in the land. That decision was the true inaugural of the first President ever elected by a sectional vote in the country. The result of that decision is the loss of respect, in all manly minds, for a republican tribunal which, in spirit, decides against humanity, and, consequently, against God.

58. AN ACCOUNT OF THE MORMON WAR

*Although Utah had officially been made part of the United States in 1850, in prac-
tice it operated as an enclave controlled entirely by the Mormon Church. Brigham
Young, as territorial governor, made sure that federal appointees had little power
and threatened them with unpleasant consequences if they crossed him. Frightened appointees fled back to Washington claiming that the Mormons had defied
federal rule in Utah. Hoping to unite Northerners and Southerners against the
threat in Utah, and divert attention from the question of slavery, President James
Buchanan sent twenty-five hundred men to stop the rebellion, but they traveled
slowly and were forced to spend the winter on the Green River, east of Salt Lake
City. The following spring, when the army continued its march, the city's Mormon
population fled. However, the delay gave negotiators a chance to convince Brigham
Young to come to terms. He backed down and accepted the authority of federal
officials. This document, a set of letters from Jesse A. Gove, a captain in the Utah
Expedition, sent to his family in New Hampshire, reveals how close the country
came to a civil war. What did Gove understand to be the army's role in Utah?
What evidence did he see of a Mormon rebellion? Was Gove, like Lawrie and
Hoole in Kansas, acting out of his own political and moral convictions?*

Jesse A. Gove
Letters from Utah
1857–58[1]

Army for Utah,
Harris Fork, Camp Winfield, U. T.,
Sept. 30, 1857.

Dear Maria and children:

I sent you letter no. 12 from the ford below by an opportunity that presented
itself through the kindness of Lt. Tallmadge of the artillery. . . . We shall stay
here until further orders. Drills commenced today as skirmishers, and you do
not know how pleased I am with my company. I have so few men that are
recruits that I can put one in each group of four men and go on as though they
were old men. I have my company perfectly organized, and never should want
any better men for a desperate fight. . . .

Mormons continue to hover around us, and the first one that shows his head
will get it cracked to a dead certainty. The enormity of their oppression here in
this country is heart rending in the extreme. Murders are as common among
them, to all those who do not bow to Mormondom, as the sun rises. The ox
trains of Russell & Wharton, which were here with our supplies, have a girl of

---

1. *The Utah Expedition, 1857–1858: Letters of Capt. Jesse Gove, 10th Inf. U.S.A.*, ed. Otis Ham-
mond (Concord: New Hampshire HIstorical Society, 1928) 68–71, 176–78).

about 15 years of age who came to them for protection. They treated her worse than savages. They have 70 men whom they designate as the destroying angels. These men put out of the way any man whom they suspect of expressing any dissatisfaction of the creed. Thousands have been murdered without any other provocation than a desire to return to the States. They leave Salt Lake valley and that is the last that is heard of them. They are worse than the banditti of Italy. They have sent out circulars to induce our men to desert, and offering them $50 and a safe passage through to California or employ them in any business they wish to go into. What a comment on human nature! How changed from civilized life! They require Mormons going into the Indian country to marry squaws, and give white women to Indians with a view to obtain the friendship of the whole race of Indians. In this they have been sadly mistaken. Not any tribe of any importance has gone over to them, on the contrary they want to go with us to fight them.

Bridger, the celebrated guide who owned the fort by that name (see atlas), says that he can take the army in to the valley without going through Echo Cañon, without any trouble. It is 100 miles further. We will winter in Salt Lake valley in spite, that is certain. . . .

Camp 62, Oct. 3. We moved our camp up the creek yesterday about six miles for better grass; . . . camp pleasantly situated, weather beautiful. Last night it was somewhat cold but my little stove kept me and my little pets very warm, plenty of wood. Thousands of rabbits within gun shot of the camp. Everybody dines on rabbits. Plenty of fish, also, some splendid trout. . . .

Yesterday Brigham Young sent to the commanding officer of the troops on Harris Fork an official letter, together with his proclamation, warning all armed bodies of men from advancing into the valley, calling on the forces of the Territory to rally to the defence of the state and their creed. . . . That if we desired provisions he would furnish them upon the proper application, etc., etc. The old fool! Did you ever see such impudence, such braggadocio? Such an old idiot! We will show him on which side of his bread the butter should be spread. The 5th Inf. was at Green River last night. It will come to Harris 1st crossing today, and next day to this point. Capt. Reno's seige train is there also. . . .

Oct. 4, Sunday. Today has been truly one of rest. Sunday morning inspection this morning. I thought how I should like to have had you and dear little Charlie see Co. I under arms, with their rifles loaded, 20 rounds of ball cartridges in their cartridge boxes, all on a Sunday morning, shirts tucked into their trousers. I gave the order last night that the shirt was to be inside the trousers. Carroll and myself did the same. Drab hats with the letter "I" in front, looking sunburnt, hardy and stout. Just imagine a march of 1000 miles, and nearly 3 months time consumed, and picture then to yourself what must be the physical condition of us all. Why, we are iron men. I am as stout and strong in all my limbs as an ox. My cheek bones are not visible, I am so healthy and fleshy. I shall cut my hair tomorrow again. Weather delightful. Sent you a note yesterday as I wrote you. Be particular and date the slips of news you send me.

Camp 62, Harris Fork, Oct. 6, Tuesday. I wrote you on the 4th, Sunday. Yesterday I did not write you because I was on guard and had no good opportunity. . . .

. . . At 4 P.M. I went on guard after the hard morning's march. When we returned two men that had died in hospital were buried. The 5th Inf. and Reno's battery came in about 2 P.M. They report that two supply trains that were on Green River were attacked and burned by the Mormons. This is open war. We have, fortunately, 6 months provisions with us. The ball is opened, and attacks on our trains is their system of warfare. The excitement is tremendous. Mountaineers are leaving the Territory and everything is being burned by the Mormons to prevent our advancing. Today Col. Alexander held a council of war to decide upon what to do. . . . Col. Alexander is senior officer, and you know how much confidence we have in him. He don't know what to do. Every officer in his regiment says "take command and push on." I think he will at last do so. No time is to be lost, we want mounted troops greatly. The rascals come out on the hills boldly, knowing that we have no mounted troops. Capt. Phelps, Reno, and Col. Canby are for the advance. Col. Waite and his officers are for going into winter quarters. Tomorrow will decide it. I hope we shall go on. We are for the advance, we have got to win our colors and now is our chance. We are bound to make him assume command and go on.

Oct. 8, In Camp. Yesterday Col. Alexander assumed command and we shall go on. Good! 4 companies, 2 from the 5th and 2 from the 10th, B and H, Capts. Gardner and Tracy, were ordered on detached service to go to Green River for the purpose of ascertaining the state of the destroyed trains, and also to get all the powder and lead in the hands of the traders. They will return tomorrow. They left last night about 5 P.M. to make a night march of about 20 miles across the country, avoiding the roads. What do you think of that kind of life? . . .

Camp, 20 miles south of S. L. City, July 2, 1858.
My dear family:

We have at last found the great city, marched through it and encamped on the other side of Jordan. From Bear River the wildness of the country is extreme to the great valley of Salt Lake. . . .

Monday, 21. Left camp early. Hot and dusty. Continued our march, and when within about 2 or 3 miles of Weber River we came to the narrow pass and the Mormon fortifications. The pass is truly wild and romantic, ditched, and walls across the road and narrow passes, but of the most flimsy character. It could have been turned easily by 500 troops. There were huts standing which would accommodate probably 1000 or 1500 men. These were behind the works. On the high bluffs overhanging the road large stones were placed to throw over, just as though we were to be fools enough to go under and let them drop them on us. We could have whipped them out so easy that I regret we could not try them, especially as they now talk so wildly. . . .

26th. Left camp early. I am rear guard of our own regiment. We ascended rapidly and then descended more so. After miles of dust and wind we came to the narrow pass in Emigration Cañon, and then we came out upon the bank bordering the great valley. Here we had everything before us; 4 miles brought us into the outskirts of the city. We found the city evacuated, all had gone to Provo except a few men whom they left to burn the city if ordered. The city is 50 per cent better in structure and situation than I expected to find. It is beautifully laid out and watered at every street. Most of the description in Harper's Weekly is very correct, but the city itself is too grandly displayed.

Brigham's palace is a magnificent structure. His apartment for his wives is attached so that it is easy of access. It is said that the inside is furnished in the most elaborate style, furniture imported, two or three pianos, etc.

The people are at Provo. They are impudent and rebellious still. They say they will accept the pardon, but that the President is a fool; that they will not obey anyone but Brigham Young. They don't want the army and won't have it. Such is the result of the pardon, a miserable policy which the government ought to be damned for. We stayed on the side of the Jordan in dust and alkali for two days, then moved camp south in the direction of Provo, on the mountain benches, where we have now a beautiful camp and grass. . . .

. . . Nothing but a fight will make them understand our power and their inability to cope with us. A strong posse will go with the marshal in all cases.

We shall go from here in a few days to Cedar Valley.

There is some splendid fishing at Utah Lake.

The last letter I got from you was mailed 17th of May. It conveyed to me the afflicting intelligence of the death of brother George. I cannot say that I was unprepared for it, but the reality of such news never struck me with that earnest force until it indeed was so. How it must rend the hearts of my father and mother! You must write them often. I shall write them this mail. Truly my father's house has been one of death. I cannot realize that I shall never see George again. When I saw him last he was hale and hearty. Truly in the midst of life we are in death. . . .

. . . You must write every week. Send via St. Joseph, Mo. Send me papers and letters often.

I approve of Mrs. Alexander being Godmother to Jessie, and of Hannah standing for her. Tell Hannah to hurry up matters if she wants me as the God-father of the first. The same to Ann. Tell them to buy a barrel of rice. Eat freely and don't despair.

Love to all. Kisses to mine. Hoping to see you all soon. . . .

FURTHER READING

Arrington, Leonard J., and Davis Bitton. *The Latter-Day Saints.* Champaign: University of Illinois Press, 1992.

Bagley, Will. *Blood of the Prophets: Brigham Young and the Massacre at Mountain Meadows.* Norman: University of Oklahoma Press, 2004.

Bigler, David, and Will Bagley. *The Mormon Rebellion: America's First Civil War, 1857–1858.* Norman: University of Oklahoma Press, 2012.

Brooks, Juanita. *The Mountain Meadows Massacre.* Stanford, CA: Stanford University Press, 1950.

Etcheson, Nicole. *Bleeding Kansas: Contested Liberty in the Civil War Era.* Lawrence: University of Kansas Press, 2004.

Faragher, John Mack. *Eternity Street: Violence and Justice in Frontier Los Angeles.* New York: Norton Books, 2016.

Hyde, Anne F. *Empires, Nations, and Families: A New History of the North American West, 1800–1860.* New York: Ecco Books, 2012.

May, Robert E. *Manifest Destiny's Underworld: Filibustering in Antebellum America.* Chapel Hill: University of North Carolina Press, 2004.

Stampp, Kenneth M. *America in 1857: A Nation on the Brink.* New York: Oxford University Press, 1990.

Dakota hanging, Fort Snelling, Minnesota, 1862. This image, which appeared in a popular illustrated magazine, was seen by millions of Americans. As punishment for a violent and initially successful uprising, thirty-eight Dakota men were hanged in public. A detailed *New York Times* article described the entire event, including the tears of some observers and the cheers of others. Does the image depict this as a military or civilian event? What are the logistics of a "mass execution"? Who is in the crowd?

From a sketch by W. H. Childs, *Frank Leslie's Illustrated Magazine.*

Civil Wars Spread Over the West

14

The West, which played an important role in events preceding the Civil War, did not recede from national attention once war began. After guns were fired on Fort Sumter, off the coast of South Carolina, on April 12, 1861, Northerners, Southerners, and Westerners joined the army. Northerners fought to preserve the Union and abolish slavery, Southerners fought to preserve slavery and support the doctrine of states' rights, white Westerners fought to protect their own vision of a West full of opportunity and empty of Indians, and Native Westerners battled to protect their homelands. Everyone wanted to settle the question of slavery in the territories, and all assumed that the war would be short and that one side would give in. However, the events of the 1850s and the bitter reaction to them should have impressed on people the vicious holding power of these issues. Four years of bloody military engagement to bring the Confederacy back into the Union would only begin to end slavery and would bring on protracted Indian War.

The Union and Confederate armies focused their attention on battles east of the Mississippi, but the West continued to figure in military and political strategy in important ways. As Southern states began to secede from the Union after the election of Abraham Lincoln as president in 1860, both the Union and the new Confederacy worried about the loyalty of the border states and of the West. Ultimately, only Texas joined the Confederacy, but strong secessionist sympathies nevertheless emerged in California, New Mexico, Utah, Kansas, and Indian Territory, threatening Union control in those areas. Missouri suffered bitter civil war within its borders as the proslavery governor and legislature fled to the Confederate state of Arkansas, where they declared a government in exile. Union supporters established a temporary government in St. Louis, and Missouri remained officially in the Union, although guerrilla warfare raged there for much of the war. That the border states (Missouri, Kentucky, Maryland, and Delaware) and the West remained in the Union proved to be an enormous strategic advantage.

When the border states stayed with the Union, the Confederacy looked for other ways to increase its power. Expansionistic and ambitious Confederates, especially Texans, imagined a grand slaveholding empire spreading across the American Southwest and into Mexico. Parts of New Mexico, Arizona, and California were strongly pro-Confederacy and offered a springboard for Confederate action in the Southwest. Early in the war, troops from Texas invaded New Mexico and Arizona and called the region Confederate Arizona. In the winter of 1861–62, troops headed north up the Rio Grande valley hoping to seize the gold mines of Colorado. The Confederates won an important victory at Valverde in southern New Mexico, the largest US Civil War battle in the West. They then took the territorial capital at Santa Fe. In March, however, at Glorietta Pass, to the north of Santa Fe, after another Confederate victory, Union troops and volunteers from Colorado and New Mexico destroyed their supply train, forcing a retreat. By summer, the Confederates had to march back to Texas, ending hopes of a western empire.

The Union also eyed the political potential of the West. President Lincoln consolidated western support by creating new territories in the Dakotas, Colorado, Nevada, Idaho, Montana, and Arizona. Concern about maintaining control over gold- and silver-producing regions, especially California, Nevada, and Colorado, prompted the federal government to create and subsidize mail service, the Pony Express, transcontinental telegraph service, and finally railroads. These communication lines linked east and west in powerful ways and created an infrastructure that made mining the resources of the West possible.

Native peoples, having spent much of the 1850s in destructive war against the United States in the Pacific Northwest and on the Great Plains, found themselves especially challenged by the situation created by the Civil War. Gold in California, Colorado, Dakota, and Montana and silver in Nevada brought hundreds of thousands of miners across Indians lands and into direct conflict over rivers, trails, fishing and hunting sites, and gold. Tension over resources combined with a culture of violence among frustrated white miners resulted in genocidal binges of Indian killing in California and Oregon. A long era of drought on the central and southern plains, combined with huge amounts of traffic on the Santa Fe and Oregon Trails, decimated bison populations and brought waves of epidemic disease to the Great Plains.

In such difficult situations, some Native nations chose to fight back. In August 1862, after Dakota Indians had suffered decades of broken treaties with the United States government, undergone relentless invasion of their land by Minnesota emigrants, and been starved and cheated by military officials, their leader Little Crow agreed with other leaders they had had enough. They insisted that their people must fight an all out war with the white settlers and the US Army. After six weeks of fighting, the burning of hundreds of white settlers' homes, the kidnapping of hundreds of women and children, and the killing of dozens, the great Dakota uprising was smashed. The violence and the carefully planned rebellion surprised and frightened many white Americans. In the end, thousands of Indians were taken prisoner by the US Army, and 303 Dakotas were sentenced to death. President Lincoln, in the midst of the Civil War, stepped in to save the lives of 265 of the condemned men, but in the end, 38 Dakota men swung from nooses in a public hanging, the largest government-sanctioned execution in US history. After the execution, all of the Dakota were expelled from Minnesota and the US Congress abolished their reservations.

Two years later, in November 1864, a large group of Colorado Cheyenne and Arapaho, tired of fighting, marched through the barren winter landscape to turn themselves in to federal authorities. After Black Kettle's villages set up camp near a US Army fort, a group of Colorado militia and US Cavalry marched into the sleeping camp and killed more than a hundred people. In this terrible massacre, the troops shot everyone they could see, regardless of age or gender, and rode triumphantly back to Denver. This episode, called the Sand Creek massacre, convinced all Plains nations that fighting was their only option. The region spiraled into two decades of brutal Indian War.

The documents in this chapter illustrate the full import of the Civil War as it ranged across the entire continent and the different ways Westerners—white, black, native, and newcomer—experienced that war. Correspondence between Confederate military leaders reveals their hopes about the West, while a letter from a Texas soldier about the battle of Glorietta Pass shows how quickly those hopes faded. Letters from a Dakota prisoner, Four Lightning, lay out his reasons for taking on the US Army. Finally, two accounts of the Sand Creek massacre, one a newspaper report in Denver and the other a letter written by a guilt-ridden soldier to a friend, demonstrate the moral complexity of the past.

59. THE CONFEDERACY IMAGINES A WESTERN EMPIRE

In March of 1861, before the outbreak of the US Civil War, the citizens of what is now southern New Mexico and Arizona declared their allegiance to the Confederacy. Once the war started, Confederate military leaders, who wanted to enlarge this thin vein of western support, sent troops led by Lieutenant Colonel John Baylor from Texas into New Mexico territory. After a brief battle in late July 1861, Baylor marched into the region and seized control, declaring himself the military governor of Arizona on August 3, 1861. This initial success alerted Union leaders to the seriousness of the Confederate threat in the West. The following document includes Baylor's report on the battle and its aftermath, as well as his proclamation to the citizens of Arizona informing them of the military occupation of southern New Mexico and Arizona by the Confederacy. Was Baylor surprised by the ease of his victory? Why did he put so much emphasis on the guns and ammunition captured by his troops? What political purposes might his proclamation have served?

John Baylor
Reports on Taking Arizona
1861[1]

> Picacho, Mesilla Valley,
> *Arizona, August 3*, 1861.

Sir: I have the honor to report that I had an engagement with the U.S. forces, numbering over 500 cavalry and infantry with four pieces of artillery, at Mesilla, on the evening of the 25th of July, in which the enemy were repulsed with a loss of 3 killed and 7 wounded.

On the 27th I captured at San Augustine Springs the entire command of the enemy under Major Lynde, consisting of eight companies of infantry, three of Mounted Rifles, with four pieces of artillery, together with all their transportation, arms, ammunition, commissary and quartermaster's stores; all of which, with Fort Fillmore, are now in my possession.

Too much praise cannot be given to the officers and soldiers under my command, and especially to Captain Hardeman and company, who were the only part of the command engaged with the enemy.

I have thought proper to release upon parole the entire command of officers and men, as I could not, with less than 300 men, guard over 600 and meet another force of 240 of the enemy that is looked for daily.

I have the honor to be, respectfully,

> *JOHN R. BAYLOR,*
> *Lieut. Col., Comdg. Second Regiment Mounted Rifles, C. S. A.*

---

1. "Report of Lieut. Col. John R. Baylor, Aug. 3, 1861," in *The War of the Rebellion: A Compilation of the Official Records of Union and Confederate Armies*, vol. 4 (Washington: Government Printing Office, 1882), 16–21.

Headquarters,
Doña Aña, Ariz., September 21, 1861.

Sir: I have the honor to submit the following report of the engagement at Mesilla on the 25th of July; the capture of the United States forces the day after the next succeeding at San Augustine Springs, in the Organ Mountains, Territory of Arizona, and of my operations in the Territory up to the present time:

On assuming command at Fort Bliss I ascertained that the United States forces were concentrating in strong force at Fort Fillmore, and from the proximity of that post I supposed that the object of the enemy was to attack the forces under my command at Fort Bliss. . . . I accordingly took up the line of march in the night of the 23d of July with 258 men, and in the night of the 24th succeeded in taking a position on the river near Fort Fillmore. The surprise of the enemy would have been complete but for the desertion of a private from Capt. T. F. Teel's company, who reported to Major Lynde our strength and position. . . .

. . . I reached Mesilla in the afternoon of the 25th, and was soon informed that the enemy were marching to attack us. I posted my men in position and awaited the arrival of the enemy. At about 5 o'clock I discovered their cavalry approaching the town by the main road, and soon after the infantry came in sight, bringing with them three howitzers. They formed within 300 yards, and were, as near as I could tell, about 600 strong. A flag was sent in to demand the "unconditional and immediate surrender of the Texas forces," to which I answered that "we would fight first, and surrender afterward." The answer was followed by the enemy opening on us with their howitzers. After four or five rounds of bombs, grape, and canister, the cavalry formed and marched up within 250 yards, preparatory to making a charge. Captain Hardeman's company, being in position nearest the enemy, was ordered to open on them with his front rank, to see if they were within range of our guns. The fire was well directed and proved effective, killing 4 of the enemy and wounding 7. The cavalry was thrown into confusion and retreated hastily, running over the infantry. In a few moments the enemy were marching back in the direction of their fort; but supposing it to be a feint, intended to draw me from my position, I did not pursue them, but kept my position until next morning, the 26th, expecting that they would attack us under cover of night.

The enemy not appearing, I sent my spies to reconnoiter, and discover, if possible, their movements. The spies reported the enemy at work at the fort making breastworks, and evidently preparing to defend themselves. . . .

After getting water for my men I started in pursuit of the enemy, who had passed through San Augustine Pass. . . . Upon gaining the summit of the Pass, a plain view of the road to the San Augustine Springs was presented. The road for 5 miles was lined with the fainting, famished soldiers, who threw down their arms as we passed and begged for water. At the Springs the enemy had drawn up in line of battle some 200 or 300 strong. I ordered Major Waller to charge with Captain Hardeman's company until he reached the end of the line of straggling soldiers, then to form and cut them off from the main body. I followed, disarming the enemy, and as fast as our jaded horses could go. On reaching Captain Hardeman's company, who were formed, I saw Major Waller and Captain Hardeman riding into the enemy's lines. I was in a few moments sent for by Major Lynde, who asked upon what terms I would allow him to surrender. I replied that the surrender must be unconditional. To this Major Lynde assented, asking that private property should be respected. The articles of capitulation were signed, and the order given for the enemy to stack arms. . . .

The accompanying abstracts of quartermaster's, subsistence, medical, and ordnance stores will show but a part of the property captured, much of it having been stolen and destroyed while I was awaiting the enemy at Picacho and some since I have left the command to Major Waller. A number of muster rolls are lost, the remainder only showing about half of the prisoners captured; also the correspondence with the commanding officer in reference to his regimental colors was lost. I regret the loss of these papers, but in the hurry and excitement it was unavoidable. I can only give the number of the enemy as it was reported to me by the officers captured.

On the 10th of August an express reached me from Fort Stanton, stating that the news of the capture of Major Lynde's command had created a stampede among the United States troops, who hastily abandoned the fort after having destroyed a considerable portion of their supplies and Government property of all kinds, and all would have been destroyed but for a storm of rain, which extinguished the fire intended by the enemy to destroy the fort. The few citizens living near the fort took possession of it, and saved a valuable lot of quartermaster's and commissary stores. The Mexicans and Indians in large numbers demanded the right to pillage the fort, which was granted. The citizens, being too weak to resist, not knowing that they would get aid from me or not, were forced to abandon the fort to the Mexicans and Indians. . . .

Believing that the interest of Arizona demanded imperatively some form of government, I issued my proclamation, of date 1st of August, 1861, to the people, a copy of which I forward you.

I cannot conclude this report without alluding to the courage, fortitude, and patriotism of the officers and soldiers of my command and to those citizens who participated with us. All did nobly their part. I cannot make distinction between men so willing and ready to do their whole duty. To the courage of my officers and men the country is indebted for the success of our arms and the acquisition of a Territory valuable in many respects.

I have the honor to be, very respectfully, your obedient servant,

JOHN R. BAYLOR,
Lieut. Col., Comdg. C. S. Forces in Arizona.

Capt. T. A. Washington,

Asst. Adjt Gen., C. S. Army, San Antonio, Tex.

Proclamation

To the People of the Territory of Arizona:

The social and political condition of Arizona being little short of general anarchy, and the people being literally destitute of law, order, and protection, the said Territory, from the date hereof, is hereby declared temporarily organized as a military government until such time as Congress may otherwise provide.

I, John R. Baylor, lieutenant-colonel, commanding the Confederate Army in the Territory of Arizona, hereby take possession of the said Territory in the name and behalf of the Confederate States of America.

For all the purposes herein specified, and until otherwise decreed or provided, the Territory of Arizona shall comprise all that portion of New Mexico lying south of the thirty-fourth parallel of north latitude.

All offices, both civil and military, heretofore existing in this Territory, either under the laws of the late United States or the Territory of New Mexico, are hereby declared vacant, and from the date hereof shall forever cease to exist.

That the people of this Territory may enjoy the full benefits of law, order, and the protection, and, as far as possible, the blessings and advantages of a free government, it is hereby decreed that the laws and enactments existing in this Territory prior to the date of this proclamation, and consistent with the Constitution and laws of the Confederate States of America and the provisions of this decree, shall continue in full force and effect, without interruption, until such time as the Confederate Congress may otherwise provide. . . .

Given under my hand at Mesilla this 1st day of August, 1861.

JOHN R. BAYLOR,

Gov. and Lieut. Col., Comdg. Mounted Rifles, C. S. Army.

60. THE BATTLE OF GLORIETTA PASS

When Confederate troops led by General Henry Hopkins Sibley of Louisiana occupied Santa Fe, largely without resistance, early in 1862, the far West suddenly appeared vulnerable to a Confederate invasion. Western states loyal to the Union recognized the threat and quickly organized volunteers. The first troops to reach New Mexico were members of the First Colorado Volunteer Regiment, whose members had marched 450 miles from Denver to Fort Union, just north of Santa Fe, in only thirteen days. Meeting the unsuspecting Texans in Glorietta Pass on March 26, 1862, some of the Colorado troops engaged the Texans, while others destroyed the Confederate's supply train, forcing the rebels to retreat. This letter, written by a Texas soldier to his wife and found by a member of the Colorado regiment, was published in the Denver Times *when the troops returned home in a blaze of glory. These same troops later participated in the*

1864 Sand Creek massacre (see document 61). His letter describes the surprise of the Texas troops and how quickly the battle turned into a rout. How were the conditions surrounding these Confederate troops different from the ones in the battle in southern Arizona described in the preceding document? Why was Brown so angry with General Sibley? Why was this battle seen as a turning point for Confederate ambitions in the West?

George M. Brown

An Account of Fighting in New Mexico
1862[1]

Socorro, April 30th, 1862.

My Dear Wife—Having an opportunity to do so, I write you a letter by James Davis, who leaves here tonight for home, and who will probably get there some months before I can, for if I can get work in this country, I think I had better stay until winter at least, when I hope this war will be over. Well, here I am, with fifty-two others, on our way south, all afoot, with but three wagons that have been furnished us by our enemies to go home with. When we will get there the Lord only knows. With what a different feeling we pass through these Mexican towns now, from what we did two months ago. Then we felt like heroes, having had a fight at Fort Craig, scaring the Mexicans to flight, and driving the regular soldiers into the Fort, and getting past with our whole army and cutting off all supplies and relief to the Fort; we were marching up the country with the fixed determination of wrenching this country from the United States Government and we all thought it would soon be in our hands. But what a mistake. Having marched to within eight miles of Fort Union, we were again met by the enemy from Fort Union, and after three battles with them, all of us who were not killed or taken prisoners were obliged to destroy everything they had, and flee to the mountains for their lives, and get out of the country, the Lord only knows how. We were among those who were taken prisoners. John White, your cousin, was killed at the battle of Fort Craig. He fell by my side, and then I first thought of what you had told me, but it was too late. I had a finger shot off, but went on up the country with the rest.

Our company, with the Second and Third regiments, reached Santa Fe the 16th or 17th of March. In two days our regiment came up. We were to wait a short time, and then march on to take Fort Union, which we thought ours already, and then New Mexico would belong to the new government of the South, and it then would be so easy to cut off all comunication from California. On the 22d, six hundred of us were ordered to march to Apache canon to stand picket. . . . On the twenty-

---

1. "George M. Brown to His Wife, April 30, 1862," in Ovander J. Hollister, ed., *Boldly They Rode: A History of the First Colorado Regiment* (Lakewood, CO: Golden Press, 1949), 166–70.

sixth, we got word that the enemy were coming down the canon, in the shape of two hundred Mexicans and about two hundred regulars. Out we marched with two cannon, expecting an easy victory, but what a mistake. Instead of Mexicans and regulars, they were regular demons, that iron and lead had no effect upon, in the shape of Pike's Peakers from the Denver City Gold mines, where we thought of going to about a year ago. As I said, up the canon we went for four miles, when we met the enemy coming at double quick, but the grape and shell soon stopped them, but before we could form in line of battle, their infantry were upon the kills, on both sides of us, shooting us down like sheep. The order was given to retreat down the canon, which we did for about a mile. . . . This was no sooner done than up came the cannon with the enemy at their heels, but when they saw us ready to receive them, they stopped; but only for a short time, for in a few moments they could be seen on the mountains, jumping from rock to rock like so many sheep. They had no sooner got within shooting distance of us, than up came a company of cavalry at full charge, with swords and revolvers drawn, looking like so many flying devils. On they came to what I supposed certain destruction, but nothing like lead or iron seemed to stop them, for we were pouring it into them from every side like hail in a storm. In a moment those devils had run the gauntlet for half a mile, and were fighting hand to hand with our men in the road. . . .

It was a grand sight. We were shooting as fast as we could, and to see that handful of men jump the ditch, and charging on us; we expected to shoot the last one, before they reached us. But luck was against us, and after fighting hand to hand with them, and our comrades being shot and cut down every moment, we were obliged to surrender.

Now who do you suppose it was that came charging and nearly running over me, with a revolver pointed at my head, and ordered me to lay down my arms and consider myself a prisoner—which I did—for I knew the next moment would be my last if I did not? It was George Lowe, brother-in-law of Mr. Whitney, that keeps store in Portage, Wisconsin. You know him very well. I knew him as soon as I saw him, but he did not recognize me and I was very glad of it. I tried to get a chance to see him after we got to Union, but never could. I expect to see him at Fort Craig. I think he will be some surprised to see who it was that he came so near shooting. George Turner was also among the Pike's Peakers. He left Wisconsin last summer. I saw him after the fight, and he told me that he had received a letter from your folks last February, and that they were all well, and your brother had joined the Wisconsin Volunteers and gone to the war. How one of these men that charged us ever escaped death will ever be a wonder to me. Our men who were fighting with them in the road, were soon obliged to retreat, and the fight was over.

About eighty of us that were taken prisoners were soon marched off towards Fort Union. How many were killed and wounded, I don't know, but there must have been a large number. Such a sight I never want to see again. As I was marched off the field, I saw some men lying with their heads shot nearly off., and some with their arms or legs shot off, and one poor man that belonged to our company, I saw lying against a tree, with his brains all shot out. Henry Asher had an arm shot off, but made out to escape. He was standing by my side when he was shot. The men that charged us seemed to have a charmed life, for if they had not they could never have reached us alive. In a few days our number was increased by more of our men, who told us that they were reinforced after the night after the first battle by 1,300 men, under Col. Scurry, from Santa Fe. The Pike's Peakers were also reinforced, and on the 28th day they fought another battle near the same place as the first. After fighting all day both armies retreated. Our army marched back to Santa Fe for provisions, as our whole train of seventy wagons was burned by the enemy. In one of the wagons was that trunk of clothing you sent me while I was at Fort Fillmore. It was burned up with the rest. . . . I have been told by some of the men who were in both battles, and were taken prisoners to Santa Fe, that there were between four and five hundred killed and wounded. Our men were soon driven out of Santa Fe and Albuquerque, and made to stand at Peralta. Here they had another battle, but were again obliged to retreat, as the Pike's Peakers had made a junction with a large number of the enemy from Fort Craig. In a few days after this, they were obliged to burn the rest of the train and flee to the mountains. I hope they have reached Texas in safety. One of the men that was taken prisoner a few days after they left Peralta tells me that out of the 3,800 men and 327 wagons that were with us when we left Fort Fillmore, only 1,200 men and thirteen wagons remained together when they were obliged to flee to the mountains. The rest of the men must have been killed, wounded, or taken prisoner. Some of the prisoners were sent to the States; the rest of us have been started home this way, by swearing never to take up arms against the United States again, which I was very glad to do, and I hope the day is not far distant when Gen. Sibley will be hung. If brother John has not joined the volunteers yet, keep him away for God's sake. Give my love to all the folks and kiss the baby for me. Had it not been for the devils from Pike's Peak, this country would have been ours. If I can get work here I will write to you again as soon as I can.

Your Affectionate Husband,
GEORGE M. BROWN.

61. DAKOTA WAR IN 1862

The terrible Dakota uprising of 1862 nearly emptied Minnesota of its white set-tler population and left dozens of towns, forts, and farms burned. After 38 Dakota men were hanged, the other 265 prisoners were marched in shackles to Camp McClellan in Iowa, where they stayed four years. A missionary named Stephen Riggs had operated schools for the Dakota and now served as their chaplain in prison. He taught them to write in Dakota as a first step to learning English. This letter, originally in Dakota, was written to General Henry Sibley, the Minnesota military man and soon-to-be governor, who had beaten them in war. Four Lightning, a Dakota prisoner, begs Sibley to care for his Dakota relatives, who had been banished from their Minnesota homeland. Sibley received the letter, but it wasn't translated until very recently. What worried Four Lighting the most about the Dakota's situation in 1863? Does he apologize for the uprising? What case does he make to Sibley about the Dakota's right to their homeland?

"Letter from A Prisoner"
1863[1]

Four Lightning (David Faribault) Writes to
Minnesota General Henry Sibley
Four Lightning/David Faribault, Jr., May 18, 1863

Davenport Iowa
Camp McClellan May 18th 63

Gen. H. H. Sibley

Dear Sir I will write you this letter in the Sioux Language again and you will please to excuse us for writing you so often about this matter.

DAKOTA VERSION: Wopetonhanska—Taku wanji wanna onkini oiyapa tuka ake nahanhin wowapi oniçupi wicaxta owasin yuwitawa hecen uncinpi Wicaxta taku wanjidan eciyapi he owotanna tuka wowapi onicagapi unkan wicaxta wanjidan Caskedan eciyapi he S. R. Riggs wowapi qu hecen he token eya exta wicake xni. hehan wicaxta kaxka unkanpi kin witaya token wacinunyapi he wanna nayarun. tuka wicaxta ihdawa qa dakota tona om takan yakonpi kin hena wikopapi okini taku wanzigzi on xicaya cajaonyatapi nace onkecinpi heon akihde wowapi oniçupi hena anwicayaroptanpi kte xni iyececa ondakapi. he de taku ondapi tuka ninarin uncinpi tuka he taku waxte ece uncinpi. Waziyata eyaye cin hena om tacan onwanjipidan

qa takuwicunyapi tuka iye kagapi qa dehan iyotahaniyeonkiyapi qa mdoke-hantahan hokxiopa winurinca takuwicunyanpi wahdag onkicakijapi qa terike ondapi tuka iye he takuwicunyanpi apa kagapi qa wicoran xica wan dehan yux-tag onkakijapi—takomni he ikcewicaxta wicoran kin he yuxicapi—qa owasin onṭapi iyececa tuka dehan niunkanpi unkiyepi xni tuka dena heca wiuncaxtapi nakaex—waxicun owasin ontapi cinpi tuka akex onxiundapi qa dehan

1. National Archives Record Group 393, Western Division, Part I, Dept. of NW.3481, in Clifford Cancu and Michael Simon, trans. and eds., *Dakota Prisoner of War Letters, Dakota Kaskapi Okicize Wowapi* (Minneapolis: Minnesota Historical Society Press), 6–9.

xkanxkan onyakonpi—hecen heon unkix taku waxte wanji ecawiconkicunpi
onkokihipi kinhan he ecen econqonpi uncinpi—qa waxicun iyepi on etanhan
owasin unṭapi kta iyececa heon etanhan ece econqupi iyececa—undakapi qa
heon ota onkeyapi—wicaxta den kaxka unkanpi dena waziyata aye cin onupapi
kinhan om wounhdakapi kta iyececa

qa iye takan yakonpi qa tona om dapi kte cin hena tohinni om wohdakapi
kte xni nacece ecin hena wicahnayanpi kta kecinpi kte cin heon heunkiyapi
qaix hecen wokiyapi xni kinhan isantanka token ṭapi kinhan unkix dena owasin iyecen ontapi uncinpi—takuwicunyanpi xta tokawicunyanpi kte waxicun
om etanhan owasin unṭapi kinhan tankaya caje onkotanipi kta qa hecen wanji
unipi kinhan wicaxta iyecen onyakonpi kte—hehan decen unkanpi qa unipi
xta tohini waxteondakapi kte xni kin heon terikaondapi—tuwe waunyakapi qa
taku onkeyapi kta xta xunka iyecen wacinunkiyuzapi kte cinhe sdononkiyapi—
takuwicunyanpi wanna Minixoxa ohnayan wicahnakapi hena iye nipi uncinpi
qa mdokehanna wiconṭe erpeunkiyapi qa wicaxta ṭa iyecen tacan tawaiçiye xni
unkapi—

okini he hecen ecanupi kinhan naunjicapi kta waxicun ikopapi xta tohini
hokxiopa erpeya nawicunjicapi kte xni hecen he ikoyapapi kte xni Waxicun
kizapi uncinpi kinhan mdokehan en unkupi kte xni tuka—waxicun ehna unki-
cagapi qa tacan wanjidan om onkihdawapi iyecen unyakonpi kin heon kici
onkicizapi uncinpi xni qa en itoheya anawicunpapi tuka teriya iyeonkicizapi
tuka taku waxte wanji ecunqonpi onkokihipi he ecunqonpi uncinpi kin
heceedan—nix nixnana Wakpa minisota ohna initancan qa dakota wicoran
tayan sdonwicayaye heon nina wacinuniyanpi—qa heon wanna nupa wowapi
nicupi qa ninarin hecen uncinpi—Dakota takan yakonpi he ecadan om waun-
kiciyakapi kta keonkiciyapi qa nakun waxicun heyapi tuka token onkeniciyapi
heceedan owacin unkanpi—

TRANSLATED ENGLISH VERSION
Dear Sir I will write you this letter in the Sioux Language again and you will
please to excuse us for writing you so often about this matter.

General Henry H. Sibley—All the men are together on this, and we wanted
to write this letter about the news that has just come out. There's a man named
"That One" we are writing about—he's an honest and straight man, but there's
one named "First Born Son," who wrote a letter to S. R. Riggs, no matter what
he says, he's not truthful. These men sitting here in prison together depend
upon you, and now you have heard us. But there's some men who consider
themselves friends of those on the outside, but the Dakota are afraid of them,
we are thinking, maybe they said something bad about us, that's why we are
continually writing to you. In our opinion, you shouldn't listen to those per-

sons. There's one thing we really want and are asking for, and it's only good. Those that have gone north, we remain one body with them.

Our relatives have caused the war, but now we are experiencing great difficulty because of it. Since last summer, we have not seen our children, wives, and relatives, and we feel it's too difficult of a burden to bear. Some of our relatives [Mdewakanton] have done bad deeds, now we're defeated and suffering because of it. They have already ruined the work of the common man, for that we will probably all die. Indeed, we are all alive at this time because we're not like them, but we are men. At first the white people wanted to kill all of us, but since then, they relented and have compassion on us, and we're able to move around. For that reason, if there's one thing good we can do for them, we want to do this. The white men think we should have all been killed because of what happened, but we were not, so in our opinion, we should go ahead and do it. And many of us are saying we should. There are some men imprisoned here, if allowed, two of us can go with those going north and speak to the authorities on our behalf.

Those on the outside that are going north and those going with them probably will not speak up for us, we are saying this because those on the outside will think the white people will just fool them again; or if there's no peaceful relations, then, in what manner the soldiers die, we ourselves want to die in the same way. Although the white men are not our relatives but our enemies, if we were to die with them, our name will become greatly known. Therefore, if one of us can stay alive, we can, eventually, live free like other people. Although we are alive right now, they will never like us, and for us that's too difficult to live with. We realize that whoever sees us, and no matter what we say to try to defend ourselves, the white people will think of us as dogs. We want our relatives now imprisoned at the Missouri River [Crow Creek] to remain alive. Last summer we left death behind and with no freedom to do what we wanted, we were like dead men.

The white men were maybe afraid we would try to escape, but we would never do that, because we would not leave the children behind, so you don't have to be fearful of that. If we wanted to fight the white people, we would have never come in last summer, also we consider ourselves as one body with them, because we grew up with them, so we would never fight them. We are much like them, therefore, we would never fight them, instead we run to them for protection. They're the ones who fought us, causing great difficulty for us; if there's one good thing we can do, we want to do that. You alone, General H. H. Sibley, are the Commander in the Minnesota River area and know the Dakota custom well, that's why we depend upon you. We are serious about wanting peace, that's why we've written twice. We said to one another, we will soon see each other and be with those on the outside. The white men said to us, no matter what, think only about what we've said to you.

The different bands—every one will do just as these will say—

We think that's the only way we can do something good. And all the elderly common men here will sign their names.

Big Eagle		Lightning Cloud, Red Cap's Son
Iron Elk		Good Day Red Owl's Son
Kick the Earth, Son of Cloud Man		Walks with Stone Short First Son
Scarlet Boy	Comes Home Openly	Lays Violent Hands On
Blowing Wind	White Cloud Man	Great One, Son of Walks on Pine
	Throw	
Hears the Wind		Iron Track Shooter Splits with Knife
Red Star Crow band		
Yellow Medicine Man	Walks Among the Clouds	
	Scarlet Second Son	
	His Big Fire	
	His Sacred Nest	

62. ACCOUNTS OF SAND CREEK MASSACRE, 1864

After the Colorado Gold Rush began in 1859, Indian life in the mountains and plains of Colorado changed dramatically. Emigrant traffic on trails passed through Indian winter camps and through summer hunting areas. Such contact created inevitable tension as Native people stole horses and food from white travelers and raided new settler communities. By 1864, destructive cycles of raiding and retaliation made travel into the new territory nearly impossible. While army officials knew that only a few bands of Cheyennes, Arapahos, and Lakotas were causing the trouble, white Colorado settlers demanded that all Indians be rounded up. In this atmosphere of fear and hatred, the US Army and local militia marched into a large camp of Native people who had already surrendered and slaughtered them. Even at the time, individuals viewed the episode in very different ways. The first report of the dreadful night at Sand Creek, published in the Denver Rocky Mountain News, *describes it as a triumph. A letter from a participant who refused to let his troops join the brutal killing provides an entirely different perspective. Why would Denver residents in 1864 inevitably consider this a justifiable battle? What troubled Cap-*

tain Soule about the situation from the beginning and why did he decide not to participate? What does Soule want the army to do know?

Rocky Mountain News
Dec. 8, 1864

"Great Battle with Indians!"

The Savages Dispersed!

500 INDIANS KILLED

Our Loss 9 Killed, 38 Wounded

Full Particulars

H'dqters, District of Colorado

This noted, needed whipping of the "red skins, by our "First Indian Expedition" particulars of which appear elsewhere, was the chief subject of comment and glorification through town today. The members of the Third, and First and First of New Mexico, who collectively "cleaned out" the confederated savages on Sand Creek, have won for themselves and their Commanders, from Colonel down to corporal the eternal gratitude of the dwellers on these plains. This brave beginning will bring down the "*hauteur*" of the treacherous tribes, all around, so that, should there not be even a similar defeat enacted on them through this season, our people may rest easy in the belief that outrages by small bands are now at an end, on routes where troops are stationed. Having tasted of the "bitter end," the news of which will quickly be dispatched among the others, the supremacy of our power will be seriously considered . . . This plan of attacking them in their villages is the only one available and while it is certainly as advantageous to the Indians as they justly dare desire, if they're in for a fair fight.

Captain Silas Soule
Letter to Edward Wynkoop
December 14, 1864[1]

Fort Lyon, C.T.
December 14, 1864

Dear Ned:

Two days after you left here the 3rd Reg't with a Battalion of the 1st arrived here, having moved so secretly that we were not aware of their approach until they had Pickets around the Post, allowing no one to pass out! They arrested Capt. Bent and John Vogle and placed guards around their houses. They then declared their intention to massacre the friendly Indians camped on Sand Creek.

---

1. Original in Denver Public Library, cmss rbv59 m67–1163 WH/GEN stx 6; published in *Colorado Magazine* 41 (Fall 1964).

Major Anthony gave all information, and eagerly Joined in with Chivington and Co. and ordered Lieut. Cramer with his whole Co. to Join the command. As soon as I knew of their movement I was indignant as you would have been were you here and went to Cannon's room, where a number of officers of the 1st and 3rd were congregated and told them that any man who would take part in the murders, knowing the circumstances as we did, was a low lived cowardly son of a bitch. Capt. Y. J. Johnson and Lieut. Harding went to camp and reported to Chiv, Downing and the whole outfit what I had said, and you can bet hell was to pay in camp.

Chiv and all hands swore they would hang me before they moved camp, but I stuck it out, and all the officers at the Post, except Anthony backed me. I was then ordered with my whole company to Major A- with 20 days rations. I told him I would not take part in their intended murder, but if they were going after the Sioux, Kiowa's or any fighting Indians, I would go as far as any of them. They said that was what they were going for, and I joined them. We arrived at Black Kettles and Left Hand's Camp at daylight. Lieut. Wilson with Co.s "C", "E" & "G" were ordered to in advance to cut off their herd.

He made a circle to the rear and formed a line 200 yds from the village, and opened fire. Poor Old John Smith and Louderbeck ran out with white flags but they paid no attention to them, and they ran back into the tents. Anthony then rushed up with Co's "D" "K" & "G" to within one hundred yards and commenced firing. I refused to fire and swore that none but a coward would. for by this time hundreds of women and children were coming toward us and getting on their knees for mercy. Anthony shouted, "kill the sons of bitches" Smith and Louderbeck came to our command, although I am confident there were 200 shots fired at them, for I heard an officer say that Old Smith and any one who sympathized with the Indians, ought to be killed and now was a good time to do it.

The Battery then came up in our rear, and opened on them. I took my Comp'y across the Creek, and by this time the whole of the 3rd and the Batteries were firing into them and you can form some idea of the slaughter.

When the Indians found there was no hope for them they went for the Creek and got under the banks and some of the bucks got their Bows and a few rifles and defended themselves as well as they could. By this time there was no organization among our troops, they were a perfect mob—every man on his own hook. My Co. was the only one that kept their formation, and we did not fire a shot.

The massacre lasted six or eight hours, and a good many Indians escaped. I tell you Ned it was hard to see little children on their knees have their brains beat out by men professing to be civilized. One squaw was wounded and a fellow took a hatchet to finish her, and he cut one arm off, and held the other with one hand and dashed the hatchet through her brain. One squaw with her two children, were on their knees, begging for their lives of a dozen soldiers, within ten feet of them all firing—when one succeeded in hitting the squaw in the thigh, when she took a knife and cut the throats of both children and then killed herself. One Old Squaw hung herself in the lodge—there was not enough room for her to hang and she held up her knees and choked herself to death. Some tried to escape on the Prairie, but most of them were run down by horsemen. I saw two Indians hold one of anothers hands, chased until they were exhausted, when they kneeled down, and clasped each other around the neck and both were shot together. They were all scalped, and as high as half a dozen taken from one head. They were all horribly mutilated. One woman was cut open and a child taken out of her, and scalped.

White Antelope, War Bonnet and a number of others had Ears and Privates cut off. Squaws snatches were cut out for trophies. You would think it impossible for white men to butcher and mutilate human beings as they did there, but every word I have told you is the truth, which they do not deny. It was almost impossible to save any of them. Charly Autobee save John Smith and Winsers squaw. I saved little Charlie Bent. Geo. Bent was killed.

Jack Smith was taken prisoner, and murdered the next day in his tent by one of Dunn's Co. "E". I understand the man received a horse for doing the job. They were going to murder Charlie Bent, but I run him into the Fort. They were going to kill Old Uncle John Smith, but Lt. Cannon and the boys of Ft. Lyon, interfered, and saved him. They would have murdered Old Bents family, if Col. Tappan had not taken the matter in hand. Cramer went up with twenty (20) men, and they did not like to buck against so many of the 1st. Chivington has gone to Washington to be made General, I suppose, and get authority to raise a nine months Reg't to hunt Indians. He said Downing will have me cashiered if possible. If they do I want you to help me. I think they will try the same for Cramer for he has shot his mouth off a good deal, and did not shoot his pistol off in the Massacre. Joe has behaved first rate during this whole affair. Chivington reports five or six hundred killed, but there were not more than two hundred, about 140 women and children and 60 Bucks. A good many were out hunting buffalo. Our best Indians were killed. Black Kettle, One Eye, Minnemic and Left Hand. Geo. Pierce of Co. "F" was killed trying to save John Smith. There was one other of the 1st killed and nine of the 3rd all through their own fault. They would get up to the edge of the bank and look over, to get a shot at an Indian under them. When the women were killed the Bucks did not seem to try and get away, but fought desperately. Charly Autobee wished me to write all about it to you. He says he would have given anything if you could have been there.

I suppose Cramer has written to you, all the particulars, so I will write half. Your family is well. Billy Wilker, Col. Tappen, Wilson (who was wounded in the arm) start for Denver in the morning. There is no news I can think of. I expect we will have a hell of a time with Indians this winter. We have (200) men at the

Post—Anthony in command. I think he will be dismissed when the facts are known in Washington. Give my regards to any friends you come across, and write as soon as possible.

Yours, SS
(signed) S.S. Soule

FURTHER READING

Arenson, Adam, and Andrew Graybill, eds. *Civil War Wests: Testing the Limits of the United States.* Berkeley: University of California Press, 2015.

Berg, Scott W. *38 Nooses: Lincoln, Little Crow, and the Beginning of the Frontier's End.* New York: Vintage Books, 2013.

Frazier, Donald S. *Blood and Treasure: Confederate Empire in the Southwest.* College Station: Texas A&M Press, 1995.

Green, Jerome A., and Douglas Scott. *Finding Sand Creek: History, Archeology, and the 1864 Massacre Site.* Norman: University of Oklahoma Press, 2006.

Kelman, Ari M. *A Misplaced Massacre: Struggling Over the Memory of Sand Creek.* Cambridge, MA: Harvard University Press, 2013.

Ortiz, Roxanne Dunbar. *An Indigenous Peoples' History of the United States (ReVisioning American History).* Boston: Beacon, 2015.

Ostler, Jeffrey. *The Plains Sioux and U.S. Colonialism from Lewis and Clark to Wounded Knee.* Cambridge: Cambridge University Press, 2005.

Sleeper-Smith, Susan, Juliana Barr, Jean M. O'Brien, Nancy Shoemaker, and Scott Manning Stevens. *Why You Can't Teach United States History without American Indians.* Chapel Hill: University of North Carolina Press, 2015.

Ho for Kansas!

Brethren, Friends, & Fellow Citizens:

I feel thankful to inform you that the

REAL ESTATE

AND

Homestead Association,

Will Leave Here the

15th of April, 1878,

In pursuit of Homes in the Southwestern
Lands of America, at Transportation
Rates, cheaper than ever
was known before.

For full information inquire of

Benj. Singleton, better known as old Pap,

NO. 5 NORTH FRONT STREET.

Beware of Speculators and Adventurers, as it is a dangerous thing
to fall in their hands.

Nashville, Tenn., March 18, 1878.

African American migration to Kansas, 1878. This flyer announces preparations for westward migration by black Southerners at the end of Reconstruction in the late 1870s. As the federal government pulled out of the South, thousands of former slaves looked to the West as an escape destination from economic obstacles, terrible memories, and constant danger of violence from whites. The West, especially Kansas, began to resemble the Promised Land, at least in the dreams of many of those eager to test their new freedom. How would you sum up the feelings embedded in this flyer? Does it give you any sense of life in the South, the life that so many African Americans wished to escape but few could? How did this Kansas land suddenly become empty and available for new settlers?

Library of Congress.

War and Reconstruction

15

Limiting the Empire for Liberty

As Americans tried to piece their lives together after the US Civil War, many turned to the West for a new start. New opportunities beckoned, from the Great Plains to the Pacific. European immigrants and Mormon converts, Northerners and Southerners, went west in greater numbers. The federal government played a central role by aggressively taking up arms against many Indian nations that now struggled to protect traditional homelands, or to adjust to new reservation lands, but till lived in areas that white settlers expected to possess.

The federal government and its taxes sponsored massive public works projects that reshaped the western landscape. US politicians, eastern and western business people, and new western residents had long wanted a railroad. Long, expensive government expeditions in the 1850s had mapped out four potential routes over western rivers and mountain ranges: one far to the north, linking Minnesota to Seattle, Washington; another from Omaha, Nebraska, to San Francisco; a third that went south of the main range of the Rocky Mountains; and, finally, a southern route that linked New Orleans to Southern California. The choice became a political nightmare and the entire railroad project was scrapped.

However, once the war started, with Southern opposition gone from the nation's capital, Congress passed and President Lincoln signed three measures of tremendous significance in the coming decades. On May 20, 1862, the Homestead Act became law. It granted 160 acres of unclaimed public land to any adult, including immigrants intending to become citizens, who worked the land for five years and built a house, which entitled them to the title to the land. Only six weeks later, on July 1, Lincoln signed the Pacific Railway Act providing land and government loans to construct the first transcontinental rail line. The next day he signed the Morrill Act, which allotted public lands to states to finance colleges dedicated to agricultural education and research, an especially pressing need given the semi-arid West's great challenges to farmers. The vision of productive Americans sending farm goods and mineral resources to a worldwide market was compelling indeed.

Among these new farmers were newly freed African American slaves. Nearly twenty thousand of them moved onto the plains and prairies opened by Indian war and the Homestead Act. Although the vast majority of the former slaves who left the South after the Civil War went to northern cities, which were undergoing rapid industrialization, these new citizens also gazed west. One significant group viewed the West in religious terms, equating it (or parts of it) with the biblical Promised Land. They took to calling themselves "Exodusters," because they felt a religious and experiential kinship with the ancient Israelites and their exodus into the Sinai desert as they founded new communities in the West.

Despite their hopes for these new farming communities, African Americans would discover the West to be far from idyllic. Finding homes where they could live and work free of the shadow of former slaveholders might have been salvation enough. Unfortunately, however, the South did not hold a monopoly on racism; many African Americans found their paths in the West blocked by prejudices that were often as entrenched and as ugly as any they had faced in the South. While black emigrants carved out new lives in the broad fields of the Kansas plains, they faced fresh torment at the hands of white Westerners, who attacked them and destroyed their property. Some of these attackers were no doubt members of the Ku Klux Klan, the extremist band made up of former Confederate soldiers, which continued to wage the Civil War through its violence against African Americans. Former slaves who migrated to cities like Denver, San Francisco, and Seattle faced similar obstacles and disappointment: carefully worded laws and constant threats of violence made it impossible for them to buy land or own houses or businesses.

Freedom for some and new opportunity for many, however, came at great cost to others. Because of the Homestead Act, Native Americans had their land carved up, crossed by railroads, and mined and deforested by large corporations. This great storehouse of land and resource wealth was created by war and relocation. Two thousand African American soldiers fought in the US Army against Native peoples in the West throughout the latter decades of the nineteenth century. One irony of life in the post–Civil War West is that African American soldiers, often denied civil rights because of their race, appeared more patriotic, more American in the eyes of the nation by helping to subdue the first Americans. "Buffalo soldiers," as they were called by Native Americans, who thought their hair resembled the dense coat of the bison, fought in skirmishes and full-scale battles and guarded Native American prisoners over a large area from the eastern Great Plains, west into Utah, and south to the Mexican border.

One example, among many, many hard stories, was the Navajo War in the Southwest. At the same moment that Colorado soldiers slaughtered sleeping Cheyenne and Arapaho villagers at Sand Creek and as Dakota warriors rose up against the US Army in Minnesota, the Navajo faced forced removal from their homeland in an isolated and mountainous part of the Southwest. In the incident called the Long Walk by Navajo people, who still discuss it regularly, the US Army rounded up eight thousand Navajos in 1864. Led by frontiersman and longtime New Mexican sheep rancher, and now army officer Kit Carson, they marched three hundred miles to a desolate, almost waterless place in eastern New Mexico called the Bosque Redondo. The site, hastily chosen by the military, turned into a death camp for the Navajo. The bad water killed their sheep and made their children and old people sick. Comanches and Ute raiders stole horses and children. Worms ate their corn, and all the available wood was gone by the end of the first winter. After four long years, a third of the Navajos had died. Finally, because the government no longer wanted the expense of guarding and maintaining the camp, the Navajo marched back to their western New Mexico and Arizona homeland, now the largest Indian reservation in the United States.

As white settlers moved onto lands opened by the conquest of Indian nations and as Native peoples reorganized and regathered in new places in the West, how to govern these complicated places became a challenge. If citizens were defined as white men, that meant few western territories had enough people to meet the federal requirements to become a state. Some places decided to count Hispanic, Native, and mixed-blood men as citizens, and others decided to consider white women citizens. In 1848, white male legislators in Washington Territory became the first to introduce a women's suffrage bill. That Washington bill was narrowly defeated, but similar legislation succeeded elsewhere, especially after the Civil War. Wyoming Territory was the first to give women the vote in 1869, quickly followed by Utah Territory in 1870. However, granting citizenship meant giving new groups of people new rights, which was always a rocky road. What happened in the western state and local governments that granted rights and then took them away, as new communities experimented with the complicated range of peoples and ideas they now included, was always a bellwether for the rest of the nation.

The documents in this chapter survey not only the impact of the Civil War on the West but also the aspirations of westerners as the war ended. The West became a place of experimentation for a newly powerful federal government, which had good and bad consequences for the region. A new vision for the

West that combined small farms and giant corporations is laid out in the Homestead Act and the Pacific Railway Acts. The US Army and civilian groups offered up new ideas about managing Native people that had a devastating impact on the Navajo nation. Legislators in Wyoming experimented with allowing women to serve on juries and received a storm of criticism from newspaper editors everywhere.

63. THE GOVERNMENT CREATES THE WEST

In 1862, in the midst of the US Civil War, the Homestead Act offered up a vision of peace and plenty. Soldiers imagined taking their families to small farms. Women, widowed by the war or single by choice, could imagine creating homes in the West. The 160 acres was not accidental. Tied to Thomas Jefferson's 1785 legislation that created the system of surveying land, the 160 acres was a logical division of the one-square-mile section—640 acres—used to measure land everywhere. Even though 160 became a magic number as the amount a family could farm in the well-watered East or Midwest, it little sense in the arid or mountainous parts of the West. The Pacific Railway Act was equally optimistic. The route began in Nebraska and followed much of the old overland trail over the South Pass, in what is now Wyoming, and through northern Nevada and across the Sierra Nevada to Sacramento. No one knew how to build a railroad over the deserts and high mountain passes, but the Railway Act created several new large corporations eager to try. Because the act offered up the greatest government subsidy and land deal ever offered to wealthy US investors, it offered vast profits and big engineering challenges. What were the political and military advantages of creating these two pieces of legislation in 1862? What kinds of aspirations does the wording in both of these pieces of legislation indicate about the kind of place the West might become? Are there limitations in the Homestead Act? Why does the Railroad Act lay out the details of the route so carefully?

The Homestead and Pacific Railway Acts[1]
Homestead Act
1862

CHAP. LXXV.—An Act to secure Homesteads to actual Settlers on the Public Domain.

Be it enacted by the Senate and House of Representatives of the United States of America in Congress assembled, That any person who is the head of a family,

---

1. Act of May 20, 1862, Public Law 37–64, 05/20/1862; and Pacific Railway Act, July 1, 1862; Enrolled Acts and Resolutions of Congress, 1789–1996, both in Record Group 11; General Records of the United States Government; National Archives.

or who has arrived at the age of twenty-one years, and is a citizen of the United States, or who shall have filed his declaration of intention to become such, as required by the naturalization laws of the United States, and who has never borne arms against the United States Government or given aid and comfort to its enemies, shall, from and after the first January, eighteen hundred and sixty-three, be entitled to enter one quarter section or a less quantity of unappropriated public lands, upon which said person may have filed a preemption claim, or which may, at the time the application is made, be subject to preemption at one dollar and twenty-five cents, or less, per acre; or eighty acres or less of such unappropriated lands, at two dollars and fifty cents per acre, to be located in a body, in conformity to the legal subdivisions of the public lands, and after the same shall have been surveyed: Provided, That any person owning and residing on land may, under the provisions of this act, enter other land lying contiguous to his or her said land, which shall not, with the land so already owned and occupied, exceed in the aggregate one hundred and sixty acres.

SEC. 2. And be it further enacted, That the person applying for the benefit of this act shall, upon application to the register of the land office in which he or she is about to make such entry, make affidavit before the said register or receiver that he or she is the head of a family, or is twenty-one years or more of age, or shall have performed service in the army or navy of the United States, and that he has never borne arms against the Government of the United States or given aid and comfort to its enemies, and that such application is made for his or her exclusive use and benefit, and that said entry is made for the purpose of actual settlement and cultivation, and not either directly or indirectly for the use or benefit of any other person or persons whomsoever; and upon filing the said affidavit with the register or receiver, and on payment of ten dollars, he or she shall thereupon be permitted to enter the quantity of land specified: Provided, however, That no certificate shall be given or patent issued therefor until the expiration of five years from the date of such entry; and if, at the expiration of such time, or at any time within two years thereafter, the person making such entry; or, if he be dead, his widow; or in case of her death, his heirs or devisee; or in case of a widow making such entry, her heirs or devisee, in case of her death; shall prove by two credible witnesses that he, she, or they have resided upon or cultivated the same for the term of five years immediately succeeding the time of filing the affidavit aforesaid, and shall make affidavit that no part of said land has been alienated, and that he has borne rue allegiance to the Government of the United States; then, in such case, he, she, or they, if at that time a citizen of the United States, shall be entitled to a patent, as in other cases provided for by law: And provided, further, That in case of the death of both father and mother, leaving an Infant child, or children, under twenty-one years of age, the right and fee shall ensure to the benefit of said infant child or children; and the executor, administrator, or guardian may, at any time within two years after the death of the surviving parent, and in accordance with the laws of the State in which such children for the time being have their domicil, sell said land for the benefit of said infants, but for no other purpose; and the purchaser shall acquire the absolute title by the purchase, and be entitled to a patent from the United States, on payment of the office fees and sum of money herein specified.

SEC. 3. And be it further enacted, That the register of the land office shall note all such applications on the tract books and plats of, his office, and keep a register of all such entries, and make return thereof to the General Land Office, together with the proof upon which they have been founded.

SEC. 4. And be it further enacted, That no lands acquired under the provisions of this act shall in any event become liable to the satisfaction of any debt or debts contracted prior to the issuing of the patent therefor.

SEC. 5. And be it further enacted, That if, at any time after the filing of the affidavit, as required in the second section of this act, and before the expiration of the five years aforesaid, it shall be proven, after due notice to the settler, to the satisfaction of the register of the land office, that the person having filed such affidavit shall have actually changed his or her residence, or abandoned the said land for more than six months at any time, then and in that event the land so entered shall revert to the government.

SEC. 6. And be it further enacted, That no individual shall be permitted to acquire title to more than one quarter section under the provisions of this act; and that the Commissioner of the General Land Office is hereby required to prepare and issue such rules and regulations, consistent with this act, as shall be necessary and proper to carry its provisions into effect; and that the registers and receivers of the several land offices shall be entitled to receive the same compensation for any lands entered under the provisions of this act that they are now entitled to receive when the same quantity of land is entered with money, one half to be paid by the person making the application at the time of so doing, and the other half on the issue of the certificate by the person to whom it may be issued; but this shall not be construed to enlarge the maximum of compensation now prescribed by law for any register or receiver: Provided, That nothing contained in this act shall be so construed as to impair or interfere in any manner whatever with existing preemption rights: And provided, further, That all persons who may have filed their applications for a preemption right prior to the passage of this act, shall be entitled to all privileges of this act: Provided, further, That no person who has served, or may hereafter serve, for a period of not less than fourteen days in the army or navy of the United States, either regular or volunteer, under the laws thereof, during the existence of an actual war, domestic or foreign, shall be deprived of the benefits of this act on account of not having attained the age of twenty-one years.

SEC. 7. And be it further enacted, That the fifth section of the act entitled "An act in addition to an act more effectually to provide for the punishment of certain crimes against the United States, and for other purposes" approved the third of March, in the year eighteen hundred and fifty-seven, shall extend to all oaths, affirmations, and affidavits, required or authorized by this act.

SEC. 8. And be it further enacted, That nothing in this act shall be construed as to prevent any person who has availed him or herself of the benefits of the first section of this act, from paying the minimum price, or the price to which the same may have graduated, for the quantity of land so entered at any time before the expiration of the five years, and obtaining a patent therefor from the government, as in other cases provided by law, on making proof of settlement and cultivation as provided by existing laws granting preemption rights.

APPROVED, May 20, 1862.

Pacific Railway Act
1862

An Act to aid in the Construction of a Railroad and Telegraph Line from the Missouri River to the Pacific Ocean, and to secure to the Government the Use of the same for Postal, Military, and Other Purposes.

Be it enacted by the Senate and House of Representatives of the United States of America in Congress assembled . . . hereby created and erected into a body corporate and politic in deed and in law, by the name, style, and title of "The Union Pacific Railroad Company;" and by that name shall have perpetual succession, and shall be able to sue and to be sued, plead and be impleaded, defend and be defended, in all courts of law and equity within the United States, and may make and have a common seal; and the said corporation is hereby authorized and empowered to layout, locate, construct, furnish, maintain, and enjoy a continuous railroad and telegraph.

. . . SEC. 2. And be it further enacted, That the right of way through the public lands be, and the same is hereby, granted to said company for the construction of said railroad and telegraph line; and the right, power, and authority is hereby given to said company to take from the public lands adjacent to the line of said road, earth, stone, timber, and other materials for the construction thereof; said right of way is granted to said railroad to the extent of two hundred feet in width on each side of said railroad where it may pass over the public lands, including all necessary grounds for stations, buildings, work-shops, and depots, machine shops, switches, side tracks, turntables, and, water stations. The United States shall extinguish as rapidly as may be the Indian titles to all lands falling under the operation of this act and required for the said right of way and; grants hereinafter made.

SEC 3. And be it further enacted, That there be, and is hereby, granted to the said company, for the purpose of aiding in the construction, of said railroad and telegraph line, and to secure the safe and speedy transportation of the mails, troops, munitions of war, and public stores thereon, every alternate section of public land, designated by odd numbers, to the amount of five alternate sections per mile on each side of said railroad, on the line thereof, and within the limits often miles on each side of said road, not sold, reserved, or otherwise disposed of by the United States, and to which a preemption or homestead claim may not have attached, at the time the line of said road is definitely fixed: Provided, That all mineral lands shall be excepted from the operation of this act; but where the same shall contain timber, the timber thereon is hereby granted to said company. And all such lands, so granted by this section, which shall not be sold or disposed of by said company within three years after the entire road shall have been completed, shall be subject to settlement and preemption, like other lands, at a price not exceeding one dollar and twenty-five cents per acre, to be paid to said company.

SEC. 4. And be it further enacted, That whenever said company shall have completed forty consecutive miles of any portion of said railroad and telegraph line, ready for the service contemplated by this act, and supplied with all neces-sary drains, culverts, viaducts, crossings, sidings, bridges, turnouts, watering places, depots, equipments, furniture, and all other appurtenances of a first class railroad, the rails and all the other iron used in the construction and equipment of said road to be American manufacture of the best quality, the President of the United States shall appoint three commissioners to examine the same and report to him in relation thereto;

. . . SEC. 7. And be it further enacted, That said company shall file their assent to this act, under the seal of said company, in the Department of the Interior, within one year after the passage of this act, and shall complete said railroad and telegraph from the point of beginning, as herein provided, to the western boundary of Nevada Territory before the first day of July, one thousand eight hundred and seventy-four: Provided, That within two years after the pas-sage of this act said company shall designate the general route of said road, as near as may be, and shall file a map of the same in the Department of the Inte-rior, whereupon the Secretary of the Interior shall cause the lands within fif-teen miles of said designated route or routes to be withdrawn from preemption, private entry, and sale; and when any portion of said route shall be finally located, the Secretary of the Interior shall cause the said lands hereinbefore granted to be surveyed and set off as fast as may be necessary for the purposes herein named: Provided, That in fixing the point of connection of the main trunk with the eastern connections, it shall be fixed at the most practicable point for the construction of the Iowa and Missouri branches, as hereinafter provided.

SEC. 8. And be it further enacted, That the line of said railroad and telegraph shall commence at a point on the one hundredth meridian of a longitude west from Greenwich, between the south margin of the valley of the Republican River and the north margin of the valley of the Platte River, in the Territory of Nebraska, at a point to be fixed by the President of the United States, after actual surveys; thence running westerly upon the most direct, central, and practicable route, through the territories of the United States, the western boundary of the Territory of Nevada, there to meet and connect with the line of the Central Pacific Railroad Company of California.

SEC. 11. And be it further enacted, That for three hundred miles of said road most mountainous and difficult of construction, to wit: one hundred and fifty miles westwardly from the eastern base of the Rocky Mountains, and one hundred and fifty miles eastwardly from the western, base of the Sierra Nevada mountains, said points to be fixed by the President of the United States, the bonds to be issued to aid in the construction thereof shall be treble the number per mile hereinbefore provided, and the same shall be issued, and the lands herein granted be set apart, upon the construction of every twenty miles thereof, upon the certificate of the commissioners as aforesaid that twenty consecutive miles of the same are completed. And between the sections last named of one hundred and fifty miles each, the bonds to be issued to aid in the construction thereof shall be double the number per mile first mentioned, and the same shall be issued, and the lands herein granted be set apart, upon the construction of every twenty miles thereof, upon the certificate of the commissioners as aforesaid that twenty consecutive miles of the same are completed: Provided, That no more than fifty thousand of said bonds shall be issued under this act to aid in constructing the main line of said railroad and telegraph.

. . . SEC. 12. And be it further enacted, That whenever the route of said railroad shall cross the boundary of any State or Territory, or said meridian of longitude, the two companies meeting or uniting there shall agree upon its location at that point, with reference to the most direct and practicable through route, and in case of difference between them as to said location the President of the United States shall determine the said location; the companies named in each State and Territory to locate the road across the same between the points so agreed upon, except as herein provided. The track upon the entire line of railroad and branches shall be of uniform width, to be determined by the President of the United States, so that, when completed, cars can be run from the Missouri River to the Pacific coast; the grades and curves shall not exceed the maximum grades and curves of the Baltimore and Ohio railroad; the whole line of said railroad and branches and telegraph shall be operated and used for all purposes of communication, travel, and transportation, so far as the public and government are concerned, as one connected, continuous line; and the companies herein named in Missouri, Kansas, and California, filing their assent to the provisions of this act, shall re-ceive and transport all iron rails, chairs, spikes, ties, timber, and all materials required for constructing and furnishing said first-mentioned line between the aforesaid point, on the one hundredth meridian of longitude and western boundary of Nevada Territory, whenever the same is required by said first-named company, at cost, over that portion of the roads of said companies constructed under the provisions of this act.

. . . SEC. 14. And be it further enacted, That the said Union Pacific Railroad Company is hereby authorized and required to construct a single line of railroad and telegraph from a point on the western boundary of the State of Iowa, to be fixed by the President of the United States, upon the most direct and practicable route, to be subject to his approval, so as to form a connection with the lines of said company at some point on the one hundredth meridian of longitude aforesaid, from the point of commencement on the western boundary of the State of Iowa, upon the same terms and conditions, in all respects, as are contained in this act for the construction of the said railroad and telegraph first mentioned; and the said Union Pacific Railroad Company shall complete one hundred miles of the road and telegraph in this section provided for, in two years after filing their assent to the conditions of this act, as by the terms of this act required, and at the rate of one hundred miles per year there-after, until the whole is completed: Provided, That a failure upon the part of said company to make said connection in the time aforesaid, and to perform the obligations imposed on said company by this section and to operate said road in the same manner as the main line shall be operated, shall forfeit to the government of the United States all the rights, privileges, and franchises granted to and conferred upon said company by this act.

. . . SEC. 18. And be it further enacted, That whenever it appears that the, net earnings of the entire road and telegraph, including the amount allowed for services rendered for the United States, after deducting all, expenditures, including repairs, and the furnishing, running, and managing of said road, shall exceed ten per centum upon its cost, exclusive of the five per centum to be paid to the United States, Congress may reduce the rates of fare thereon, if unreasonable in amount, and may fix and establish the same by law. And the better to accomplish the object of this act, namely, to promote the public interest and welfare by the construction of said railroad and telegraph line, and keeping the same in working order, and to secure to the government at all times (but particularly in time of war) the use and benefits of the same for postal, military and other purposes, Congress may, at any time, having due regard for the rights of said companies named herein, add to, alter, amend, or repeal this act.

SEC. 19. And be it further enacted, That the several railroad companies herein named are authorized to enter into an arrangement with the Pacific Telegraph Company, the Overland Telegraph Company, and the California State Telegraph Company, so that the present line of telegraph between the Missouri River and San Francisco may be moved upon or along the line of said railroad and branches as fast as said roads and branches are built; and if said arrangement be entered into and the transfer of said telegraph line be made in accordance therewith to the line of said railroad and branches, such transfer shall, for all purposes of this act, be held and considered a fulfillment on the part of said railroad companies of the provisions of this act in regard to the construction of said line of telegraph. And, in case of disagreement, said telegraph companies are authorized to remove their line of telegraph along and upon the line of railroad herein contemplated without prejudice to the rights of said railroad companies named herein.

SEC. 20. And he it further enacted, That the corporation hereby created and the roads connected therewith, under the provisions of this act, shall make to the Secretary of the Treasury an annual report wherein shall be set forth-

First. The names of the stockholders and their places of residence, so far as the same can be ascertained;

Second. The names and residences of the directors, and all other officers of the company;

Third. The amount of stock subscribed, and the amount thereof actually paid in;

Fourth. A description of the lines of road surveyed, of the lines thereof fixed upon for the construction of the road, and the cost of such surveys;

Fifth. The amount received from passengers on the road;

Sixth. The amount received for freight thereon;

Seventh. A statement of the expense of said road and its fixtures;

Eighth. A statement of the indebtedness of said company, setting forth the various kinds thereof. Which report shall be sworn to by the president of the said company, and shall be presented to the Secretary of the Treasury on or before the first day of July in each year.

APPROVED, July 1, 1862.

64. INVENTING THE RESERVATION: ELDERS REMEMBER THE NAVAJOS' LONG WALK, 1864–68[1]

These stories were collected and published in the 1990s as Navajo people realized their own stories of the Long Walk in 1864 and the Navajo return in 1868 were disappearing. People who had heard those stories at home for generations but had been forced to give up their Navajo language were reluctant to tell these crucial histories. Groups of Navajo speakers now interviewed elders and their children and grandchildren for vivid and detailed accounts of what had happened. Some scholars remain critical of oral histories, but when used with care they provide access to pieces of history that have been entirely lost to us. We can see patterns in the accounts of the Long Walk told by Helen Begay, Esther Benally, and Joe Redhorse Benally. They show us the terrible realities of being in a foreign place, the constant danger from Plains Indian raiders, and the dangers children faced. How do these three people explain why the Navajo were forced to leave? What seemed most difficult about the camp at Bosque Redondo?

Helen Begay's Account

> Helen Begay is from Lake Valley, New Mexico. She is eighty years old and is of the Nooda'f (Ute) clan. Her grandmother told her this story.

The Navajo people traveled to Hweeldi because of the enemies. This would not have happened if the Navajos had not stolen from the Naakai (Mexicans), Nooda'f (Utes), Naalan i (Comanches), and Beehai (Jicarilla Apaches). This raiding by the Navajo People led to fighting with the enemies. I do not know if the Navajos stole livestock from the white men or not.

At night, the Navajos stole livestock such as sheep and goats from the Mexicans and other tribes. In the morning, the Mexicans would find tracks of cattle and horses which had been herded out of the corrals. Some Navajos did not steal because they did not want to get involved with the enemies. Other Navajos had livestock of their own, so they did not need to steal any livestock. Some people stole because they did not have any livestock.

This is the reason the Navajos brought the war upon themselves. Even the people who did not get involved were killed or taken to Hweeldi.

The Navajos were gathered by the enemies and taken to Tsehootsoof (Fort Defiance), Arizona, and from there they departed for Hweeldi. Only the elderly

---

1. "Helen Begay's Account," "Esther Benally's Account," and "Joe Redhorse Benally's Account," collected in Patty Chee, et. al, *Oral History Stories of the Long Walk*, by the Diné of the Eastern Region of the Navajo Reservation; stories collected and recorded by the Title VII bilingual staff, Patty Chee, Milanda Yazzie, Judy Benally, Marie Etsitty, and Bessie C. Henderson. Crownpoint, N.M.: Lake Valley Navajo School, 1990. Government Printing Office, 1991.

women and men and children were allowed to ride in the wagons. I do not know how many years they lived at Hweeldi. On the journey a woman sang a song about her donkey called, "I Have a Donkey." At Hweeldi some of the Navajo families lived in branch shelters made from trees. They would run from the shelter if the enemies attacked them. Some families would put their shoes in one pile every night and when the enemies attacked, they would grab their shoes and run from the enemies. There is a story about a man who grabbed a horse blood sausage thinking it was his shoes. He did not notice it until he was far away from the enemies.

At Hweeldi the people were gathered with their Navajo leaders to hear news about when they would be allowed to return to their homeland. I only remember two Navajo leaders at that time. They were Hastiin'ch'il Haajini (Manuelito) who was a big chief and Ch'ohyja deez' j"i (Man Looking Up The Douglas Fir Tree). I do not remember the other Navajo leaders.

The Navajos promised the white men that they would put their children in schools, which were provided by the United States government. When the people got back to Fort Defiance, food was again distributed among the Navajo families. Some of the food included flour, bacon, and coffee. The people did not know how to prepare these foods. Some people ate the bacon raw and the flour without mixing it, and they chewed the coffee beans without boiling them. Many Navajos got sick from the improper preparation of this foreign food.

My grandfather, who was my mother's father, went on the journey to Hweeldi. His Navajo name was Hastiin Ts'ish'zho'di (Big Tree Man). He traveled to Fort Sumner when he was only a child the age of six. Mrs. Helen Begay's grandfather was born at home in a tree branch shelter home. People used to live in this type of shelter in those days.

One time when my grandfather was a baby, he was left behind leaning against the wall of a tree shelter while everybody went to hide from the enemies who had come to raid the place. The people had hurriedly escaped into the forest to hide from the enemies, and the mother had forgotten her baby in the confusion. A woman named Dine neez be'esdzaa' (Tall Man's Wife) was being chased by the enemies when she saw the baby leaning against the Unazti (tree branch shelter). She rode by the baby and bent down and reached for the headboard of the baby's cradleboard. Then she pulled the baby up to her lap and rode away into the woods. She found the mother and gave back her baby.

Mrs. Begay said, "If that woman had not saved my grandfather's life, I would not be sitting here telling you this story."

Esther Benally's Account

My maternal great-grandmother used to tell stories about the Long Walk. The story began when there was starvation among the Dine (Navajos). My great-grandmother had gone on the long journey to Hweeldi (Fort Sumner). Staple foods such as flour and coffee were not available during that time. TA'ohazihii (Mormon tea), ch'ilgoweW (lesperma garcile), and bl'oh azihii biak&i'ool (Mormon tea roots) were used for coffee. The only sources of food were U'ohsahbinaa, tl'oh dei binaa', and tl'oh dei ntl'iz. Seeds were gathered in large goat skins which had been sewn together. The skin was spread underneath a seed bush. Then the bush was hit with a stick so that the seeds would fall into the skin. After the seeds were gathered, the tse'daashjee' (millstone) was used to grind them, Ygnacio Pesquiera's Sonoran Responseand they were boiled in clay pots on tset'ees, (stone grills). Hashk'aan (bananas), which grew on tsa'aszf (yucca), and chiiichin (sumac) were other sources of food found only in the mountains.

The camps of the Dine were usually attacked unexpectedly by the Naaianf (Plains Indians) and N6oda'f (Utes) on horseback. The Dine would run to the Chuska Mountains to hide in bear dens. When the Dine were attacked, they would run for their lives leaving everything behind, even children and belongings. Some Navajos were rounded up around Naatooh sik'ai'i (Grants) including my great-grandmother. The journey to Hweeldi began from there. A large number of women and their families were running from the enemy. Wagons and horses were their transportation, but the wagons slowed down travel so that they left them behind and traveled on horseback. Things got worse, and they lost all their horses just before they were captured.

About that time my great-grandmother and two other women were traveling together. They realized that they were the only women left from the group that had begun the journey. It was only a few days before they were captured. At the age of fifteen, my great-grandmother experienced her first menstruation while she was at Hweeldi. Kinaalda (the puberty ceremony) was performed. The fall after the Kinaalda, the Navajos were released. Upon their return home, a Blessingway Ceremony was performed. The people had to build an Unazt'i" (tree branch shelter) on top of DzlLna'oodUii (Huerfano Mountain).

Joe Redhorse Benally's Account

> Joe Benally is of the Tl 'aashchi 1 (Red Bottom People) clan. He will be eighty years old in August, 1990. His grandmother told him stories about the journey to Hweeldi. This is the way she told her story.

We started from a place called Liba seke hi (two grey hills sitting by each other) which is near Toadlena, New Mexico. We were herded by the white people. There were many of us who made the journey. We lived in Hweeldi for four years. The reason for this journey was that some people had stolen sheep, but innocent people who did not raid also had to suffer for the actions of the raiders. The journey to Hweeldi was made on foot, except for the children who rode with some of the horseback riders. The people who rode the horses were most likely the white people. The journey took many days, probably about a month.

At Hweeldi we received food to last about two days. A small amount of flour and a small piece of meat were given to us to eat. While at Hweeldi, the Comanches attacked us. Early one morning, we heard a strange sound, and we asked each other, "What is that sound?" The noise was coming from the sound of many hoof beats. Against the early dawn light, we could see the outline of the Comanches. We went into a honooji (rugged area) following a lady. The lady was singing a protection song as she led us. We hid there while watching the Comanches. A squaw dance had just been completed the night before, and the chaha'oh (shade houses) were still up. The Comanches surrounded the shade houses where some of the people had taken shelter.

There were two women who were not shy at all who ran out to them. They were instantly killed. We could just see their red blankets lying on the ground from where we were hiding. Some of the Comanches got off their horses and scalped the two women in the back of the head. They put the scalps on a stick, and they left holding up the sticks as they went. We all went back to our places after the incident. The two ladies were the only two people killed that day. We spent four years at Hweeldi, and then we returned to our homeland at Liba selce he.

65. EXODUSTERS: OKLAHOMA AND KANSAS

In the political turmoil of Reconstruction, Republicans and Democrats traded charges and countercharges about the treatment of recently freed slaves in the North, South, and West. Democrats claimed that Republicans urged former slaves to migrate out of the South solely to create a Republican majority in the western regions. Republicans responded that freed people moved to places like Kansas only because they had suffered violence and oppression in the former states of the Confederacy. In 1879, Congress initiated an investigation of the causes of African American migration. Senators interrogated whites and blacks alike about conditions. The following document excerpts the testimony of four African American witnesses. Best-known among these witnesses was former slave Benjamin "Pap" Singleton, who had played an instrumental role in urging "Brethren, Friends, & Fellow Citizens" to leave the South for the West since the end of the Civil War. His efforts led to the founding of a number of African American colonies. H. Ruby, B. F. Watson, and John Milton Brown offer a arrange of views about freedom, the poverty of Exoduster emigrants, the lure of the West and the failed dreams of emigrants to Texas. How do Reconstruction politics come to light in these testimonies? In what ways were the people of the West still fighting the Civil War?

Accounts of the Black Movement West to Texas and Oklahoma: Benjamin Singleton, H. Ruby, B.F. Watson, and John Milton Brown, Testimony before the US Senate
1879–80[1]

[Topeka, Kansas, June 25, 1879]
[BENJAMIN SINGLETON (colored) sworn and examined. . . .]

Q[uestion]. Mr. Singleton, you say there is no party spirit in this movement of emigrants to Kansas?—*A[nswer].* Well, there was not; I have always been a Grant man myself.

Q. Among these people out there in Kansas, who are helping it on, are there any Democrats?—A. In Kansas?

Q. Yes.—A. Let me tell you, as a positive man, I don't know nothing much about the committee; but let me tell you, right now, one thing, in behalf of my colonies, that the Democrats are just as good to my people there as anybody else.

Q. O, yes, as kind to you personally; but are any of these people in the societies there that are formed to encourage this emigration of your people and pay their way and get them out of their Southern homes—are any of these Democrats?—A. Just let me tell you right now that I don't know of any white people there that is encouraging this emigration. . . .

Q. The Kansas Relief Association that is organized for the purpose of aiding emigrants to come out there I am referring to; is there anybody connected with that, either as a member or officer, who is a Democrat?—A. Not that I know, sir; I don't know, sir, about that.

Q. Well, are any of these branch relief associations there conducted by Democrats?—A. I don't know, sir, at all; if I knew I would tell you.

Q. As far as you know they are conducted by Republicans?—A. As far as I know, I suppose they are. You ask me for facts, and I carry them with me to give to the people.

Q. You carry only the facts with you to give to the people. Well, that is right.—A. My people that I carried to Kansas ever since 1869 have generally, sir, come on our own resources, and generally went on our own workings. We have tried to make people of ourselves. I tell you to-day, sir, this committee is outside of me, for I don't know nothing about it hardly; my people depends upon their own resources.

Q. Then you don't know anything about bulldozing in Mississippi and Louisiana?—A. Didn't I tell you I have never been there?

---

1. Report and Testimony of the Select Committee of the US Senate to Investigate the Causes of the Removal of the Negroes from the Southern States to the Northern States," 46th Congress, Senate Report 693, Part 2:338–65, Part 3: 391–426

Q. But you talked very hard about them—called them scoundrels, rascals, and so on?—*A.* I have heard about it, and if the men there bulldozes and wears these false-faces, they ain't nothing else but what I called them; they ain't right, nohow.

Q. Do you believe it?—*A.* It is the proof of fifty or sixty thousand of them, and it occurs to me that every one of them can't lie about it.

Q. But it is all hearsay with you?—*A.* I told you I have not seen it myself. You don't think fifty or sixty thousand of them could all tell a lie, do you—you don't think they are all cheating?

Q. O, yes; there are instances where whole nations have lied.—*A.* Well, mebbe these have lied. I know what I have seen. I have seen women and children in wagons and teams come in, and they said they was run in by the Kuk-lux into Nashville, and the Democrats have housed them there and given them victuals, and administered to them and cared for them; I have seen that.

Q. Well, that is clever.—*A.* I am a man of realities; I am a man that will live in a country where I am going to cope with the white man, where the white man will lift himself to the level of justice; but when the white man will think that equal rights under the law to the colored man is a violation of his (the white man's) dignity, then I am going to leave. Suppose now that out in the country there the colored man goes to law to get his contract carried out with a white man; if the Democrats don't say anything, there is a lot of men there that will go around and run that black man out of the country because he took that gentle-man up to the law; and suppose he beats that gentleman; why, it is a violation of his dignity, they think, and they won't stand it. . . .

Q. I say, did you never hear the Republican speakers tell the colored people that they would be put back into slavery if the Democrats got into power, and if they did not vote against the Democrats?—*A.* I have heard something about that.

Q. What have you heard?—*A.* Well, these threats I have heard myself—I have heard the Democrats stand right up, that is, when the colored man was getting the rights of suffrage, and say, "You damned niggers, we've got you now, and we don't ask you for your suffrage, we don't care for it." Well, that was a chill on them. And there is another thing—

Q. But what was the threat? I don't see what your meaning is.—*A.* Why, that's threat enough; "You damned niggers, we've got you now."

Q. You called that a threat, did you?—*A.* Yes; that was enough to scare us. *Q.* Did that scare your people?—*A.* Well, that scared *me.* Then there's another thing. They have got up and looked up in these upper galleries, you know, where they see these stacks of arms, and they ask, "What are those stacks of arms put up there for?" And they tell them, "They are not for *you*," and they keep wondering what they are there for and that excites us, and makes us want to get away.

Q. Well, you are scared without cause; "The wicked flee when no man pursueth."—*A.* Mebbe that's it. . . .

[Washington, D.C., April 22, 1880]

H. RUBY (colored) sworn and examined. . . .

Question. Please state where you live, Mr. Ruby.—*Answer.* I am residing in Kansas.

Q. At what point?—A. Oswego, Southern Kansas.

Q. Where has been your home for the past few years?—A. For the last ten years I have lived in Texas.

Q. What part of Texas?—A. From the county of Galveston to as high up as McLennan County.

Q. Where were you born?—A. I was born in New York City.

Q. Did you come from New York to Texas?—A. I went from Central America to Texas.

Q. Did you emigrate from Texas to Kansas?—A. Yes, sir.

Q. Did any others go with you?—A. Yes, sir; ten families went when I did.

Q. You had some reason for going, I suppose; what was it?—A. Well, sir, last July there was a colored man's conference held at Houston, and I was a delegate from my county. The county delegation from my district elected me as a commissioner of emigration; and these colored men that wanted to leave got me to go and pick out locations for them.

Q. You attended the convention at Houston?—A. Yes, sir.

Q. What was the desire among these people to emigrate?—A. The call for the convention was issued the 20th of May, and in the call it was stated that it was a convention for the colored men to take into consideration the religious, political, and educational interests of their race.

Q. Were any complaints made at that convention as to their treatment in Texas?—A. Yes, sir; a majority of the delegates claimed that there were reasons for leaving; and the idea was to impress on the people to get away from there on account of the obnoxious laws of the State.

Q. What features of the laws did they complain of?—A. They complained of this law making qualifications for jurors—that they must be freeholders and know how to read and write.

Q. That is to say, they must own lands?—A. Yes, sir; be a freeholder or house-holder; then they also complained of the inefficiency of the school law.

Q. Does that jury law apply to whites and blacks alike?—A. Yes, sir; the colored men rent houses and lands but they are not freeholders.

Q. Were there any complaints?—A. Well, they go on to complain that as they did not put the colored man on the juries a good many of them were prosecuted wrongfully and convicted because the white people did not like the blacks. . . .

Q. Do you know anything of the Skull Creek colony?—A. Yes, sir; it is west of Columbus and was established about six years ago. There have been several established in Texas but they have been broken up. The only one I know in operation is at Fort Bend County, in the Senegambian settlements. This Skull Creek colony was composed of some of the best people in these counties. They went there thirty or forty years ago, but last June a crowd of men went down there and killed one of the leading men as he was coming from town with his cotton money and groceries. The people heard the reports of the guns and went out and found him riddled with buckshot and one of his mules gone. They made all kinds of threats against them, and when they could not run them out that way they put up placards telling them to "leave this neck of timber or we will make you."

Q. These placards were addressed to whom?—A. To the colored people of that colony.

Q. What was the result?—A. Some of the young men said they would not go away, but a few weeks afterwards they had to go; their fences were burned and so were their cotton houses and cribs; they were all burned in that colony except two houses, one belonging to a poor white person and another one in which a white man lived.

Q. How many were there in that colony before that?—A. There were twelve families, I think. The only drawback and the fault we find in Texas is that we do not know whether we are safe when we get a homestead. That is what some of them complained of from Lee County.

Q. Tell us what you know about that.—A. In that case even the good people around Giddings say that the outrages were uncalled for. They say that the cowboys went in there and killed these people at that place.

Q. How many people were there living there?—[A.] There were two hundred and fifty or three hundred living there, but they broke up the colony and went back on the farms where they were before. . . .

Q. What about the treatment of colored women down there?—A. That is one of the main grievances of the colored people, and causes of their going out of the South. Another of the main wants of the colored people is education for their children, and in leaving the South they are actuated by the same motives that the colonists were actuated by one hundred years ago. They do not say to the white people, "we will fight you," but they say, "we will leave you." They have to talk up for themselves, or else be like the Indian and be driven from the country. And that which you spoke of is one of the great troubles that is causing them to leave the South. They say that their daughters and mothers and wives are not safe; that they are liable to be insulted at any time, and if a colored man talks up for his family, he is either shot down or taken out at night and bushwhacked or killed. I have talked with them about it, and I have said that if I had any women-folks, and they were insulted, they would have to kill me before I would stand it. But they said to me, "if you lived down there, you have got to take what we give you." I lived ten years among them and did take a good deal. The fact is, the colored people must leave there because of their want of education and of protection for their women, and if a man wants to stay, and buys lots, he pays for the lot four times before he owns it.

Q. Is there much political trouble down there on account of your people now?—A. No, sir; not now. They have devices now for keeping the men from voting. It is a kind of bulldozing the same as they have in the North. Sometimes they deceive them by saying that the day of election is changed, or that the next day after the real day is the day of election, and many times the colored people are fooled in that way. . . .

Q. I do not suppose your race expects or wants the Government of the United States to elevate you over the heads of the whites—only to give you a fair chance?—A. That is all we want.

Q. In the matter of schools you say you have a fair chance, the same as the whites?—A. Yes, sir.

Q. Will you get any advantage over the whites, when you go to Kansas?—A. No, sir.

Q. Will you not have some disadvantages there?—A. I do not know.

Q. Do you not know that the constitution of the State of Kansas says that black men shall not vote?—A. Vote how?

Q. At the ballot-box. The word "white" is used in the constitution of Kansas, in describing the qualification of voters.—A. You have asked me a great many questions, now I would like to ask you one: Admitting that the constitution of Kansas does say that, does not the Constitution of these United States say that all men are born free and equal, endowed by—

Q. No, the Constitution of the United States does not say that; that is in the Declaration of Independence; it was Thomas Jefferson, a slaveholder, who said that.—A. Well, notwithstanding that was put in there, has not our race been hewers of wood and drawers of water for the white race for two hundred years, up till the time of the surrender?

Q. Yes; and since then you have been hewers of wood and drawers of water for the Radical party.—A. I don't allow that; I never let the radical party use me for a monkey to pull their chestnuts of [sic] the fire. . . .

[Washington, Friday, March 26, 1880]

B. F. WATSON (colored) sworn and examined:

Question. State your place of residence.—Answer. Kansas City, Mo.

Q. How long have you resided there?—A. Since November, 1878.

Q. Where did you reside prior to that?—A. In Omaha, Nebr.

Q. Were you born in Omaha?—A. No, sir; I am a minister by profession, and we receive our appointments at various parts from year to year.

Q. What is your native place?—A. The State of Missouri.

Q. To come to the point itself, what, if anything, have you had to do with assisting the emigrants who have come to Kansas, or to Missouri, from the Southern States?—A. I have been caring for them since last March, in the way of supplying them with food and clothing, and shipping them to Kansas, Nebraska, and Iowa.

Q. From Kansas City?—A. Yes, sir.

Q. In what capacity have you performed that labor? Has it been in connection with any society?—*A.* We organized a society in Kansas City last spring, but since its first meeting the society has not tried to do anything. Mr. Armor, one of our bankers, raised a fund of $2,000 in Chicago, and requested me to see to its use. There was no committee about it.

Q. Have you seen any considerable number of these emigrants?—*A.* I have shipped from May to the last of August about 2,500 of them, and have their names.

Q. Where did they come from?—*A.* From Mississippi and Louisiana. They arrived at Saint Louis and took the boat for Kansas City, and I would meet them there, and send them out to different places.

Q. Was there any money raised to help them except the amount that you speak of?—*A.* No, sir; not by me.

Q. How was that raised?—*A.* On hearing of the suffering of those parties who were arriving there at Wyandotte, Mrs. Armor went there, and her brother, who has a packing-house in Chicago, on her solicitation, went out and raised $2,000 for them. They seemed to be so destitute that Mr. Armor thought they had better try to relieve their suffering.

Q. Do you know whether any number of these people have found places?—*A.* Generally they have; the most of them that we sent to Topeka. More than two hundred were sent to Nebraska, and I have letters from Nebraska and Colorado and as far east as Illinois.

Q. From whom were those letters?—*A.* They were from people who desired this kind of labor.

Q. How many applications have you of that kind?—*A.* Four or five hundred still pending.

Q. Not supplied?—*A.* Not supplied.

Q. Have you had any before, that you have supplied?—*A.* Yes, sir; a great number.

Q. From all you know, is there a great demand for this kind of labor?—*A.* Yes, sir; throughout Missouri they want a good many, but they don't desire to stop there.

Q. Why not?—*A.* Because it has been a slave State, and they want to get to Kansas.

Q. What do you know of any political burdens that are moving them in their coming there?—*A.* I have conversed with a good many of them, but some of them give that as a reason. . . .

Q. What stories did they tell?—*A.* Various stories; generally, that their lives were insecure; that they had no chance for making a living; that no protection was given them in the South, and that many of them had to run away, the same as they did before the war, when they would slip out at night and make for the free States. A man by the name of George Washington, from Louisiana, told me that when he started from home he had to leave at twelve o'clock at night and carry his budget on his head to the river, and that then they were followed, but having met up with their crowd of friends they managed to protect themselves. A good many of them stopped on the banks of the river for many weeks before they could get a boat to take them up the river. Many of those from Mississippi stated that they had no trouble in their section, but that they were having it all around them and they did not know when it would come to them. Last summer I assisted an excursion from Kansas City to Topeka, made up of bull-dozers and colored people who came from Canton to Topeka. I saw a man by the name of Matthews, from Copiah County, and a man by the name of Bunch, from Yazoo; they were white men. They had heard that the bones of these colored people were bleaching on the fields out there, and they brought some of the colored people to see the sight and go back home and tell the news.

Q. What do you say was the object of that excursion?—A. It was to disgust these representative colored men, and to show them how badly they were treated in Kansas. They had been told that they were doing well out there, and they wanted to show them the bones of their fellow men who had come ahead. They came back and told me that if I saw any of these colored people who wanted to go back to Mississippi they could come free of charge. There was an agent in Kansas City all last summer to furnish transportation and provisions to those who wanted to go back. . . .

Q. These colored people have heard of John Brown and Kansas before?—A. Yes, sir; and they know more about Kansas than any other State. They know that it is the land of freedom.

Q. And it is a land of freedom they are looking for?—A. Yes, sir; and it is not only from the South that they are coming but from counties in Missouri also. . . .

Q. You spoke also of a man named George Washington, from Louisiana, who had to run away in order to get to Kansas.—A. Yes, sir.

Q. What part of Louisiana did he come from?—A. I cannot tell without my book here. I put down the names of persons, but I remember him because I nick-named him "President," and he told me how he would have to go through swamps twenty-five miles to get to the river and the boat in order to get away.

Q. Do you think that these people were being killed down there for coming away?—A. Yes, sir.

Q. Do you think that the white people loved them so much that rather than see them go away they preferred to kill them?—A. Yes, sir; rather than for them to leave there.

Q. You say they all told you that their lives were insecure and their political privileges denied them, and that they were leaving the South on that account?—A. Yes, sir.

Q. And you gave an opinion that the exodus would not stop until the people wiped out their miserable laws down there?—A. Yes, sir. I understand they are trying to pass a law in Mississippi—whether they did or not I do not know, but they had in other States—that no meeting of the colored people for the purpose of emigration shall be held, and that the leaders of them should be punished. . . .

[Washington, Friday, March 26, 1880]
JOHN MILTON BROWN (colored) sworn and examined. . . .

Q. Then the cold weather of Kansas, their exposure to storms, their sufferings from destitution, and all that, they prefer to endure rather than what they left behind them in the South?—A. Yes, sir; they love the Southern soil; they enjoy its climate; but it is the greatest horror of their lives to mention the idea of their going back there to suffer what they have suffered in the past. They will not go back. They will be the first.

Q. What is your idea, from the communication and intercourse that you have had with these colored men, who have come into Kansas since this exodus commenced, of the probable future of the movement?—A. I think it will increase rapidly all the time, unless speedy action is taken on die part of the white people of the South. If the Southern white people would give the colored people there the same rights and the same treatment which they receive in Kansas, they could stop the whole thing inside of six months.

Q. Other things being equal, that is, if given the same rights and privileges and protection in the one place as in the other, where would the colored people prefer to live, in Kansas or in the South?—A. I never yet met a colored man or woman but what said they would rather live in the South, two to one, than in Kansas, if they could have the same rights there that they have in Kansas.

Q. In your opinion, then, the only remedy for the exodus is different treatment of the colored people by the white people of the South?—A. It rests in the hands of the Southern white people altogether.

Q. What, in your belief, will be the extent of the exodus if that treatment is not changed?—A. It will continue to go on for the next twenty years, and until all, or a very large majority, of the colored people get out of the South. They will go to the Indian Territory, which from present appearances will before long be opened up to white immigration; they will go to other Western States besides Kansas, and to the Western Territories; they will be scattered all over the Northern States. . . .

66. WOMEN'S SUFFRAGE IN WYOMING

The nation watched with great interest as Wyoming Territory gave women the vote in 1869. The recognition of equal rights under the law included the right to serve on juries, at least for a time. Wyoming Chief Justice Howe insisted that if women were citizens they should serve as jurors. The first grand jury in the United States to include both women and men was convened in Laramie City, Wyoming, in March 1870. This news of a "mixed jury" shocked the nation, and editorials described this as a threat to propriety and even to civilization itself. Though Justice Howe and other suffrage advocates saw the experiment as a success, after Howe left the court in 1871, women in Wyoming were not called for jury service again until 1950. Why did this experiment in women serving on juries concern people? What dangers did the editorial writers see? How did Howe defend his decision? Was this moment a turning point for women's rights?

New Orleans Times
March 3, 1870

"LADY JURORS."—Confusion is becoming worse confounded by the hurried march of events. Mad theorizings take the form of every-day realities, and in the confusion of rights and the confusion of dress, all distinctions of sex are threatened with swift obliteration. When Anna Dickinson holds forth as the teacher of strange doctrines in which the masculinity of woman is preposterously asserted as a true warrant for equality with man in all his political and industrial relations; when Susan B. Anthony flashes defiance from lips and eyes which refuse the blandishment and soft dalliance that in the past have been so potent with "the sex"; when, in fine, the women of Wyoming are called from their domestic firesides to serve as jurors in a court of justice, a question of the day, and one, too, of the strangest kind, is forced on our attention.

Must man, as the anointed head of the animal creation, be turned from the easy tenor of his way by the railings of these tell-tale women. Yes, verily; he must pause and consider. . . . Though there might be something sensational and novel in the fact that half a dozen merry masculines are liable to be locked up as jurors with an equal number of the wives and daughters of their neighbors . . . [e]ach gentle juror would be a spy upon her neighbor and the hope of obtaining a harmonious conclusion on any legal question, would in all human probability be defeated by the green-eyed monster or some other spirit of misrule.

Our conclusion, from a careful review of all the surroundings, is that the Wyoming experiment will lead to beneficial results. By proving that lady jurors are altogether impracticable—that they cannot sit as the peers of men without setting at defiance all the laws of delicacy and propriety—the conclusion may be reached that it will be far better to let nature alone in regulating the relations of the sexes. We believe in the glories and graces of women, but we want woman where she was left by nature and nature's God.

The Philadelphia Press
March 8, 1870

"WOMEN AS JURORS."—Now one of the adjuncts of female citizenship is about to be tested in Wyoming. Eleven women have been drawn as jurors to serve at the March term of the Albany County Court. It is stated that immense excitement has been created thereby, but the nature of the aforesaid excitement does not transpire. Will women revolutionize justice? What is female justice, or what is it likely to be? Would twelve women return the same verdict as twelve men, supposing that each twelve had heard the same case? Is it possible for a jury of women, carrying with them all their sensitiveness, sympathies, predilections, jealousies, prejudices, hatreds, to reach an impartial verdict? Would not every criminal be a monster, provided not a female? Can the sex, ordinarily so quick to pronounce pre-judgments, divest itself of them sufficiently to enter the jury-box with unbiased minds? Perhaps it were best to trust the answer to events. Women may learn to be jurymen, but in so doing they have a great deal to learn.

Letter from Wyoming Chief Justice
J. H. Powell to Mrs. Myra Bradwell, Editor,
Chicago Legal News, Illinois
April 4, 1870

DEAR MADAM: I am in receipt of your favor of March 26, in which you request me to "give you a truthful statement, over my own signature, for publication in your paper, of the history of, and my observations in regard to, women as grand and petit jurors in Wyoming." I will comply with your request, with this qualification, that it be not published over my own signature, as I do not covet newspaper publicity, and have already, without any agency or fault of my own, been subjected to an amount of it which I never anticipated nor conceived of, and which has been far from agreeable to me.

I had no agency in the enactment of the law in Wyoming conferring legal equality upon women. I found it upon the statute-book of that territory, and in accordance with its provisions several women were legally drawn by the proper officers on the grand and petit juries of Albany county, and were duly summoned by the sheriff without any agency of mine. On being apprised of these facts, I conceived it to be my plain duty to fairly enforce this law, as I would any other; and more than this, I resolved at once that, as it had fallen to my lot to have the experiment tried under my administration, it should have a fair trial, and I therefore assured these women that they could serve or not, as they chose; that if they chose to serve, the Court would secure to them the most respectful consideration and deference, and protect them from insult in word or gesture, and from everything which might offend a modest and virtuous woman in any of the walks of life in which the good and true women of our country have been accustomed to move.

While I had never been an advocate for the law, I felt that thousands of good men and women had been, and that they had a right to see it fairly administered; and I was resolved that it should not be sneered down if I had to employ the whole power of the court to prevent it. I felt that even those who were opposed to the policy of admitting women to the right of suffrage and to hold office would condemn me if I did not do this. It was also sufficient for me that my own judgment approved this course.

With such assurances these women chose to serve and were duly impanelled as jurors. They were educated, cultivated eastern ladies, who are an honor to their sex. They have, with true womanly devotion, left their homes of comfort in the States to share the fortunes of their husbands and brothers in the far West and to aid them in founding a new State beyond the Missouri.

And now as to the results. With all my prejudices against the policy, I am under conscientious obligations to say that these women acquitted themselves with such dignity, decorum, propriety of conduct and intelligence as to win the admiration of every fair-minded citizen of Wyoming. They were careful, painstaking, intelligent and conscientious. They were firm and resolute for the right as established by the law and the testimony. Their verdicts were right, and, after three or four criminal trials, the lawyers engaged in defending persons accused of crime began to avail themselves of the right of peremptory challenge to get rid of the female jurors, who were too much in favor of enforcing the laws and punishing crime to suit the interests of their clients. After the grand jury had been in session two days, the dance-house keepers, gamblers and *demi-monde* fled out of the city in dismay, to escape the indictment of women grand jurors! In short I have never, in twenty-five years of constant experience in the courts of the country, seen more faithful, intelligent and resolutely honest grand and petit juries than these.

A contemptibly lying and silly dispatch went over the wires to the effect that during the trial of A. W. Howie for homicide (in which the jury consisted of six women and six men) the men and women were kept locked up together all night for four nights. Only two nights intervened during the trial, and on these nights, by my order, the jury was taken to the parlor of the large, commodious and well-furnished hotel of the Union Pacific Railroad, in charge of the sheriff and a woman bailiff, where they were supplied with meals and every comfort, and at 10 o'clock the women were conducted by the bailiff to a large and suitable apartment where beds were prepared for them, and the men to another adjoining, where beds were prepared for them, and where they remained in charge of sworn officers until morning, when they were again all conducted to the parlor and from thence in a body to breakfast, and thence to the jury-room, which was a clean and comfortable one, carpeted and heated, and furnished with all proper conveniences.

The cause was submitted to the jury for their decision about 11 o'clock in the forenoon, and they agreed upon their verdict, which was received by the court between 11 and 12 o'clock at night of the same day, when they were discharged.

Everybody commended the conduct of this jury and was satisfied with the verdict, except the individual who was convicted of murder in the second degree. The presence of these ladies in court secured the most perfect decorum and propriety of conduct, and the gentlemen of the bar and others vied with each other in their courteous and respectful demeanor toward the ladies and the court. Nothing occurred to offend the most refined lady (if she was a sensible lady) and the universal judgment of every intelligent and fair-minded man present was and is, that the experiment was a success.

I dislike the notoriety this matter has given me, but I do not shrink from it. I never sought it nor expected it, and have only performed what I regarded as a plain duty, neither seeking nor desiring any praise, and quite indifferent to any censure or criticism which my conduct may have invoked.

Thanking you for your friendly and complimentary expressions, I am very respectfully yours, J. H. HOWE.

FURTHER READING

Armitage, Sue. *Shaping the Public Good: Women Making History in the Pacific Northwest.* Corvallis: Oregon State University Press, 2015.

Denetdale, Jennifer Nez. *Reclaiming Diné History: The Legacies of Navajo Chief Manuelito and Juanita.* Tucson: University of Arizona Press, 2007.

Painter, Nell Irvin. *Exodusters: Black Migration to Kansas after the Civil War.* New York: W. W. Norton, 1992.

Reid, Joshua. *The Sea Is My Country: The Maritime World of the Makahs.* New Haven, CT: Yale University Press, 2015.

Richardson, Heather Cox. *West from Appomattox: The Reconstruction of America after the Civil War.* New Haven, CT: Yale University Press, 2008.

West, Elliott. *The Last Indian War: The Nez Perce Story.* New York: Oxford University Press, 2012.

White, Richard. *Railroaded: The Transcontinentals and the Making of Modern America.* New York: W. W. Norton, 2011.

Index

Note: *Italic* page numbers indicate illustrations.